In the Beginning God

Modern Science and the
Christian Doctrine of Creation

Regent's Study Guides

In the Beginning God

Modern Science and the
Christian Doctrine of Creation

John Weaver

Regent's Park College, Oxford

with

Smyth & Helwys Publishing, Inc.
Macon, Georgia

For Sheila

ISBN (UK) 0-9518104-2-1
ISBN 1-880837-82-X

In the Beginning God
Modern Science and the Christian Doctrine of Creation

by John Weaver

Copyright © 1994
John D. Weaver and Regent's Park College, Oxford
Published by Regent's Park College, Oxford OX1 2LB UK
in association with Smyth & Helwys Publishing, Inc.
Macon, Georgia31207USA

The paper used in this publication meets the minimum requirements of
American National Standard for Information Sciences—Permanence of
Paper for Printed Library materials, ANSI Z39.48-11984.

Library of Congress Cataloging-in-Publication Data

Weaver, John
    In the beginning God: modern science and the Christian doctrine of
creation / John Weaver
    vii + 210 pp.   6" x 9" (15 x 23 cm.)
    Includes bibliographical references and index.
    ISBN 1-880837-82-X   (UK) 0-9518104-2-1
    1. Creation. 2. Religion and science. I. Title. II. Series.
    BL240.2.W37   1994   94-13425
    231.7'65—dc20   CIP

Contents

Acknowledgements

Quotations from *The Hitch-Hiker's Guide to the Galaxy* by Douglas Adams, copyright 1979 Douglas Adams, are reprinted by kind permission of Pan Books Ltd., London.

The text figures 1:1 and 1:2 from *Religion in an Age of Science* by Ian G. Barbour, copyright Ian G. Barbour 1990, are reprinted by kind permission of SCM Press, London.

The text figure 6:1 from 'Information, Physics, Quantum: the Search for Links' by John Wheeler, copyright 1990 John Wheeler, in *Complexity, Entropy and the Physics of Information* (ed.) W. H. Zureck, is reprinted by kind permission of the author.

Preface

Imagine a nine-year-old boy in Junior School who was asked to learn to write his own address, and who then wondered just how complete he could make it. So he began to write:

> John David Weaver
> 58 Park Avenue
> Whitchurch
> Cardiff
> Glamorganshire
> South Wales
> Wales
> Great Britain
> Europe
> Northern Hemisphere
> The World
> The Solar System
> The Milky Way
> The Universe
> ????

Those question marks bothered me; where was the universe? What could I write next? Could I liken the universe to our goldfish pond—was the universe a pond in God's back garden? Scientific questioning continued with chemical experiments in my early teens: growing copper sulphate crystals and halite crystals. But all this experimentation was brought to an abrupt end when my experiments with rocket fuel resulted in an explosion that shattered our neighbour's window. So I moved on into the safer field of physics, building three radio receivers, a pursuit motivated by the desire to listen to pop music on Radio Luxemburg when I should have been sleeping or studying. But the real life-changing experience came in the Spring of 1961—or was it the Autumn of that year?

Two experiences that were to shape the rest of my life took place in that year. In the Spring of 1961 the School Scientific Society received a visit from Emlyn Evans, the Schools' Officer for the Geology Department of the National Museum of Wales, in Cardiff. He spoke about rocks, minerals and fossils, and ended his talk by showing us 'potato stones' from the Triassic rocks of Penarth, near Cardiff. These were concretions, about the size of a large potato, which were filled with crystals. He offered to break one open and invited someone to come and see. I volunteered; as he broke it open he said, 'You are the first person to see inside this nodule, since the moment it was formed, in fact, ever!' From that moment I was hooked; geology was to dominate my interest through school, university, and my first employment as a lecturer in geology.

In the Autumn of that same year I was baptised at Bethel Baptist Church, Whitchurch, Cardiff. The warm loving faith of Christian parents was something that then became my own personal experience, and for seventeen years these two strands of my life, geology and Christian faith, would run in parallel, but only occasionally intersecting.

Geology led to fossil hunting, caving, to beaches, quarries and coal mines. I devoured information, read books, attended lectures, and went on field courses. I had caught the bug and longed to study the subject for real. During this time my Christian faith was somewhat slower in its development. I belonged to a traditional Welsh non-conformist church, I attended services regularly, taught in the Sunday School, and tried spasmodically to read my Bible and spend time in prayer.

When I went to university these two pathways in my life came into collison for the first time. The private world of faith was questioned by the public world of scientific argument in the form of a fellow student who said, 'How do you reconcile your Christian belief in a six day creation with your geological understanding of an Earth that is at least 4,500 million years old?' I was forced to consider exactly what I did believe. Six days of creation was out of the question for a geologist, but at least the general shape of the Genesis account made sense. I could, for the time being, live with 'In the beginning God . . .' and leave my geology to look after the next 10 billion years or so, while my faith dealt with the implications of the 4,000 years or so of Bible and Church history.*

Studying geology in the late 1960s was exciting as the implications of the theory of Plate Tectonics began to unfold; it was clear that this model of the Earth's crust (made up of six plates which move apart, alongside, and under each other) had a great deal to say about the evolution of the Earth. My own doctoral research and lecturing over the next ten years was focussed on this area: geotectonics and structural geology. Alongside this work my spiritual journey took another significant step, with the recognition that the Christian faith was lived out in seven days a week discipleship and not only when the church met together. This recognition encouraged me to look again at the relationship of my research and teaching interests to my faith in the Bible, and in particular to the accounts of creation in Genesis 1 and 2. I recognised that this could become a useful apologetic for the Christian faith and I took the opportunity of giving a number of talks to schools and colleges, on the subject of science and faith.

While training for the ordained Baptist Ministry at Regent's Park College in the University of Oxford from 1978 to 1981, my study of the Old and New Testaments and of the development of Christian doctrine enabled me to put some flesh on the bones of my views of creation. During the eleven years in pastoral ministry that followed, my interest in a constructive dialogue between science and Christianity grew, mainly as the result of coming into contact with people inside the church who are afraid to face the discoveries of science, and people outside the church who find science (as they imagine it to be) a stumbling block to faith. During many talks in schools and churches I found a breadth of interest that went beyond my scientific specialization in the area of geology. The publication, in 1988, of *A Brief History of Time* by Stephen Hawking, the Lucasian Professor of Mathematics at Cambridge, heightened public interest in physics, and in particular in the origin of the universe. Such was the interest in this book and the work of Paul Davies, then Professor of Theoretical Physics at Newcastle University, who had in 1983 written *God and the New Physics*, that the BBC produced a radio series on Science and Christianity. During one of these broadcasts there was a long discussion with Paul Davies, who discussed the Big Bang, the fine tuning of the universe and the Anthropic Principle, in which purpose and design could be detected in the universe. Here, with the addition of some serious theological thinking, was a basis for a meeting of science and theology, and a basis for an apologetic that could be used with the many young people that I was meeting outside the church.

This book is an attempt to develop that apologetic through the fields of cosmology, geology, biology, and natural theology. It is a journey of discovering facts and theories about the world, and of developing a reasonable belief about creation.

John Weaver
Oxford 1994

* Editor's note: American readers should observe that the author follows the British pattern of counting wherein the next denomination after a million is a thousand million, not a billion. Hence, 10 billion (British) would be equivalent to 10 trillion (American).

1

'I applied myself to the understanding of wisdom'[1]

The Methods of Science and Theology

In his book *The Hitch-Hiker's Guide to the Galaxy,* a satiric version of science fiction based on a successful radio and television series, Douglas Adams writes:

> There are of course many problems connected with life, of which some of the most popular are Why are people born? Why do they die? Why do they want to spend so much of the intervening time wearing digital watches?

This reflection leads him into telling the story of two programmers on a distant planet who switch on the greatest galactic computer ever built and assign it its very first task:

> 'O Deep Thought Computer,' [said Fook], 'the task we have designed you to perform is this. We want you to tell us . . .' he paused, '. . . the Answer!'
> 'The Answer?' said Deep Thought. 'The Answer to what?'
> 'Life!' urged Fook.
> 'The Universe!' said Lunkwill.
> 'Everything!' they said in chorus.
> Deep Thought paused for a moment's reflection.
> 'Tricky,' he said finally.[2]

In the following pages we shall be looking at the search of human-kind for that answer through science. We shall consider both the questions asked and the answers given in the light of the Christian faith; and we shall allow Christianity and science to enter a dialogue with each other in developing a doctrine of creation. During the course of our investigation we shall be dipping into a good deal of history to understand how we have arrived at where we are in science and religion. We shall consider the historical development of the sciences and the history of philosophical discussion about knowledge of God presented by the universe ('natural theology'). In the scientific realm we shall draw evidence from the fields of cosmology, physics, biology, palaeontology, and geotectonics, and we shall consider in detail the questions posed to theology by the works of Stephen Hawking, Roger Penrose, Paul Davies, John Barrow, and Richard Dawkins. In the area of theological thought, we shall seek to develop a clear understanding of the purpose and meaning of the biblical accounts of creation, focusing our attention on Genesis 1:1-2:4a; we shall draw out the relevance and also the deficiencies of natural theology and consider the place of the natural world within the scope of God's self-revelation. At the end of all these investigations and explorations, we shall discuss the place of apologetics as the Christian church encounters the modern scientific world-view.

1. Chalk and Cheese?

We might question whether it is possible at all for one book to bring together the fields of science and theology. Are they not too disparate? Do they not speak different languages and use different methodology? In short, are they not as different as the proverbial chalk and cheese? But if we believe that God is the creator of the whole of 'life, the universe and everything', then we must see his involvement in the domain of scientific research and not merely confine God-talk to the church and theological college. Lesslie Newbigin has rightly attacked the division between the public world of scientific facts and the private world of beliefs and values.[3] Scientists have their own beliefs, doubts, questions, and certainties; and the world of public decision-making clearly needs the values, ethics, morality, and perspective that an understanding of the Christian faith might bring to it.

It is the scientist who is now posing the questions to which only theology has any meaningful answers. Modern cosmologists are posing questions about the beginning and end of the universe, about the place of *Homo sapiens* within it, and the reasons for apparent design and purpose within the evolution of the cosmos. On Christmas Eve 1968, as the first astronauts orbitted the Moon, Frank Borman read the opening verses of Genesis chapter 1, and all the world was able to hear his beliefs. Yet at this juncture we need to stress a point that will be made many times during the course of this book, namely that God's existence is not proved by scientific discovery. Let us not forget that some years before Borman, the first man in space, the Russian astronaut Yuri Gagarin, had declared that he did not find God in the heavens.

The heavens have, however, held a fascination for human beings, and many of the scientists of the early eighteenth century considered that they were discovering there something of the wonder of God's creation. This is captured in Joseph Wright's painting, *The Orrery*, which forms the cover of this book. Joseph Wright of Derby (1734–1797), like many English artists of his period, sought to capture the mood of the age in which he lived, and a number of his paintings reflect the fascination that people felt for the most recent discoveries of science. He was inspired by the wonder and awe that accompanied the birth of the industrial age, with its science and technology. *The Orrery*, painted in Derby in 1766, shows the philosopher demonstrating the movements of the planets to a group of interested children. It combined the painter's interests in scientific demonstrations and the dramatic use of light and shade. Among his other paintings are *A Philosopher Lecturing on the Orrery* and *An Experiment on a Bird in the Air Pump*. I chose the picture for the cover of this book because I should like to encourage others to share those children's excitement as the truths of God's universe are discovered through scientific research.

The modern popularity of science is shown by the plethora of books dealing with human life and the universe; many books that were originally published in hardback for the scientific market have been reprinted in paperback versions for a wider readership. Such books include Stephen Hawking's *Brief History of Time*, Paul Davies' *God and the New Physics* and *The Mind of God*, Roger Penrose's *The Emperor's New Mind*, Richard Dawkins' *The Selfish Gene* and *The Blind Watchmaker*, and Stephen Gould's *Wonderful Life*. The interest in these books reflects the modern concern with questions of the origins, purpose, and meaning of life. The growth of the Green Movement and New Age religion can also be seen as part of this search with their central concerns for the environment of the planet and the use of its resources, together with monistic beliefs in a world soul and the interconnectedness of human life with the whole of the cosmos.

Albert Einstein was right to state that 'religion without science is blind, and science without religion is lame', but the decisive factor will be the way in which these two areas are brought together. Science is presenting an ever-clearer picture of the universe of which we are a part. We are understanding more and more of the complex patterns and structures of the galaxies, of human life, and of the sub-atomic particles that compose all things. Cosmologists speak of the discovery of 'design' and pose questions about 'purpose'. There is a growing weight of evidence to suggest that human life could only have developed on this planet through a unique set of parameters that were established at the birth of the universe itself, which again suggests purpose, but with the additional possibility that humankind might actually be central to it. The fragile conditions that enabled life to develop are now seen to be adversely affected by human activity, leading to the pollution of the environment, the exhaustion of natural resources, and the destruction of the protective ozone layer. With the same totally anthropocentric attitude that led to the present state of affairs, people are seeking to solve the world's problems through lobbying of governments and through legislation, most of which is beneficial to the rich nations, but takes little account of the 'four-fifths' world.

Where can we look for answers to the world's questions and problems? We need to bring the fields of scientific discovery and Christian values together. In doing this we will need to recognise that while there are some fundamental differences, there is also a great deal of sympathy and comparison between science and theology. The fundamental difference lies in the place of the human observer. For theologians, God is the subject and the centre of their deliberations, and information about him comes initially by means of revelation. For scientists, humankind is the subject and centre of their investigations, and information comes initially from observation. In the world of science, where observation, measurement, and analysis define all studies, observable nature replaces the invisible God, and the scientists who understand nature's ways and can interpret them easily become a new priesthood. They replace the Christian priesthood, who understand and interpret the God revealed in the Scriptures.

In our discussions we will find ourselves walking on a tight-rope when discussing the place of humankind. We will be aware of the anthropocentric scientific world-view that has been behind the successes of technology and medicine, and also behind the life or world-threatening dangers inherent in nuclear warfare, pollution, exploitation of resources, and genetic engineering. As Paul Davies has pointed out, science 'has spawned some horrific children.'[4] Yet we shall discover science confirming the central place of human beings in creation, which is the theological view described in the first chapters of the Bible. The tight-rope lies between recognising human beings as the crown of God's creation, and the morally and spiritually dangerous view that we have everything under our control, with no need of reference to God and with no need of respect for the rest of creation.

The success of science in industrialised society has been matched by a corresponding decline in traditional religious observance. There has been, in more recent times, a turning away from the received wisdom of a biblical faith to the pseudo-scientific 'religions' of UFOs, ESP, and New Age, exemplified in the film industry's output of the Star Trek series and the Star Wars trilogy. Similar manifestations have been interest in the Bermuda Triangle and crop circles, and the writings of Hal Lindsey. We therefore need to consider the methodology and discoveries of science, both to inform our understanding of its relation to theology and as a yardstick by which to measure the claims of pseudo-science.

2. The Wonderful World of Science

Scientific research over the last couple of centuries has seen a cone of expansion, which grows ever larger. Stephen Hawking remarked, 'A lot of [Nobel] prizes have been awarded for showing that the universe is not as simple as we might have thought.'[5] Scientific studies take place for a number of reasons. There is basic human curiosity; there are the benefits that come from use of the Earth's resources and from technological advances; and there is the search for meaning and truth about the world in which we live. Science is involved in a rational exploration of the universe; it is a search for an understanding of the nature and patterns of the physical world. Science is only effective because it seriously seeks to describe things the way they are. Scientists have confidence that the discovery of the physical laws that govern the universe, such as gravity, are part of objective reality; they are objective truth and not the invention or imagining of some scientist. The whole field of science is thus motivated by discovery and not by construction; there is an honesty and integrity in the search for explanation. Scientific results are frequently cross-checked and validated or questioned when other workers repeat the same experiments. In this context I shall not hesitate in this book to speak of 'laws of nature', though I am well aware that theologians are often uncomfortable with this concept. I do not disagree that 'laws of nature' are 'observed regularities', but this does not make the idea of a law any less useful.

This search for objective truth must, of course, be immediately qualified by recognising certain actualities in the situation. Investigators look through the spectacles of a scientific world-view, which will include various presuppositions. This will mean that all facts are, to a greater or lesser extent, interpreted facts. There will be both the personal commitment of the scientists in their search for truth and the personal judgement of the individual researcher. This may mean the eliminating of background information that is not relevant to the particular work but which later research may prove to be of vital importance. The possibility of any objective observation at all has been questioned; for example, Michael Polanyi[6] has emphasised the central part played by personal judgement in scientific research. We certainly have to recognise that scientific experiment or observation can be both 'fact-laden' and 'theory-laden'; for any collection of data there may be more than one possible solution, or the theory may be in the mind of the observers before they conduct the experiment. Moreover, scientists employ 'models' that they recognise to be limited and often inadequate ways of expressing what cannot be observed directly, though they believe them to represent the truth of how things are. (We shall explore the place of models further below.) Yet for all this, to understand the scientific enterprise we must be clear that the one goal that drives its investigations is the desire for knowledge, to understand better the way the world is.

Scientists speak of a rational beauty in the universe; the universe appears to be marvellously, rationally transparent. Paul Davies says that the miracle of science is that it works[7]; human beings have rational minds that are able to unlock the secrets of nature. One of the earliest and important discoveries of science was that the universe is mathematical. The language of nature is essentially mathematics. Mathematics is a specific ability that belongs to *Homo sapiens*, and it is through the intelligibility of the physical world that we gain insight. Our minds reflect the nature of the universe and point us towards a sense of transcendence.

There has been a revolution in our understanding of the physical world over the last 300 years. Copernicus and Galileo pointed us to a universe that was not centred on Earth, and Kepler and Newton pointed us toward the physical laws by which the universe operated. At that time, however, the universe was envisaged as being infinite with no beginning or end, a machine operating under predictable laws with God safely positioned on the outside as a machine minder. With Einstein space and time became interwoven, and measurements were relative to the position of the observer. Time was no longer uniform. Hubble's investigation of the light emanating from distant galaxies revealed the fact that they are moving away from us at very high speeds. Studies since then have confirmed an expanding universe, which can be traced backwards to an explosive beginning at a single point, some 10-20 billion years ago. Palaeontologists and biologists have discovered an enormous diversity in living organisms. Darwin proposed natural selection to account for the development, variety, and complexity of living things, and Mendel and later Crick and Watson, through their work in the field of genetics, showed the biological mechanism by which evolution might occur. There is also the complexity of the particles that make up every physical and living part of the universe: molecules, atoms, protons, neutrons, electrons, quarks, and gluons. In this quantum world of sub-atomic particles we will find that prediction is far from certain. On the large scale we have discovered a universe in which there are over one thousand million galaxies, like our own Milky Way, and each of these galaxies contains between one thousand million and one million million stars, like our own Sun. The universe is of a size and age that the figures become almost meaningless, and yet with all this size and complexity it demonstrates a unity and simplicity of laws, principles, and relationships.

The patterns of the physical world are intriguing; there is an order that is both beautiful and exciting, and scientists are often heard to use words like 'wonder' and 'awe' when considering their researches and results. One of the greatest surprises that these patterns and results are showing is that the present state of the universe depends on a 'fine tuning' of the initial conditions that brought it into existence. This is what is generally known as the 'Anthropic Principle'. It is being suggested that a universe that contains the evolution of conscious human life must have been 'designed' to reach that end result. In other words, science is discovering something like purpose in the world, and while scientific use of expressions like 'design' and 'purpose' do not in themselves necessitate a Supreme Mind or purposeful Designer behind the universe, they do at least suggest the possibility of a Creator God. We shall discover that the universe has to be the size it is, the age it is, expanding in the way it is, with the initial level of entropy that it had, to have seen the development of the rich diversity of life that we experience. For example, every atom of carbon, in every living thing, was once part of the nuclear furnace of a star, which later exploded to disperse those atoms so that they could be assimilated into planet Earth. This appears to require the size and age of universe that science has discovered.

Science has a number of things to say to theology. Of course, physics itself does not allow us to build metaphysical models; science will not allow us to go beyond our empirical knowledge. Yet to the eye of faith, the history of the universe is pointing to a God who does not work by magic, but who has been patiently at work, over a long period of time, in an evolving cosmos. There is a picture of the outworking of divine love here, which we will have to consider later in some detail. Science reveals an interplay of chance and necessity within the evolution of the universe, which points us toward another aspect of divine love, namely freedom. Science presents us with a universe that has a beginning and which will have a definite end in which carbon-based life will be extinguished. This points to the Christian conviction that the universe has a story given to it by God. Lastly, it is the human mind that is able to observe, investigate, and understand the world that we experience. Scientific research has demonstrated that the mind does not function as a computer. It may be possible to reduce everything else to sub-atomic particles, acting under the laws of physics, but there are aspects of the mind, namely those of personhood, which do not compute. Once more we are pointed toward the possibility of a personal God as the ground of all personality.

3. Theology: Getting the Whole Picture

Theology, like science, is a search for truth in our understanding of the reality of the universe; like science, it is a search to understand the way the world is. Theology has its information on which it builds, but this is of a different kind from that of science. The kind of theology I am commending depends upon Scripture, tradition, and the reasoning of the community of faith—a collection of source materials that is often referred to as 'the Anglican Triad',[8] all of which contain the element of experience. Scripture is witness to the self-revelation of God in the history of Israel and in the experience of the first Christians. The documents that make up the Bible are themselves interpretations of events under the inspiration of God's Spirit, and they have been sifted and tested in the light of the experience of the community of faith. Tradition takes that interpretation and testing a stage further as the community of faith, in the light of continuing experience, has developed formulations of doctrine. Finally, in every age the community of faith must apply critical reason, in the light of its own experience of the world and God, to Scripture, doctrine, and their interpretation. All of this is seen by Christians as the work of the Holy Spirit, the presence of God, bringing enlightenment to the whole of life within the world, both material and spiritual.

There is an important difference between the place of experience in science and theology. Science can repeat experiments in order to recreate experiences, but Christian experience is personal and each instance therefore has its own uniqueness. Such a uniqueness is exemplified above all in the Incarnation, Crucifixion, and Resurrection of Christ. Yet there is still something universal about the character of religious experience, since persons exist in relation with others. John Polkinghorne[9] is surely right to point to Christian mystical experience as one of the strongest indicators of the validity of the claim that religion is in touch with reality. Experiences of conversion, inspiration, guidance, and healing are not universal in the sense of happening to everyone or happening in a uniform way, but they have some common characteristics wherever they happen as well as a uniqueness. For example, there is a sense of being challenged by an 'Other' beyond the self, an encounter that can bring radical change to life. Rather like the enterprise of scientific research, Christian experience of God and understanding of his self-revelation are constantly being examined within the community of faith, where experiences are shared.

Theology, however, takes a further step of interpretation than science does. It takes our ability to understand the rational universe that science affirms, and sees in this a deeper rationality at the heart of the cosmos. It was this step that led Anselm and Aquinas to attempt proofs for the existence of God. Theology 'sees' creation as an expression of the purposes of God. It sees the universe as an act of God's free will. The contingent nature of the universe (it need not have been the way it is) is seen as an expression of love. The laws of nature are seen as signs of God's faithfulness and reflect his character. Conscious human life is seen as the crown of God's creation, entering into the care and control of the world. Human free will and the role of chance within physical and biological processes are seen as expressions of God's self-denying love.

Polkinghorne is right to comment: 'The world created by the God of love and faithfulness may be expected to be characterised both by the openness of chance and the regularity of necessity.'[10]

Theology therefore welcomes the Anthropic Principle as evidence of the work of the creator. A finely tuned universe offers two possible explanations: Either there are many universes, and this is the one that by chance produced human life that is able to observe it; or there is a well-defined purpose behind creation, which theology locates in the will of God. Both of these explanations can only be argued for on various philosophical grounds, as this is the only universe we know about; but personal Christian experience will confirm this universe and our place in it as the result of God's loving purpose. The whole universe is filled with creativity, and we see the workings of both chance and necessity within it. In a deterministic, predictable universe there could be no creativity, except possibly the remote creative act of a God who lit the blue touch-paper of the Big Bang and stood back to see the show explode into life. But then if the universe was too much open to chance, human life would be but one of a million of scenarios, as suggested by Stephen Gould.[11] What science has observed is a universe in which chance and necessity both play a part. In the evolution of life there are animals and plants that mutate and survive and those that do not, but there is a 'guiding mechanism' of some kind that leads to the possibility of human beings; in physics there is uncertainty in the behaviour of the smallest particles and unpredictability in some systems (known as chaotic), but overall they operate within the framework of dependable physical laws. In all this the theologian sees the faithfulness of God, his planning, and his self-limiting love that allows a universe with free will.

Theology reflects upon the experience of the people of God in the Old Testament, New Testament, and the Church of Jesus Christ, and so builds a picture of the providential activity of God in the universe, as well as in human life. The regularities of nature, in the laws of physics, the motion of the sun and planets, the processes at work in the Earth's crustal layers, the weather systems and climate are all to be seen as demonstrations of God's providential ordering and care. The Bible points us towards seeing God as the source of order and towards seeing God intimately involved with his creation. Christian theology is the exciting enterprise of working out what it means to believe that this Creator God has made himself known in Jesus Christ. Theological reflection on the

Genesis account of creation draws out the insight that God has put relationship at the heart of the universe. Human beings are commissioned to care for the creation and to worship their creator, and since they are declared to be in the image of God we can see that God himself is in dynamic relationship with his creation. This comes into clear focus in Jesus Christ, where the divine takes human flesh and shares our life. Theology notes that the social sciences have recognised a human longing for ultimate reality and affirms that this longing finds its rest in the Christ of the gospel, whose resurrection is the ground, foretaste, and guarantee of life beyond death. Here is the disclosure of ultimate reality and purpose for humankind.

Yet theology, constructing this picture into which everything fits, is not without its difficulties. Theology seeks to make sense of the whole universe, but in doing this it is confronted by suffering and evil. We are forced to face questions such as, 'Does a creation that includes a Holocaust or a Bosnia demonstrate the work of a loving God?' Suffering presents us with a mystery, but Christianity meets this mystery at the profoundest level in the Cross of Christ. It is here that God involves himself in the suffering of the world, and this is a perception that we shall be working out in more detail in the course of this book.

Theology addresses science in a number of places. First of all, while science deals with the minutiae of particles or the mega-theories of the universe, theology attempts (as we have seen) to pull the whole of human experience together in its physical, mental, emotional, and spiritual aspects, producing a holistic view of the universe in which we exist. Secondly, theology aims to bring answers to the questions that science is posing. Theology, for instance, hears the questions raised by the fine-tuning of the universe and the Anthropic Principle and attempts to describe what it might mean to see the guiding hand of God within these. Lastly, theology speaks of the way that nothing lies outside the will of God and so is able to bring together all the large questions of meaning—the purpose of the universe, the meaning of life, and the question of what lies beyond death or beyond the end of the universe's life. Thus theology attempts to bring together the issues that affect both science and itself. Just because the theological view of the world is a total all-embracing view, Polkinghorne is right to conclude that there must be a consonance between science and theology.[12]

4. *'Let's Talk Together'*

Both theology and science are seeking to make sense of the world that they experience, and their methodologies are not totally different. In each case the reasonable search for understanding is motivated by a desire for truth and by certain beliefs (or theories). As such there must be a common ground for dialogue. Science is able to investigate the universe because human beings have a measure of transcendence over the world, and theology is able to bring a greater degree of understanding because it recognises the transcendence of God, who reveals his purposes to humankind.

Understanding the world in which we live is an undertaking that unites science and theology, and the search for truth will not succeed without a commitment to belief and a readiness for testing, confirmation, and correction. In his recent Gifford Lectures, Ian Barbour helpfully draws parallels between the methods of science and theology.[13] He points out that while a popular view of science is that it begins with observation and experimental data and produces concepts and theories out of them, in fact there is no such simple inductive approach. On the diagram he offers (reproduced in text figure 1:1) there is no direct upward arrow, but rather the path from observation to theory is only made by way of 'acts of creative imagination for which no rules can be given'.[14]

A scientific theory, once it has been developed, needs to be tested in order to be useful, and the vertical downward arrow in Barbour's diagram represents this process of moving from theory to observation by way of deduction. We can never test a theory on its own, however, since any

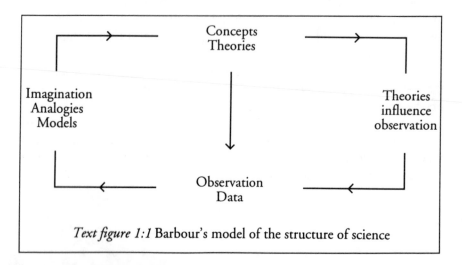

Text figure 1:1 Barbour's model of the structure of science

theory is also part of a network of theories and concepts that make up the store of scientific knowledge and tradition, and this influence is shown on the right-hand side.

Barbour rightly points us to the fact that there is no theory-free observation or experiment. The form of questions we ask will to a certain extent determine the answers we receive, as any national opinion pollster knows. For example, take the question of Sunday Trading, recently decided by the British Parliament; if in the run-up to that decision we had asked, 'Do you think that you should be denied the opportunity to buy D.I.Y. materials on a Sunday?' we would have obtained a completely different answer from that obtained by asking, 'Do you think that it would be right for the nation to lose a day for family time and rest, through Sunday being treated like any other day of the week?' The first question was the kind asked by the pro-Sunday opening lobby and the second by those against Sunday trading. A more neutral question would be 'Should all shops be free to open or remain closed on a Sunday?' We need to recognise that our preconceptions may determine our questions, and as a result our conclusions are always incomplete, tentative, and subject to revision. To take a scientific example, early geologists would not have sought to link the occurrence of earthquakes and volcanoes with fold mountain belts or deep sea trenches because they had no concept of plate tectonics and the movement of continents. So we see that there is an interconnection between models, concepts, theories, and observation and experiment.

Barbour suggests that the picture in theology is similar, with beliefs replacing theories and data coming in the form of religious experiences, ritual, and the traditions of the faith. I reproduce Barbour's corresponding diagram in text figure 1:2,[15] though I would want to add 'intuition' to the left-hand side. Barbour marks the downward arrow as a dashed line, as the testing of religious beliefs is more problematic than the testing of scientific theories. He does nevertheless think there are criteria for judging the adequacy of beliefs, and I shall be developing one general criterion myself shortly.

We must agree with Barbour that, like scientific observations, there are no uninterpreted religious experiences. The Christian experiences of conversion, God's presence, guidance, courage, peace, healing, moral obligation, or recognition of the universe as the ordering of God, can be put down to psychological feelings and needs, wishful thinking, coincidence, and irrational faith by those who do not hold such religious belief. Critics will be drawing upon different analogies and models to interpret the experience and will be influenced by different beliefs and worldviews. For this reason religious experiences need to be checked against the accepted beliefs of the community of faith over the past centuries and in the present.

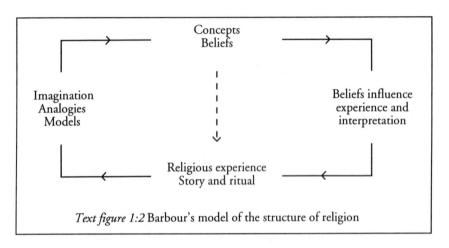

Text figure 1:2 Barbour's model of the structure of religion

Both science and theology use models to present meaning and to evoke understanding. Science collects data and builds a model that may form the basis of a theory. To take an example from what used to be my own professional area, geologists collect the data of earthquake epicentres, fracture patterns, oceanic topography, subsurface structures, distribution of volcanoes, igneous and metamorphic rocks, together with fossils and evidence of past climates contained in sedimentary rocks, and then produce a plate tectonics model of the Earth's crust: see text figure 4:1. The model (in this case a patchwork of six 'plates') displays what cannot be observed directly and is therefore usually regarded with what has been called a 'critical realism'[16]; there is some caution about how far, how adequately, and in what ways it describes the phenomenon it is portraying (as with the model of light travelling in waves or particles), but it is still believed to represent what is really there. It helps understanding, promotes the development of theories, and can be confirmed or modified by further information arising within the scientific community.

In a similar way, theology presents models of God, which are largely derived from the images and metaphors contained in biblical accounts of people's experience of their relationship with God and his unveiling of himself to them. For example, we develop the model of God as Father, which has its main basis in the unique experience of Sonship by Jesus Christ who in turn taught his disciples to address God as 'Father'; this model is tested through our own personal experiences and those of the community of faith through the ages. The model of 'Father' may, of course, be difficult to use for those who have had an experience of human fathers that was destructive or dominating, and so it is critical that all models of God should be received and understood in the context of the whole community of faith and not individualistically. The community preserves the witness to God's revelation of himself that re-defines all human concepts of relationship; in this case, the way that Jesus revealed the Fatherhood of God challenges all human ideas of patriarchy. Religious models thus help our understanding but also have the additional function of evoking a response from people. In this sense they have an important role in evangelism.

In commenting upon Barbour's two diagrams (or 'models'), I have been indicating my appreciation for their illuminating quality. My aim in this book, however, is to work towards an integration of a scientific and theological view of the world, and so I venture to include a third diagram, which is indebted to the other two but which attempts to express the interactions between the approaches of science and theology to the world. It is the first of several diagrams in this book where I attempt to bring a theological and scientific world-view into one perspective (see also text figures 5:1, 7:1, 7:2).

In spite of comparisons between science and theology, there have been, and still are, conflicts between these two fundamental sources of human knowledge about the world. The conflict is at its most acute between the scientific materialist and the biblical literalist, and these ways of thinking are represented on the 'integrated model' (text figure 1:3) by the upward vertical arrow. Both derive from an attempt to make direct inductive arguments, from either religious experience or observed data, without being sensitive to the part played by models, imagination, and analogies. From the scientific side, science is seen as the only source of reliable, factual knowledge, while religion is seen to be subjective, emotional, traditional (i.e. old-fashioned), and superstitious. From the side of

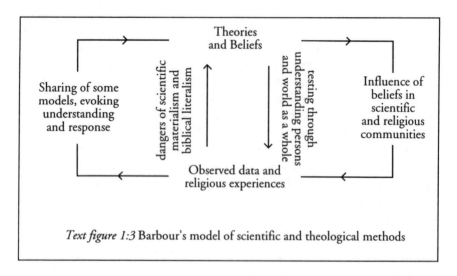

Text figure 1:3 Barbour's model of scientific and theological methods

biblical literalism, science is seen as deceived and deceiving, and centred upon sinful human beings, while uncritical biblical study provides the only sure truth. Biblical literalism confronted Galileo, Newton, Lyell, and Darwin and has continued as a force in the Church, first in the United Kingdom, and more recently in the United States of America through 'creation science'. The lack of understanding of what science is actually saying leads many Christians to fall back on a dogmatic presentation of the Bible and to have a total disengagement with the discoveries of modern science. Scientists, likewise, with an inadequate understanding of why the Bible was written and of what it is actually saying, may dismiss the claims of theology and operate as if the material world were the sum total of reality.

Recent disasters in the field of science have led to a questioning of the unchecked optimism and reliability associated with scientific and technological advancement. The development and use of nuclear bombs, the risks associated with nuclear power, the environmental pollution associated with industry, disastrous side effects of drugs such as Thalidomide, and the ethical questions raised by advances in genetics and embryology have all contributed to a growing distrust of science. Theology has also had its problems in recent times. Publicity is given to scholarly arguments about the resurrection of Christ, the ordination of women, divorce and the family, and abortion. But the debate is rarely conducted in a way that contacts the real concerns of people in their daily lives, and so the impression is given that theology is a rarified and abstract exercise and that no reliable conclusions can be reached about Christian truths. On the one hand, then, there is a decline in church attendance in Britain as in other Western industrialised societies. On the other, the failure of science to produce 'Utopia' and its emphasis on observed facts may account for the present lack of interest in science and technology in schools in Britain. It is significant that people have sought satisfaction of their spiritual hunger in movements that tend to hold human beings and the world together in some sort of harmonious relationship—neo-paganism, New Age, and Western versions of Eastern religion.

For the sake of both science and religion, there is therefore a clear need for dialogue between the Christian faith and the scientific enterprise. In our age science has found a new humility through failure, blunder, and the recognition of a universe that is not infinite, but which has a beginning and an end. Western theologians and the Western Church have also begun to recognise that there are serious questions being asked of it by cosmology, medical science, and by ordinary people outside the church, who, although wanting something in which to believe, are no longer content unquestioningly to accept the propositions of the Christian faith. While science is popularly seen as objective, public, and factual, and theology is seen as subjective, personal, and related to feelings, there is a recognition that human beings have a psychosomatic unity that requires a holistic world-view. The possibility of a bringing together of science and theology exists today, more than ever before, in the questions raised by modern cosmologists, and the readiness for discussion of these issues is underlined by the popularity of their publications.

In the 'integrated model' I offer (text figure 1:3), the vertical downward arrow represents this coming together of the scientific and the theological approaches to the world. Scientific theory and religious belief can be tested against data and experience through their adequacy in explaining the world as a whole, in its physical, moral, and spiritual dimensions. Neither can do this on its own, though in openness to each other they will do so with different emphases. Science seeks to explain the material world, to ask objective questions, and to present proofs that are demonstrated in repeatable experiments. Rational and logical arguments are a vital part of its method. But it cannot proceed much further in being of use to humankind unless it also takes account of moral issues.

Theology does seek to explain the whole of human experience, both the material and the spiritual world; it asks questions about the existence of order and beauty in the world and seeks to address human feelings of guilt, anxiety, fear, meaning, hope, forgiveness, and wholeness (*shalom*). But it cannot include an understanding of the physical world in its total picture without the help of science. Peacocke is right to recognise that interaction is seen in

> the understanding of the human person as a psychosomatic unity in both science and religion; the interaction of biological evolutionary ideas with the sense of God as an immanent ever-working creator; or reflections on the origin of the cosmos induced by astrophysics and cosmology, on the one hand, and clarification of the Judeo-Christian doctrine of creation on the other.[17]

In linking theory with experience, the influence of networks of belief in the scientific and religious communities is a crucial context (as indicated by the right-hand side of text figure 1:3). Nor must we treat these as separate communities, but rather overlapping ones. Science flourished in a Christian culture because the Christian worldview saw creation as contingent. Nature was not a necessary extension of the being of God; it was indwelt by God who had created it, but it was not divine in itself. So human beings could observe, examine, experiment, discover, and understand. Newton began by talking about 'thinking God's thoughts after him', and the Cavendish Laboratory at Cambridge had the inscription 'To the glory of God' above the doorway; but soon God was banished to the periphery of a mechanical and predictable universe. The recognition by Darwin of a process by which life might have evolved by natural means, with no reference to God, seemed to leave no place for the conception of the divine. With the new cosmology, however, the door of opportunity for dialogue has been opened wide, because it is the scientists, and not the theologians, who are posing the questions about design, purpose, and meaning. This has also meant that there is an intriguing coming together of 'models' that evoke understanding and create response; Arthur Peacocke offers an example of the way this kind of integration can happen, giving trinitarian theology a scientific perspective within a sacramental view of the cosmos:

The world is created and sustained in being by the will of God, the will of perfect love. The Son, or Word of God (the Logos), is the all-sufficient principle and form of this created order. At every level, this order reflects in its own measure something of the quality of deity. From atom and molecule to mammal and man each by its appropriate order and function expresses the design inherent in it, and contributes, so far as it can by failure or success, to the fulfilment of the common purpose. The continuing creative power is God as Holy Spirit.[18]

Peacocke writes here as both a biochemist and a Christian theologian; but we have already noted that the physicist Paul Davies, who is not a Christian believer, is prepared to use the word 'God' as a model to express the wonder and perplexity that modern cosmologists find themselves in when faced with the questions raised by a finely tuned universe displaying an Anthropic Principle. There are certainly dangers of misunderstanding with a sharing of 'models', whether by theologians or scientists, and we must avoid a synthesis that ignores the differences between science and theology; but there is also a great deal of room for new illumination. Throughout this book, in fact, I shall be asking what kind of image of God is suggested by the models of science that we adopt or reject.

5. Cheap Tricks? and Other Dangers

We are constantly faced with the demand for instant analysis and with catchy headlines, which result in a popular science, designed not so much to inform as to sell newspapers or increase the viewing audience. Take, for example, an article that appeared in the *Reader's Digest* in 1973, entitled 'New Quest for Life in Space,' and sub-headed 'The search may yet unveil the secret of our Earth's origin—and its destiny.' The article begins with the discovery of molecules of water and ammonia in interstellar space by a team of astronomers and physicists at the University of California's Hat Creek Observatory and comments, 'If these two molecules vital to life were present in outer space, were there perhaps more?' The author goes on to discuss Black Holes and then gives his conclusion, which presupposes life elsewhere in the universe:

Further, stimulating the search for extraterrestrial life could produce tremendous rewards for mankind. Today, we have no idea where we came from or where as a species, we are heading. If we discover advanced civilizations elsewhere, we will know at least that we are part of a universal scheme of things. If we can ever get in touch with such civilizations, we may gain invaluable insights as to how far our minds and spirits can evolve.[19]

All of this was built on the discovery of water and ammonia molecules in space! But let us not be too harsh in our judgement, for this is the quick, sensational conclusion that most people want to read.

A more recent example involved the important cosmological discovery in April 1992 by NASA's COBE (Cosmic Background Explorer) satellite: Ripples were found in the background radiation at the farthest extent of the universe. The newspapers, television, and radio leapt upon the story with headlines on 24 April such as 'The secret of the universe —found' and 'God is redundant.' When John Humphries interviewed the project director, George Smoot, on Radio 4's "Today" programme and confronted him with the headlines of God's redundancy, the scientist calmly told him that the discovery was a further pointer to purpose in the origin of the universe and of human life. The ripples supported the Big Bang hypothesis of the universe's origin and were seen as the seeds from which the galaxies might have been formed. Their discovery produced a great sense of relief for many cosmologists, confirming their theory of an expanding universe. The headline 'God is redundant', however, is far more exciting and will sell far more newspapers than talk of confirming scientific theories about the initial physical conditions of the universe.

Before we go further with our exploration of science and theology we will need to recognise the short shelf-life of many scientific theories. Scientists, in their search for truth and understanding, are not afraid of suggesting hypotheses, or provisional models, which may be modified or abandoned as further research is carried out. In my own geological research[20] I was able to make new suggestions regarding a major fracture in the rocks of the South Wales Coalfield because new road cuttings and boreholes for opencast coal sites provided previously unknown information. My conclusions, however, have since had to be modified in the light of new evidence provided by the construction of a major trunk road. There will clearly be dangers in basing our theology on the latest scientific theories. This was the problem that advocates of Natural Theology encountered in the nineteenth century when, having drawn their conclusions from Newton's model of a mechanistic universe in which living things could only be explained as the designed creation of God, they were faced by Darwin's theory of evolution, whereby the variety of living things was seen to have brought itself into being through the process of natural selection.

A further danger results from a refusal to allow dialogue to take place between science and theology. This tends to show itself in one of two ways, to which we have already alluded above in considering 'scientific materialism' and 'biblical literalism'. The first is a basic distrust in the reliability or reasonable nature of Scripture, Church tradition, and Christian belief. This leads to an attitude that accepts uncritically every new suggestion made by science and seeks in some way to accommodate this into belief. This view will assume that science is right, and so where it contradicts religious belief, it is always that belief that must be altered. The second is a basic distrust in science and scientists, whether they are Christians or have no beliefs at all, based on a dogmatic attitude toward Scripture, which accepts every verse in a literal and uncritical way. I would maintain that these are the 'safe' positions to take, involving no mental struggles or heart searching—as long as you are able to hold your ground. But I believe that real theology must be worked out in the grey and uncertain areas of dialogue and interaction between science and theology. This will mean taking science seriously, seeking to understand what science is revealing and the questions and implications of its findings for the Christian faith. It will also mean taking Scripture and the doctrine of the Church seriously; it will mean listening to critical scholarship and philosophical debate and drawing a deeper understanding from seeking to address the questions and issues raised by such works.

Finally, we will have to recognise that there are no proofs for the existence of God to be found in this dialogue and voyage of discovery. As we listen to and seek to understand the more recent findings of the physical and natural sciences, we will recognise conclusions that support the reasonableness of Christian belief. For example, The Anthropic Principle demonstrates the reasonableness of believing in a creator God, whose purpose has been to bring into existence a universe in which conscious self-aware human beings have a central place. The picture of an evolving universe with the evolution of carbon-based life on Earth presents a reasonable basis for belief in a God who is intimately involved with his creation. But none of this is proof; a step of faith is required. In particular, the Christian faith accepts the God of creation revealed in nature and in the Scriptures as the same God who was incarnate in the world in Jesus Christ and who encounters believers in their experience of him.

6. A Voyage of Discovery

Carl Sagan concludes his introduction to Stephen Hawking's book *A Brief History of Time* with these words:

> This is also a book about God . . . or perhaps about the absence of God. The word God fills these pages. Hawking embarks on a quest to answer Einstein's famous question about whether God had any choice in creating the universe. Hawking is attempting, as he explicitly states, to understand the mind of God. And this makes all the more unexpected the conclusion of the effort, at least so far: a universe with no edge in space, no beginning or end in time, and nothing for a Creator to do.[21]

In passing we may note that Hawking's understanding of the space-time dimensions of the universe as indicated in Sagan's summary is rather out of step with other cosmologists.[22] But mainly I want to refer to Sagan's last phrase; the purpose of my book is quite opposite from Hawking's here. It is to present a dialogue between science and theology in which the role of the Creator becomes increasingly clear in his transcendence, immanence, and self-limiting love. There is a limit as to how far science can ever take us in our understanding of the world in which we live. The former NASA astrophysicist, Robert Jastrow, was probably correct in his assessment:

> For the scientist who has lived by his faith in the power of reason, the story ends like a bad dream. He has scaled the mountains of ignorance; he is about to conquer the highest peak; and as he pulls himself over the final rock, he is greeted by a band of theologians who have been sitting there for centuries.[23]

In the following chapters we shall begin to bring together both the mountaineering feats of the scientists and the mountaintop views of the theologians, and so seek to find a solid ground for an apologetic of Christian faith in the Creator and Sustainer of the universe. From an understanding of both science and theology we shall seek to find a way of presenting and proclaiming the gospel of Christ that will encounter people in their experience of the world at the end of the twentieth century.

Notes to Chapter 1

[1]Ecclesiastes 1:17 (New International Version).

[2]D. N. Adams, *The Hitch-Hiker's Guide to the Galaxy* (London: Pan Books Ltd., 1979) 128.

[3]L. Newbigin, *Foolishness to the Greeks—The Gospel and Western Culture* (London: SPCK, 1986) 18-19.

[4]P. Davies, *God and the New Physics* (London: Dent, 1983) 3.

[5]S. W. Hawking, *A Brief History of Time* (London and New York: Bantam Press, 1988) 78.

[6]M. Polanyi, *Personal Knowledge* (London: Routledge & Kegan Paul, 1958).

[7]P. Davies, *The Mind of God* (New York and London: Simon & Schuster, 1992) 20.

[8]L. Newbigin, *The Gospel in a Pluralist Society* (London: SPCK, 1989) 52.

[9]J. Polkinghorne, *One World—the Interaction of Science and Theology* (London: SPCK, 1986) 29.

[10]J. Polkinghorne, *Science and Creation* (London: SPCK, 1988) 52.

[11]S. J. Gould, *Wonderful Life—The Burgess Shale and the Nature of History* (London: Hutchinson Radius, 1990) 320.

[12]Polkinghorne, *Science and Creation*, 1f.

[13]I. G. Barbour, 'Models and Paradigms' in *Religion in an Age of Science,* Gifford Lectures 1989–1991, Vol. 1 (London: Harper & Row, 1990).

[14]Ibid., 32.

[15]Ibid., 36.

[16]See I. G. Barbour, *Myths, Models and Paradigms. The Nature of Scientific and Religious Language* (London: SCM, 1974) 47-48.

[17]A. Peacocke, *Theology for a Scientific Age—Being and Becoming, Natural and Divine* (Oxford: Blackwell, 1990) 5.

[18]A. Peacocke, *God and the New Biology* (London: Dent, 1986) 125.

[19]J. Miller, 'New Quest for Life in Space' in *Reader's Digest* (June 1973): 43-46.

[20]J. D. Weaver, *The Swansea Valley Disturbance,* unpublished Ph.D. Thesis (Swansea: University of Wales, 1972).

[21]C. Sagan, 'Introduction' in *A Brief History of Time,* by S. W. Hawking (London and New York: Bantam Press, 1988) x.

[22]He develops a mathematical model of a finite universe with no boundaries, a self-contained universe of four-dimensional space-time; this is not a concept widely shared by other cosmologists. See his *A Brief History of Time*, 116ff.

[23]R. D. Jastrow, *Reader's Digest* (October 1980): 57, quoted in D. Wilkinson, *God, the Big Bang and Stephen Hawking* (Tunbridge Wells: Monarch, 1993) 71.

2

'Lift your eyes and look to the heavens'[1]

The Witness of Physics and Cosmology

In the last chapter I mentioned the first appearance of the powerful computer named 'Deep Thought', created by Douglas Adams in *The Hitch-Hiker's Guide to the Galaxy*. Adams describes how, seventy-five thousand generations later, two more programmers stand in front of the computer, expectant to hear 'the answer to the great question of life'.

'. . . Good morning,' said Deep Thought at last.

'Er . . . Good-morning, O Deep Thought,' said Loonquawl nervously, 'do you have . . . er, that is. . . .'

'An answer for you?' interrupted Deep Thought majestically. 'Yes, I have.'

'To Everything? To the great Question of Life, the Universe and Everything?'

'Yes'. . .

'Though I don't think,' added Deep Thought, 'that you're going to like it.'

'Tell us!'

'All right,' said Deep Thought. 'The Answer to the Great Question . . . Of life, the Universe and Everything'. . . .

'Is. . . .'

'Yes??? . . .'

'Forty-two', said Deep Thought, with infinite majesty and calm.

'Forty-two!' yelled Loonquawl. 'Is that all you've got to show for seven and a half million years' work?'

'I checked it very thoroughly,' said the computer, 'and that quite definitely is the answer. I think the problem, to be quite honest with you, is that you've never actually known what the question is'. . . .

'Look, all right, all right,' said Loonquawl, 'can you just please tell us the question?'

'The Ultimate Question?'

'Yes'. . . .

Deep Thought pondered for a moment.

'Tricky,' he said.[2]

Modern scientific discoveries are providing us with many answers to
the nature of life, the universe, and everything, but the problem of the
question of ultimate meaning remains. In the eighteenth century many
scientific thinkers supposed they had finally reached all the answers, a
thought that is captured in Alexander Pope's memorable lines:

> Nature and nature's laws lay hid in night.
>   God said: 'Let Newton be.'
>   And all was light!

As we seek to discover exactly what light has been shed on our understanding of the universe by cosmological studies we will indeed look
at Newton, together with both his predecessors and his successors. We
will find that the first result of scientific research was the discovery of
order in the physical world. This order, or an appearance of repeated patterns, was formulated by scientists into laws. It seemed to them that on
both the mega-scale of the universe itself and on the micro-scale of atoms
and molecules the world of nature obeyed a small number of fundamental
laws.

In the early years of the seventeenth century, this process of discovery and formulation was accompanied by a sense of wonder among
scientists as they considered themselves to be uncovering more of the
glory of God's creation. As they made further discoveries that seemed to
contradict a literal interpretation of the Bible, or the teaching of the
Church's own philosophers, however, they increasingly found themselves
in conflict with religion. Thus God at first became the 'God of the gaps',
filling in the spaces where scientific knowledge was deficient. Then God
was pushed out of the arena of the 'real world' of factual knowledge into
the subjective world of human feelings and experience. But as we come
to the end of the twentieth century, we find a scene that is similar in one
respect and yet strikingly different in another. In continuity with earlier
convictions about physical laws, we find modern cosmologists beginning
to discuss the possibility of finding some 'super law' to explain everything in the whole of the universe; yet, as I want to show, they are more
ready than their predecessors to employ a theistic kind of language in
their theorizing, in a manner that opens up fascinating possibilities for
Christian thinking as well as some traps for the unwary apologist.

John Barrow, Professor of Astronomy at the University of Sussex, writes at the beginning of his latest book: 'The theologians think they know the questions but cannot understand the answers. The physicists think they know the answers but don't know the questions.'[3] From a Newtonian universe that seemed mathematically predictable to the physicists of today with their 'grand unifying theories', the question that is constantly asked is this: can there be a Theory of Everything? In this study I am standing with the scientists of today in affirming the continuing usefulness of the concepts of 'order' and 'law' in understanding the nature of the universe, though these are less popular categories in a great deal of contemporary theology, and I admit that they need some qualification. But with the Christian theologians I want to go on to ask: if there are such ultimate explanations, how do they affect our understanding of God and creation?

1. Discovering Order in the Universe

We begin our historical review with a Polish priest, Nicolaus Copernicus (1473–1543), who began to study the movements of the planets in 1513. He was the first person to suggest that the Sun and not the Earth was the centre of our Solar System. He set out his heliocentric theory in his work *De revolutionibus orbium coelestium*, which was published in 1543 shortly before his death. Copernicus was followed by the Italian Catholic philosopher, Galilei Galileo (1564–1642), who developed a telescope with a magnification of thirty-two, capable of observing the planets. Galileo adopted the Copernican heliocentric theory, observing the mountainous regions of the Moon, the stars of the Milky Way, the satellites of Jupiter, the phases of Venus, and Sun spots. Galileo's discoveries, however, brought him into conflict with the Catholic Church.

His translation of Copernicus' theory into Italian became popular reading in the universities, and soon rival academics were seeking to persuade the Catholic Church to ban Copernicanism. Galileo went to see the ecclesiastical authorities in Rome and argued that the Bible was not to be understood as a scientific document. In support of this approach, he pointed out that there was a long tradition of considering the Bible to be allegorical where it appeared to be in conflict with common sense. The Church authorities would not listen to Galileo and in 1616 declared that Copernicanism was erroneous and forced Galileo to recant. When in 1632 he wrote a book discussing the theories of Aristotle and Copernicus, *Dialogue Concerning the Two Chief World Systems*, he was brought before the Inquisition, who placed him under house arrest for life and again forced him to recant. But in 1638, while still under house arrest, he wrote *Two New Sciences*, which was smuggled out of Italy and published in Holland. This book more than his support of Copernicus became the genesis of modern physics.[4] Viviani, one of Galileo's students, wrote this epitaph of his master:

> With philosophic and Christian firmness he rendered up his soul to his Creator, sending it, as he liked to believe, to enjoy and to watch from a clear vantage point those eternal and immutable marvels which he, by means of a fragile device, had brought closer to our mortal eyes with such eagerness and impatience.[5]

Galileo's writings, especially in the area of dynamics, which derived in large part from his studies of ballistics, paved the way for Newton. Yet before we consider Newton, we need to look at one more of his predecessors, namely the German astronomer Johann Kepler (1571–1630).

Kepler had crippled hands and an impaired eyesight, the result of smallpox, which he caught at the age of four. This bodily infirmity, combined with a high mental aptitude was eventually considered to indicate a theological vocation! At the age of twenty-three he was persuaded reluctantly to turn aside from the Christian ministry and accept the Chair of Science at Gratz. He too had learned Copernican principles and devoted much of his attention to the orbit of Mars. Its eccentricity was a problem to the theory of planetary motion that he published in 1609. Kepler established the law of elliptical orbits of the planets and formulated important truths that applied to gravity, in particular recognising that the tides on Earth could be ascribed to lunar attraction. Kepler's demonstration that the planes of all planetary orbits pass through the centre of the Sun, coupled with his clear recognition of the Sun as the moving power of the system, entitles him to rank as the founder of physical astronomy.

Sir Isaac Newton (1642–1727), an English mathematician and physicist, probably contributed more to scientific understanding than any other man or woman before or since. His laws of motion and gravity made sense of the planetary observations of Kepler. Newton's discovery of gravity in 1666 (apples fall off trees, according to the apocryphal story) laid the foundations of a scientific world-view that has dominated western society for 300 years. Newton presented his three laws of motion in 1687 in his magnum opus: *Philosophiae naturalis principia mathematica.* Through Newton's work we have the picture of a dynamic universe, which is never at rest and is always moving. It is infinite and has no centre.

For Newton God was not at the centre of the natural process but outside, holding the whole dynamic system within a timeless and motionless framework. Newton thought of the universe as the rational design of God, with its infinite size related to the all-embracing Spirit of God. For Newton, God was the creator and the repairer of the universe. He kept the planets from crashing into each other and preserved the mechanism of the universe in good order. Newton was a deeply religious man, approaching the Bible as literal truth, and attempting to develop a Biblical chronology. His scientific view of God outside the universe, however, did not allow for the incarnation of God in Jesus Christ, and Newton's views were Unitarian and Arian in content. God was the controlling force outside the universe, keeping the boundaries, and such a God could not be on the inside as one of its participants.

Newton's work both affirmed God and at the same time limited what he could be and do. Typical of eighteenth-century thinking was the idea that God could be read out of nature in a fairly mechanical way. God guaranteed the design and the content of the universe, but no more. The possibility of miracles, revelation, or intervention by God was not possible within a universe governed by natural laws. Immediate and new actions of God would have to belong to a different sphere. Here was laid the basis of a dualism between religious experience and the scientific observation of nature that is still with us.

Newton's scientific world-view of an infinite, predictable, mechanical universe would hold centre stage for over one hundred years, until the revolutionary discoveries of Albert Einstein (1879–1955). But Albert Einstein also had some important predecessors. First there was William Thomson, Lord Kelvin, who made a study of heat and work—the field of thermodynamics. In 1848 he developed the Kelvin temperature scale and in 1851 the principles that now form the second law of thermodynamics. Those principles stated that heat can only be directly transferred from a hotter to a cooler body. For heat to be transferred from a cooler to a hotter body, work must be done. It follows therefore that it is impossible to convert heat into work without some other effect, and in an isolated system this effect is an increase in entropy, or disorder. The increase in entropy represents the energy that is no longer available for doing work in that system. It is not possible to reverse the process, and within the universe the level of entropy, or disorder, is constantly increasing. This has led to the speculative theory of the final state of the universe, known as 'Heat Death.' If the universe is an isolated system, then its entropy must tend toward a maximum, at which all energy is degraded to uniform heat, everything is totally disordered and no change is possible. In my own explorations in this study, the factor of entropy will play a significant part.

Another important predecessor of Einstein was James Clerk Maxwell, a Scottish physicist who became the first director of the Cavendish Laboratory at Cambridge. Maxwell developed the theory of electromagnetism and predicted electromagnetic radiation. These theories arguably rank in importance with Newton's theory of gravity and motion. In 1897 J. J. Thompson discovered electrons, and in 1911 Ernest Rutherford discovered the atomic nucleus with electrons in orbit. In 1900 Max Planck (1858–1947), a German physicist, proposed the quantum theory, which stated that energy is emitted in packets called photons or quanta. He introduced this theory to explain the distribution of energy across the range of frequencies radiated by hot objects. He showed that the amount of energy in each quantum increased as the wavelength of the radiation became shorter. His theory marks the divide between the classical physics of Newton, Kelvin, and Maxwell and the modern physics of Einstein. He received the recognition of his work with the award of the Nobel Prize for Physics in 1918. We have moved from the very big scale—the universe—to the very small scale—the behaviour of atomic and subatomic particles—but before pursuing this micro-world further, we need to go back to look at the universe through the eyes of Einstein and his successors.

2. Discovering the Wholeness of Space and Time

Einstein recognised that what was important was that the speed of light was always the same, no matter how you measured it. This was the basis of his Special Theory of Relativity. He stated that for observers who were not in movement the laws of physics should remain the same. The measurement of time, however, depended on one's acceleration; for example, clocks travelling at speeds close to the speed of light would appear to run slower than those that were stationary. As speed increased he discovered that mass also increases and that length contracts. In 1915 Einstein presented his General Theory of Relativity, which demonstrated that gravity is a field like a magnetic field and is described in the concept of a space-time continuum. This is the combination of three-dimensional space with the fourth dimension of time. Thus our passage through time as well as through space can be thought of as a compound motion through space-time. The gravitational field was demonstrated to limit the movement of atoms, bend light rays, stretch space, and make time work like elastic. One recent commentator on this theory has helpfully likened space-time to a rubber sheet stretched flat. If a heavy object such as a golf ball were to be placed on it, the sheet would change shape; there would be a downward curvature in the sheet.[6] This is the way that gravity affects space-time.

Einstein believed in a changeless, uncreated cosmos, with matter evenly distributed. In itself, however, the General theory of Relativity actually required an expanding universe, as in a static universe the gravitational force would be destructive, causing the whole system to collapse in on itself. Einstein therefore introduced a cosmic constant to counteract the gravitational force. The one thing that his theory did do was to undermine the Newtonian view of a universe working like a machine, composed of individual parts. Einstein's universe is an interacting whole of space and time.

God, for Einstein was manifested in the laws of nature: impersonal, sublime, beautiful, indifferent to human beings, but still important to them.[7] Einstein affirmed the religious sense of wonder and mystery when looking at creation but could not accept the idea of a personal God. God was the great unknown and unknowable. Human beings were part of the mystery; he said, 'The most incomprehensible thing about the universe is that it is comprehensible.'[8]

Einstein received the Nobel Prize for Physics in 1922 but, as a Jew, was forced to leave a Germany under the Nazi government in 1932. In 1939 he recognised the dangers of developments in atomic physics and warned President Roosevelt of the potential of nuclear energy in the hands of the Nazis. He himself became involved in the United States' own development of the atom bomb.

3. Discovering a Universe with a Beginning and an End

Within Einstein's theory there was need of an expanding force to counteract the gravitational force. It was known that a galaxy, because of its make-up of stars and gases, emits light with its own particular spectrum. Vesto Melvin Slipher, in 1912, noted that there was a shift towards the red end of the spectrum in the light received from galaxies. This indicated that they were moving away from us at speeds greater than 600 miles/sec.[9] Edwin Hubble, in 1929, extended this work demonstrating that the further away a galaxy was, the faster it was moving, up to 25,000 miles/sec. On this basis the universe had a beginning, which Hubble calculated to be about two billion years Before the Present (B.P.).

In the 1950s and 1960s there was debate between those who advocated the concept of a universe beginning with an explosive 'Big Bang' and those who held to the concept of a steady-state. Fred Hoyle, Thomas Gold, and Hermann Bondi wanted a steady state universe, where expansion was accompanied by a continuous creation of matter. Hoyle was greatly in favour of the latter and explicitly included in his reasons that it did not require a God, and was furthest away from the account of creation in Genesis chapter 1. The steady state theory gave an eternal ground to the existence of the universe, and it has been suggested convincingly by Angela Tilby[10] that it was one of the background cultural influences that led theologians like John A. T. Robinson to regard God less as personal than as 'the ultimate reality' and Paul Tillich to suggest that God was not exterior to the universe but 'the ground of our being'. There is a warning here for all theologians that they should take care in aligning theology with scientific theories, which are constantly being revised as new facts come to light.

Confirmation for the view of an expanding universe came through the field of radio astronomy in 1963 when Quasars were identified moving away at 150,000 miles/sec. The light from these must have been travelling for several billion years, and as a result of these findings the age of the universe was estimated at some 10,000 million years B.P. This work also indicated that those quasars that were further away were denser in mass, and their very high density was evidence that the universe had changed with time. The steady state theory of Gold and Bondi was finally shattered by the discovery, in 1965, of background heat radiation in the universe. This background radiation in the universe was seen to be the relic of the big-bang fireball that marked the beginning to this expanding universe. This thermal radiation has a temperature of 2.7° Absolute or -270.3° Celsius, which, although very cold, is the left-over 'heat' of the big bang itself.[11] Enormous quantities of heat would have been generated in the first moments of the universe's existence, but as the universe expanded it cooled, losing temperature by half each time it doubled in size. In 1992 the NASA Cosmic Background Explorer Satellite (COBE) detected very small variations in the background radiation at the edge of the universe. These variations showed that the distribution of matter in the universe was not uniform but 'lumpy.' Such differences in density of matter were just what was needed to explain the birth of galaxies, through condensing and attraction of particles. So we see that the universe has a biography—a beginning and an end yet to be written.

4. The Mystery of the Beginning

Into the debate come the figures of Roger Penrose (Oxford), Stephen Hawking (Cambridge), Paul Davies (formerly Newcastle, now at the University of Adelaide), and John Barrow (University of Sussex), all of whom have devoted their attention to the nature of the beginning of the universe. Hubble in the 1920s had suggested that the universe was expanding, which implied a universe with a beginning. The discovery in the 1960s of a cosmic heat radiation field had supported a hot 'big bang' at the start of it all. Einstein's theory of general relativity has been used to confirm predictions based on the point when the universe is presumed to have been one second old. Thus, there is a remarkable general agreement among scientists (although not complete understanding), about the history of the universe from one second until the present time, approximately fifteen billion years later. What remains more contestable and mysterious are the initial conditions that led to the present state of the universe. This involves high-energy physics and the ultimate structure of elementary particles of matter.[12] The problem with that first second of creation is two-fold: We need to know how elementary particles would behave under the conditions of the big bang, and we need to know the conditions of the early universe to discover how the elementary particles would behave. The search for special initial conditions for the universe looks for laws and conditions that transcend the normal experience of classical physics.[13]

The proposed Big Bang is not only the creation of matter but also of space and time. Both Aristotle among the Greek philosophers and Augustine among the Christian had maintained that before the universe came into being there was no time; there could be no concept of 'before.' God created time along with the universe. By contrast Newton had an image of transcendent absolute time, which shadowed the passage of events; time and space were infinite. Einstein seems to have returned to Augustine, linking time and space together and showing that time can never be separated from the observer. Moreover, with Einstein's general theory of relativity it is possible to have 'singularities' of space-time, which mark out the boundary of space and time. If we run the expanding universe backwards we come to a single point of infinite density—of no volume, no space, nothing outside of it—a 'singularity'—a mathematical concept of infinity.

Einstein linked energy to matter in the equation $E = mc^2$ (where 'E' is energy, 'm' is mass, and 'c' is a constant equating to the speed of light), which implies that matter can theoretically be produced from energy. This was demonstrated in laboratory experiments in the 1930s. This, of course, does not explain away creation, for we will need pre-existing energy to be converted into material. At this point Christians will need to beware of rolling in God as the 'Prime Mover' or ultimate source of energy, as the net result of such a suggestion would be Newton's God, who was outside creation. Although the concept of a 'Prime Mover' has a long tradition in Christian thinking from the early Church Fathers' use of Aristotle to Aquinas, it will always have this inherent danger of making God external to his own creation rather than a participant within it.

In 1965 Roger Penrose showed that singularities are not mere mathematical concepts, but actually exist in the real universe. He demonstrated the presence of 'black holes', which are the location of collapsed stars (destroyed in the explosive violence of a supernova) that leave a density so great that light cannot escape its gravitational pull. The matter of the star is compressed into a region of zero volume, so that the density of matter and the curvature of space-time become infinite. This is the nature of a singularity.[14] Stephen Hawking realised that the reverse would also hold true, and in 1970 Penrose and Hawking together postulated a physical singularity as the beginning of the universe. Penrose and Hawking suggested that the universe originated as a singularity—a boundary point at the beginning of space-time when the whole universe was concentrated at one point. Here, the density of the universe would be infinitely large, its size infinitely small, and its energy infinitely high. Events before the Big Bang can have no consequences, and so they should not form part of a scientific model of the universe.[15] We therefore remove any such consequences from our model and say that time had a beginning at the Big Bang.

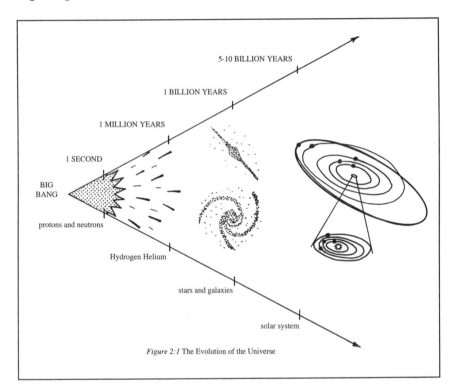

Figure 2:1 The Evolution of the Universe

At the Big Bang the universe is thought to have had zero size and so to have been infinitely hot. As it expanded, its temperature dropped. Hawking calculated that in this model about one hundred seconds after the initial big bang twenty-five percent of the protons and neutrons would have been formed into the nuclei of helium, this at a temperature in excess of one billion degrees celsius. It would be over one million years before the temperature would have dropped sufficiently for the electrons and nuclei to form atoms. As some areas cooled faster, they would stop expanding, start to collapse, develop a spin, and eventually spin fast enough to balance the attraction of gravity and form disc-like rotating galaxies. Hydrogen and helium gas in such galaxies would break up into smaller clouds, which would collapse under gravity leading to colliding atoms heating up to start nuclear fusion reactions and form stars. In some of these stars the helium would be converted into heavier elements like oxygen and carbon. Then, as the central area of the star collapsed to a neutron star or a black hole, the outer regions would be blown off in an explosion—a supernova. This in turn would produce the raw material for more stars, and also for planets. Planets would have been formed as clouds of dust and gas were pulled, by gravity, into the orbit of other stars (as shown in text figure 2:1).

5. Ultimate Explanations?

For Hawking, to be left with merely a 'singularity' as the solution to the beginning of the universe would be a frustration, as a singularity is the ultimate unknowable. I have already remarked on the understandable temptation for the Christian theologian to step in at this point where it seems that physics can go no further and to invoke creation by a transcendent God; God, it might be said, simply made the 'singularity'. But any doctrine of creation must take care to envisage God as involved in the whole process of the physical world; this means to understand creation at this primordial moment in a way that illuminates the whole continuous action of God in the universe and not just to posit once again a 'God of the gaps' who fills holes in scientific knowledge. Hawking's desire, as a scientist, is in fact to find the answer to this gap in our knowledge of the universe. He ends his book, *A Brief History of Time*, with the hope of finding a unified theory that will combine quantum physics, general relativity, and gravity. If we could find such a unified theory, we would, he claims, then be able to discern why it is that we and the universe exist. 'If we find the answer to that it would be the ultimate triumph of human reason—for then we would know the mind of God'.[16] But for Hawking 'God' here means the ultimate law or principle of the universe. The scientist's task is to explain the world without invoking the transcendent. Achieving a unified theory would be to know the mind of 'God' and so—it seems—to make a personal God redundant.

The real philosophical problem with the Big Bang is that it is a one-off happening, an anomaly. It seems impossible to get behind it or before it. Hawking is searching for what lies behind it, through trying to develop a Unified Theory. He accepts, of course, that the universe as we know it has a beginning; time ('real time') and space began with the Big Bang. But he also wants to get away from the uniqueness of a beginning and so conceives of a continual oscillation between 'imaginary time' (before creation) and 'real time' until the conditions were right for the Big Bang to occur that produced this universe we experience. Finding the equation that expresses these conditions, the Unified Theory, would be to find the law by which the other laws work and to be able to explain how the Big Bang happened. It would be the ultimate explanation.

Matching the uniqueness of the beginning of the universe is its end. Scientists are agreed that the universe will come to an end, at least as an environment for carbon-based life as we know it. The end, however, may be of two different kinds: the whole system may collapse in upon itself in a 'Big Crunch'; alternatively, the universe will go on expanding, and entropic disorder will therefore increase to the point of 'Heat Death', when all energy is degraded to uniform heat, and so life is no longer possible (though usually called 'Heat Death', this would actually be an intensely cold state). These two options are shown diagramatically in text figure 2:2.

Recent work by Stephen Hawking[17] and by Michael Hawkins[18] have suggested that continuous expansion of the universe is more likely, in their opinion, than a 'Big Crunch.' While many systems within the universe may be described as chaotic, the universe as a whole is simple, and the rate of expansion appears to be uniform in all directions, as demonstrated by the uniform nature of the background cosmic radiation left over from the Big Bang. This is constant to a factor of 1 in 10,000 in any direction. Whether the universe continues to expand or falls in on itself in a Big Crunch depends on the density of the universe. If this is greater than a critical value, then the gravitational pull between galaxies will first of all slow expansion down. Then expansion will stop altogether, and the universe will begin to contract, eventually ending in a Big Crunch singularity—a state of infinite density, at which the laws of physics would break down. If the average density is less than the critical value, then the universe will continue to expand forever. Whatever the value may be, however, Hawking believes that the universe will continue to expand for at least a further 10 billion years.[19]

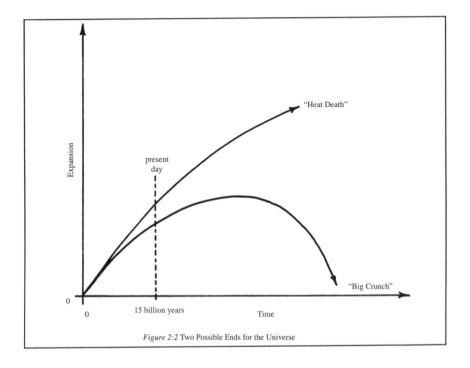

Figure 2:2 Two Possible Ends for the Universe

A major problem in seeking to discover the future of the universe is the fact that when the mass of all the stars and observable clouds of gas are added together we only have a total of one percent of the critical density value. A partial answer to this problem may be found in so-called 'dark matter', which may be present in galaxies to explain why they hold together and do not fly apart. But when we add in all the possible dark matter, we still only reach a figure of ten percent of the critical value.[20] The only solution left is that the rest of the matter is to be located in black holes. Hawkins[21] noted that the light from quasars varies in a way that has puzzled astronomers for a long time. He suggests that a large number of very dense, invisible objects lie between the quasars and the Earth. These, he maintains, have acted as 'gravitational lenses' that distort the light emitted by the quasars. He believes these compact stellar objects to be black holes. Through a study of over 300 quasars, he estimates that at least a further ten percent or more of the critical cosmological density may be found in such black holes. Hawking[22] is convinced that the density of the universe must be close to the critical value, be-cause otherwise the universe would either have collapsed back on itself within the first ten years of existence or have expanded at such a rapid rate so as to leave us with virtually empty space. Hawking is careful not to see this as evidence in support of the Anthropic Principle, as he does not want to place such importance on human beings; he would rather search for an alternative (purely scientific) solution.

Hawking's answer is an 'inflationary universe', which continues to double in size and contains sufficient dark matter to maintain the critical density. He concludes by suggesting that 'If the theory of inflation is cor-rect, the universe is actually on a knife edge.' 'So,' he says, 'I am in the well-established tradtion of oracles and prophets of hedging my bets by predicting both ways'.[23] With regard to the Earth and our own Solar Sys-tem, it is estimated that after about 5,000 million years the Sun will exhaust its nuclear fuel and will swell up to a 'red giant', absorbing the Earth and other planets into its mass, before collapsing to a 'white dwarf'. After 10,000 million years most of the present stars in the uni-verse will have met with the same fate, the larger ones becoming black holes rather than white dwarfs.

It seems that scientists, while recognising that the universe as an en-vironment for life as we know it has a beginning and an end, want to press on beyond these unique points for some other ultimates. With re-gard to the end, some want to suggest that life could take totally new forms and exist in the Heat Death of an inflationary universe or that there could be a whole cycle of Big Bangs and Big Crunches. Others have suggested parallel universes. With regard to the beginning, some, like Hawking, search for a theory that will unify the four forces that govern the universe: gravity, electromagnetism, and the weak and strong nuclear forces. Such a Grand Unifying Theory or super law will, some believe, be the ultimate answer.

It is perhaps not illegitimate for the theologian quietly to point out that the alternative is the existence of purpose in the universe, and pur-pose points to a creator. This does not mean that the beginning of our universe simply corresponds to God's act of creation *ex nihilo* or that the end as predicted by mathematics is simply the same as God's bringing of all things to fulfilment in a new creation. This would make a 'God of the gaps' indeed, and in the gospel story we have the words of Jesus to warn us against any such calculations: 'No one knows about that day or hour, not even the angels in heaven, nor the Son, but only the Father'.[24] Rather, the scientific discovery that the universe has a story with a beginning and an end points us towards a God who has a story for his creation, beginning with a loving act of origination and climaxing with a renewal of all things.[25] Whether or not the Big Bang was coterminous with God's original act of creation *ex nihilo*, the believer can be sure that God was working out his continual creative purpose through this primal event.

Paul Davies is bold enough, as a physicist, to face the question: does the chain of explanation stop with God or with some super law?[26] In an imaginary discussion between an atheist and a theist, Davies finds the conclusion to be that the origin of the universe is either 'brute fact' or 'God.' Both of these, he admits, are mysteries.[27] While Hawking suggests that the universe could be a self-contained system with no boundary conditions, and therefore no creator, we are still left to ask with Davies where the physical laws that explain the universe (even, perhaps, a super-law if it can be found) come from. We are forced to ask whether we find 'brute fact' or 'God' more convincing. Modern cosmologists can trace the universe back to when it was 10^{-43} seconds old and 10^{-33} cm in diameter, but not before. Even the following history of development presents difficulties as scientists only appear on the scene some fifteen billion years later.[28] But then we also have another critical question to ask: why do human beings have the ability to discover and understand the principles by which the universe runs?

6. The Alternatives of God or Law

Conscious human beings are a fundamental feature of the universe. Human reason comprehends the universe. The universe can be understood as being rational, so is it actually rational and what—if so—is the origin of such rationality? Is it a rational designer? Do the laws of nature reflect the nature of God himself, or are they in themselves the universal, absolute, eternal, omnipotent 'givens' of the universe? Before we can answer these related questions we have to recognise that the laws of physics do not completely describe the universe, but only our experience of it. The cosmic initial conditions lie outside those 'givens', and the fact that we see an expanding universe does not mean that it necessarily started that way. The laws, says Davies,[29] can be called 'transcendent' in terms of present reality, but came into being with the universe and therefore cannot explain the initial conditions. Only a law for the initial conditions themselves would explain how the universe came to exist in its present form.

It has been suggested that the language of nature is mathematics, and so the universe operates like a computer with the laws of physics guiding the programme. We may well need to make an exception for this, however, when it comes to the human mind; Roger Penrose[30] has argued convincingly that this does not at all function like a computer, a point that will be developed more fully in Chapter 3. But it may seem attractive to a Christian thinker, despite this qualification, to suggest that the universe is programmed with the laws of physics and the special laws for its initial state and that God is the programmer. The problem of 'God the programmer', however, is that we are back again with Newton's God who stands outside the created system. It is therefore significant for our understanding of an immanent creator that we see not only the regimented regularity of the universe but also its complexity.

So Davies rightly observes that there is cosmic significance, especially for the Christian believer, in both regular patterns and organised complexity.[31] This organised complexity goes against the arrow of increasing entropy, a point that will be developed further in chapter 3. If the universe were the 'output' of some computational process, then it must be, by definition, computable. We observe regularities in the universe, and underneath the complexity of nature lies the simplicity of the laws of physics operating even at sub-atomic levels. But the order of the cosmos is more than mere regimented regularity; it is also organised complexity. The Christian theologian may claim that it is from this phenomenon that the universe derives its openness and permits the existence of human beings with free will. It is not simply against an atheistic view of the universe that the theologian wants to maintain that it is not laws that are ultimate but God himself; a making absolute of law within a religious perspective can also lead to the view that the universe functions as a computer.

7. The Mystery of 'Fine Tuning'

The universe is either brute fact, or we must posit God. It is a feature of modern science that its investigators are as liable as theologians to speak of the universe as not only intelligible but objectively 'rational'. The logical end for non-religous belief in a rational cosmos is that the laws of physics are contingent on a 'Theory of Everything'. A genuine theory of this kind will have to explain not only why the universe came into being but also why it is the only type of universe in which conscious life could have developed. If the initial conditions had been different, then there could have been a different universe, but not one in which human life would have evolved.

These considerations lead modern cosmologists to speak of 'fine tuning', and an 'Anthropic Principle'. It is widely accepted that there is some guiding principle or even 'design' that has allowed complex human life to arise within the universe. There is the phenomenon of the organisation and the complexity of nature. There is a uniformity within nature, and there is the universality of the laws of physics. There is the uniformity of the expansion of the universe—its size and age—in excess of 100,000 billion, billion (km) and some 15-20 billion years old. It is thus a universe that is remarkably well adjusted. Biologists see the universe as biocentric—the presence of chemicals and the laws of physics making life possible. The essential element for life, carbon, is manufactured from Helium in large stars and released into the universe by supernovae explosions; if this is a mere accident, it is the luckiest of coincidences. In short, science is discovering a 'finely tuned' universe, which from the first conditions is uniquely suitable for life forms like ourselves.

We need, of course, to keep in mind that while a finely tuned universe is, in the view of modern cosmologists, indicative of 'design', this does not in itself necessarily imply a 'designer'. To believe in a divine designer is a step of faith, and so scientists who do not want to invoke a designer have an alternative; they search for a Grand Unified Theory or a Theory of Everything. The modern concept of design therefore makes faith in a designer God reasonable but cannot prove it. Darwin argued that adaption took place by random mutations and natural selection and not by divine design, an issue that we will look at in some detail in Chapter 3. But when it comes to the laws and initial conditions of the universe, we need a fine tuning and high precision that leaves a designer as a compelling suggestion. There is a universal feeling among physicists that everything that exists in nature must have a place or a role as part of some wider scheme. Each facet of physical reality should link in with others in a natural and logical way. Science is constantly unearthing a 'felicitous dovetailing'.

So we see the world as 'a marvellously ingenious and unified mathematical scheme'. Scientific observers are ready to apply words such as 'clever' to nature.[32] If the fine tuning of the laws of nature is necessary for conscious life to evolve in the universe, then for Christian believers it offers confirmation that our own existence is a central part of God's project in creation. But some cosmologists, irrespective of belief, are now seeing humanity as a central part of the universe. They especially see the presence of human consciousness as important in this conclusion, a point that will be raised again in chapters 3 and 6.

Thus we have entered a new era for the 'argument from design' in Christian belief, which theologians need to grapple with, despite all their justified suspicions of the way that the argument has been used in the past. The very use of the word 'design' may cause problems for theologians, as they read into it the problematic idea of unalterable divine plans. But scientists use the term in a much more open and flexible way. Davies, for example, freely refers to the universe as unfolding according to a 'cosmic blue print'; intelligent design is clear, but whether it really has been designed by a designer is, according to Davies, 'a matter of personal taste'.

Scientists continue to search for a Theory of Everything (T.o.E.), which may be achieved with a Grand Unified Theory (G.U.T.). Such a theory would then be the ultimate necessity for the universe, and this raises an important issue of comparison between such a kind of necessity and the Christian concept of God as 'necessary Being'. In theological tradition, to speak of God as 'necessary' has involved two inter-related ideas. In the first place, he is 'necessary' in the sense that his existence is not contingent upon any reality outside himself; he is the only self-existent being, owing his existence to nothing but himself. In the second place, it has been claimed that the origin of a contingent world (it need not be, or need not be as it is) can only be explained as the creation of a totally necessary being, who has made the world through his free choice. The framework of his creation involves the contingency of the physical laws, which govern our experience of the physical universe. There is, then, it seems a parallel claim that once cosmologists have discovered the T.o.E. or G.U.T., they will have discovered the Alpha Point, the necessity from which the whole universe is itself contingent.

We notice that a similar problem exists for the classical idea of God as necessary Being as for the scientific idea of a necessary Theory: how can a contingent universe issue from a totally necessary source? It would seem that in this case the universe itself would have to be totally necessary as well. The Christian theologian, however, can cope with this apparent impasse by re-thinking the notion of 'necessity' with regard to God. The belief in God as 'necessary' in the sense of being self-existent need not imply that he is totally self-sufficient and unaffected in the mode of his existence;[33] that is, he may freely choose to be influenced and changed by his creation and so to take contingency into himself. Such a God would be able to give his creation a genuine freedom, and this once more raises the difference between a personal God as the final explanation for the universe and a system of law as ultimate.

8. The Uncertainties and Chaos of the Universe

So far it would appear that everything within the realm of science is entirely predictable and certain, determined by well-defined laws. This is not the case at the sub-atomic level of particle physics, and it is to this that we must turn next.

The eighteenth and nineteenth centuries saw the successful application of Newtonian physics with the model of a mechanical universe, but this situation changed at the beginning of this century with the appearance of the Quantum Theory. Max Planck suggested that light, x-rays, and other waves were emitted in packets called quanta or photons. In 1926 Werner Heisenberg showed that this simple picture leads to a surprising consequence when applied to atoms and sub-atomic particles. The position and velocity of these particles cannot be determined at the same time. Particles did not have well-defined positions, but a quantum state, which was a combination of position and velocity. It was also discovered that electrons do not follow a definite path around the nucleus. At the quantum level we leave the world of objects moving along the shortest trajectory to a predetermined goal. We enter instead the quantum world of probabilities instead of certainties, which has been defined as Heisenberg's Uncertainty Principle. Quantum mechanics predicts a number of different possible outcomes and tells us how likely each possibility is. In this way it appears that unpredictability and randomness are introduced into science.

This phenomenon has led to two opposite and extreme conclusions being drawn about the idea of a Creator God. Either it is suggested that there is an ultimate randomness in the universe that excludes the possibility of a sovereign, rational creator, or it is claimed that here is the place where the universe is actually open to God, a God who works through randomness, chance, and spontaneity in his creativity. In answer to the first conclusion we should point out that the universe does not seem to be characterised by total randomness; while the activity of individual atoms may be unpredictable, the behaviour of large groups of atoms in a gas or liquid, for example, is described by deterministic laws. In response to the second suggestion we need not see areas of uncertainty as the only location for divine activity; we must agree with David Wilkinson[34] here that a God who works only with electrons at the quantum level will not do a lot. It is perfectly reasonable for Christians to accept both micro-randomness and macro-predictability as the ways in which God is at work within the universe.

More recently has come the suggestion of 'chaos' within physical systems, which again makes them far less predictable than Newtonian physics would suggest.[35] Chaos theory looks at complex phenomena that are beyond the grasp of pure determinism, such as the weather, air turbulence, fluid flow, the human heart-beat, and the electrical activity of the brain. But again when we get behind the name and look at what is meant by 'Chaos theory', we find no threat to the Christian concept of the outworking of God's purposes. Chaotic systems are systems that appear to behave in a random fashion, but which do nevertheless obey the physical laws of the universe. The reason for the apparent chaotic behaviour is that the system is very sensitive to the factors that affect its behaviour. This was recognised by Edward Lorenze, who was studying weather systems in the United States of America. In trying to produce a computerised programme for the prediction of weather patterns, he soon recognised that minute variations in air conditions in one place could completely change the predicted outcome of a whole weather pattern. This became known as the 'butterfly effect', as Lorenze suggested that some detail as small as a butterfly flapping its wings in New York could produce a tornado in Wyoming.[36] Now we at least know why the weather forecasts are often inaccurate! The unpredictability lies in our lack of complete knowledge of the initial conditions, not in the way in which the system responds to the deterministic laws of physics.

We can therefore conclude that the appearance of chaos does not conflict with the belief that God can fulfil his purposes through the universe. On the one hand, if God in his omniscience knows the initial conditions of any system, he also knows what their general conclusions will be. On the other hand, if God offers a real freedom to his creation, he will expose himself, and therefore make himself vulnerable, to a variety of chance variations within the universe that lead to the conclusions of a system in particular detail.[37] I mentioned above that both scientists and theologians are looking for a necessary, self-existent factor in the universe, but a G.U.T. will be deterministic where the idea of a personal God can allow for freedom as well as purpose in the face of 'chaos'.

9. What Kind of Creator?

What kind of God would be the creator of this universe with its unpredictability and its apparently 'chaotic' systems—at least seen from a human point of view? He will not be the God of Newton, who stands outside a mechanistic universe, nor will he be the unknowable and mysterious intelligence of nature that Einstein imagined. The God of this kind of universe is the one who accompanies creation through all its processes, a creative, dynamic God, such as we find revealed in the pages of the Bible. We will take up these issues again in chapters 6 and 7.

In our journey of discovery we have come a long way from Copernicus and his revolutionary discovery that the Earth rotated around the Sun, and not vice versa. We have uncovered a universe of almost incomprehensible proportions. Planet Earth is one of the smaller planets orbiting around a modest-sized star. This star, that we call the Sun, is one of over 100 billion stars in the galaxy to which it belongs, which we call the Milky Way, and which makes up the vast majority of the observable universe that we look out on in the night sky. The Milky Way is one of over 1,000,000,000 galaxies that make up the universe. In terms of distance, at the speed of light—i.e. 186,000 miles/sec—we could travel to the Sun in 8 minutes. To reach the edge of the Milky Way travelling at the same speed would take 100,000 years, and to reach the edge of the universe some 10-15 billion years.

But this vast universe has a story, with a beginning and an end. It is estimated that the universe is between ten and twenty billion years old and that it originated in a hot big bang explosion. When the universe was

0.01 seconds old, it had a temperature in excess of 100 billion °C and a density over a billion times that of water (a cricket-ball-sized piece of this material would weigh over a million tons).[38] The universe is also seen to have an end as an environment for life, though the end may be of two different kinds; if the density of the universe and its rate of expansion are critical enough, the force of gravity will eventually cause the whole system to collapse in on itself in a 'Big Crunch'; alternatively, it will go on expanding to the point of 'Heat Death', when all energy is degraded to uniform heat, and so life is no longer possible.

We have seen that modern cosmology in its investigations of the universe and in the questions that those studies are raising has given new scope to the old religious arguments about design. We are encouraged by the discoveries of modern cosmology to consider a universe whose initial conditions were finely tuned so as to produce human life, conscious, aware, and able to contemplate the universe of which we are a part. A recognition of something like 'design' is of course only a foundation for further steps of thought and belief, but (as we shall see in the next chapter) it is now less easy to make mere 'chance' the alternative to the presence of purpose in the universe—and so to the divine giver of purpose. The alternative must be not 'brute chance' but the 'brute fact' of design itself. So Paul Davies, while remaining agnostic about the existence of God, concludes his book *The Mind of God* with what we might describe as a modern version of Psalm 8:

> What is man that we might be party to such a privilege? I cannot believe that our existence in this universe is a mere quirk of fate, an accident of history, an incidental blip in the great cosmic drama. Our involvement is too intimate. . . . We are truly meant to be here.[39]

For the Christian theologian, however, these factors in modern cosmology are not just suggestive of the existence of God; they prompt reflection on the nature of God. At the sub-atomic level we have noted a degree of uncertainty, and in some systems apparent chaotic behaviour, which together would appear to take us away from the entirely predictable mechanistic universe of Newton, in which God could be excluded as a participant. We no longer have a God of the gaps who has to be dragged in to explain what science cannot account for, and we no longer have a God who stands outside the system. It appears that a designer of such a universe would have to be involved with the universe at all levels, from the whole to the behaviour of sub-atomic particles. We have the picture of a designer who is both necessary and contingent, that is one who is both self-existent and open to being affected by his creation.

Only a God who opens himself to contingency can be truly immanent in his creation. The ultimate difference between a G.U.T. and God is that a G.U.T. is purely necessary and not contingent at all; necessity in this scientific theory has the characteristics of the classical view of God, a merely deterministic cause and effect model. But reflection upon the nature of the universe with characteristics such as beauty and hope prompts us to think of a personal God, involved in the universe, who has taken contingency into himself.

In his book *The Creative Suffering of God*, Paul Fiddes addresses these issues with regard to the problem of suffering. He maintains that what is central to our understanding of God is God's freedom of will to choose to create a universe that is contingent in itself and to which he is also contingent. So we have a world that is not the way it is because it simply actualises God's decrees in every detail, but a world where freedom and choice will affect God himself. Fiddes discusses the nature of divine sovereignty and defends it by concluding that God can actually 'fulfil his being through the world in suffering because he chooses to do so; he chooses that the world should be necessary to him'.[40] This leads on to the further conclusion that 'God is changed by the world in suffering and that this contributes to his being, if he freely chooses that this should be so'.[41] We will consider this suggestion further when we have considered the evolution of life.

For the moment we are left with much that is unknowable. At one level we can discuss a rational, mathematical universe, and yet this is not the complete answer. There is something more than mathematical about emotions, judgements, music, and art. We cannot have a mathematical theory of everything because some things would be therefore excluded on the grounds that they were not scientific. We can compress the complexities of inanimate objects such as planets and stars into an idealised equation, but we cannot do the same thing with the complexities of human personality. John Barrow concludes his search for 'Theories of Everything' by noting that science is most at home attacking problems that require technique rather than insight. But, he says, there are prospective features to the universe such as beauty, simplicity, and truth that cannot be encompassed by laws and rules, and so no non-poetic account of reality can be complete. His final conclusion is that

> There is no formula that can deliver all truth, all harmony, all simplicity. No Theory of Everything can ever provide total insight. For, to see through everything, would leave us seeing nothing at all.[42]

Once more here the Christian thinker will find an advantage in belief in a personal God rather than a theory as final explanation. In encounter with God we know what is ultimately real, but we know him precisely as mystery. It is because he is known, not because he is unknown, that we affirm we cannot know him fully.

Having briefly mentioned the mystery of personality, divine and human, we must now move to consider in detail the development of human life in the context of the rich variety of complex, living organisms on planet Earth.

Notes to Chapter 2

[1]Isaiah 40:26 (New International Version).

[2]D. N. Adams, *The Hitch-Hiker's Guide to the Galaxy*, 135.

[3]J. D. Barrow, *Theories of Everything* (Oxford: Oxford University Press, 1990) 1.

[4]S. W. Hawking, *A Brief History of Time*, 180

[5]Viviani quoted by R. E. Peacock, *A Brief History of Eternity* (Eastbourne: Monach, 1989) 152; see also R. J. Seeger, *Galileo Galilei— His Life and Works* (Oxford: Pergamon Press, 1966).

[6]D. Wilkinson, *God, the Big Bang and Stephen Hawking* (Tunbridge Wells: Monarch, 1993) 43.

[7]A. Tilby, *Science and the Soul* (London: SPCK, 1992) 70.

[8]Einstein quoted in A. Tilby, *Science and the Soul*, 72, and P. Davies *The Mind of God*, 148.

[9]Wilkinson, 44.

[10]Tilby, 89-90.

[11]R. Penrose, *The Emperor's New Mind* (Oxford: Oxford University Press, 1989) 302-47.

[12]Barrow, 41ff

[13]Ibid.

[14]Hawking, 49-50

[15]Ibid., 46.   [16]Ibid., 175

[17]S. W. Hawking, *Black Holes and Baby Universes and Other Essays* (London and New York: Bantam Press, 1993); and 'The Future of the Universe' in *Predicting the Future,* ed. L. Howe and A. Wain (Cambridge: Cambridge University Press, 1993) 8-23.

[18]M. R. S. Hawkins, 'Gravitational Microlensing, Quasar Variability and Missing Matter', *Nature* 366/6452 (1993): 242-45.

[19]Hawking, 'The Future of the Universe', 14.

[20]Ibid.,15.

[21]Hawkins, 242f.

[22]Hawking, 'The Future of the Universe', 17-21.

[23]Hawking, *Black Holes and Baby Universes,* 155.

[24]Mark 13:32 (New International Version).

[25]The relation between a scientific and a theological 'beginning and end' is discussed further in Chapter 7.

[26]P. Davies, *The Mind of God,* 13ff.

[27]Ibid., 58-61.

[28]Wilkinson, 40.

[29]Davies, *The Mind of God,* 91f.

[30]Penrose, 447f.

[31]Davies, *The Mind of God,* 139.

[32]Ibid., 194ff.

[33]The distinction between the self-existence and self-sufficiency of God is usefully made by Keith Ward, *Rational Theology and the Creativity of God* (Oxford: Blackwell, 1982) 10, 86.

[34]Wilkinson, 57.

[35]For works on Chaos theory see J. Gleick, *Chaos* (Cardinal, 1987) and *Chaos: Making a New Science* (New York: Viking, 1988). Also see I. Stewart, *Does God Play Dice?* (Oxford: Blackwell, 1989) and J. T. Houghton, 'New Ideas of Chaos in Physics', *Science and Christian Belief,* 1 (1990): 41-51.

[36]Quoted in A. Peacocke, *Theology for a Scientific Age.* E. N. Lorenze, who is a meterologist, raised questions in 1963 concerning the degrees of freedom that existed in weather systems. See also F. C. Moon, *Chaotic Vibrations: an Introduction for Applied Scientists and Engineers* (New York: John Wiley & Sons, 1987).

[37]See Paul S. Fiddes, *The Creative Suffering of God* (Oxford: Oxford University Press, 1988) 61, 63ff.

[38]J. Houghton, *Does God Play Dice?* (Leicester: I. V. P., 1988) 23

[39]Davies, *The Mind of God,* 332.

[40]P. S. Fiddes, 68.

[41]Ibid.

[42]Barrow, 210.

3

'What are human beings that you are mindful of them?'[1]

The Witness of Biology

In Psalm 8 the ancient Hebrew writer expresses something of the cry of the modern cosmologist, when he writes:

> When I look at your heavens, the work of your fingers,
>   the moon and the stars that you have established;
> what are human beings that you are mindful of them,
>   mortals that you care for them?
> Yet you have made them a little lower than God,
>   and crowned them with glory and honour.[2]

Given the vastness of the universe, human beings ought to be insignificant items on the scene, but they seem to be playing a more major role altogether. We find Douglas Adams alluding ironically to this curious fact in his *The Hitch-Hiker's Guide to the Galaxy*, as we return to the scene where two computer programmers are baffled that the mighty computer has presented them with 'forty-two' as the answer to the 'great Question of Life, the Universe and Everything'. They realise that they actually need to know what the Ultimate Question is, and while 'Deep Thought' confesses that it cannot tell them, it goes on to predict:

> 'But I'll tell you who can. . . .
> 'I speak of none but the computer that is to come after me,' intoned Deep Thought, his voice regaining its accustomed declamatory tones. 'A computer whose merest operational parameters I am not worthy to calculate —and yet I will design it for you. A computer which can calculate the Question to the Ultimate Answer, a computer of such infinite and subtle complexity that organic life itself shall form part of its operational matrix. And you yourselves shall take on new forms and go down into the computer to navigate its ten-million-year programme! Yes! I shall design this computer for you. And I shall name it also unto you. And it shall be called . . . The Earth.'[3]

Not only for a writer of science fiction, but for some cosmologists such as Paul Davies and John Barrow, the answer to the question of a fine-tuned universe is to be seen in the evolution of human life. Einstein said that the most incomprehensible thing about the universe was that it is comprehensible. It is only with our conscious self-awareness that we are able to understand the nature of the universe in which we find ourselves.

1. Explaining the Signs of Development and Change

My father taught biology, and at an early age he introduced me to many exciting aspects of the biological sciences. He named the plants and animals that I encountered in the garden or in the countryside, and I learned their correct Latin names, species and genera, and something of the classification of the plant and animal kingdoms. I soon realised that there were huge varieties in species of grasses and trees. In our pond we had frogs, and I enjoyed the spring time when we watched frogspawn develop through the various stages of tadpole to adult frog. I learned about caterpillars becoming chrysalids and then moths or butterflies. My father had a microscope at home, and he showed me that tap water was teeming with microscopic life (which did not encourage me to drink it!) and that the hairs on my head had a particular structure. This world of life in its variety, development, and microscopic form became even more fascinating when, as a young amateur geologist, I began to discover the world of fossils. I collected brachiopods (sea shells) and trilobites, long extinct, from quarries near my home. On coal tips I discovered fossil ferns, leaves, tree roots, and tree trunks—extinct plant life that was the origin of the coal that heated our home.

It was a journey of discovery, almost like a detective story, as I began to understand something of the rich variety of life on our planet, and especially as I came to recognise that the nature of this life had changed with time. I was of course travelling a journey that others had travelled before me, and I was benefiting from their research; later I was to continue this voyage as a professional geologist. To understand the scientific conclusions about the development of life on planet Earth it will help to travel the journey of discovery made by biologists and geologists (especially palaeontologists) over the last three centuries.

In the world today there are more than 350,000 species of plants, of which approximately 250,000 are flowering plants, 10,000 are ferns and trees, and 60,000 are algae and fungi. There are 1,200,000 species of animals, of which about 900,000 are arthropods (mostly beetles and insects),

120,000 are molluscs (snails, winkles, oysters and other shells), and 45,000 are chordates, which include us. Fossil evidence of life is distributed through more than 120 kilometres of sedimentary rocks, which have accumulated in many ocean basins through geological time. It appears then that this fossil record should give vital clues to understanding the rich variety of species that we see around us today, but the history of palaeontology is marked by constant conflict with scientific and ideological dogmas and authorities, including those of the Christian church.

At first fossils seemed to verify the deluge of the Noah flood described in Genesis 7, for the finding of sea animals in the rocks underlying present-day land confirmed that this land was once covered by the sea. In 1484 Leonardo da Vinci was put in charge of a project to build canals in northern Italy, around Milan. He unearthed edible mussels, snails, oysters, scallops, shattered crabs, petrified fish, and countless other species. But there was no sea in the vicinity of Milan, and he wondered how these remains of marine life had found their way into the soil of Lombardy and how they had become petrified. Greek scientists and philosophers had made the same discoveries in the sixth century B.C., and Herodotus saw only one explanation, namely that the region in question must have at one time been covered by the sea. Leonardo was a brilliant scientist, far ahead of his time, not only in making basic designs for aeroplanes and submarines, but also in geology. He denied the possibility that fossils could have had their origin in a flood like the biblical Deluge, as rivers would have carried the dead to the sea, rather than sucking up the dead from the sea to the mountains. For Leonardo, as for the ancient Greeks, fossils were seen to be the remains of once living creatures.

During the period of the Middle Ages and the Renaissance, however, others considered that fossils were the creation of mysterious forces emanating from the stars, and there are many occult stories that relate to fossil finds in England. There were some who would later suggest, in trying to answer the evolution debate, that fossils were placed in the rocks by the devil to confuse human beings. This is only one step removed from an even more dreadful suggestion also made, that God placed fossils in the rocks to test the belief of human beings concerning creation. It seems bizzare that people who wished to hold to the literal truth of Scripture should suggest such devious activity on the part of the God revealed in those scriptures.

In 1565 Bernard Palissy, a potter, began examining fossils in the Paris area. He came to the same conclusion as Leonardo, that this had once been a bay of an ocean. He published his discoveries in a book, *Discours admirables de la nature des eaux,* which resulted in his imprisonment and subsequent death as a heretic. The majority of scholars continued to see fossils as curiosities and strongly repudiated any suggestion that they might be of organic origin. One widely held view was that of the German pastor and hymnwriter Martin Rinckhardt, who wrote in a series of poems entitled *The Christian Knights of Eisleben* in 1613 that God had scratched all sorts of figures in stone of fish, men, and forms of beasts in order to show men working in the mines that 'He is everywhere with us.' By contrast, the Chinese believed that fossil vertebrates were the remains of dragons, and many legends of giants were based on finds of fossil mammals. An elephant skull with its large nasal opening, looking deceptively like two merged eye sockets, may have been the origin of the legend of the one-eyed Cyclops.[4]

In 1695 John Woodward, professor of physics at Gresham College, wrote *An Essay Toward a Natural History of the Earth* in which he suggested that the rocks and fossils of the crust were the result of a universal flood, and that all fossils were the remains of animals that lived before that deluge. Until well on into the nineteenth century the only explanation that the Church was prepared to accept for past geological changes and the petrifaction of prehistoric organisms was the Noah flood. The positive outcome of this was that it gave impetus for the collection of fossils. In 1774 a Bavarian pastor, Johann Friedrich Esper, discovered bones of Ice Age cave bears along with unquestionable human remains. He identified the bears as bears and not as dragons and wrote in his book entitled, *Detailed Account of Newly Discovered Zooliths,* 'If human bones are also buried alongside the remains of antedeluvian animals in the mud of this cave, a man must have lived together with these animals in that period.'[5] He had discovered Cro-Magnon man. In 1746 Jean-Etienne Guettard, in France, suggested that fossils in lower sedimentary layers were older than those in higher strata. He also recognised that they represented different climatic conditions and that some were now extinct. His ideas went against the current interpretation of creation, and he was summoned before a committee of theologians at the Sorbonne and forced to recant.

2. Development through Evolution

In 1750 Georges Louis Leclerc, Comte de Buffon (1707–1788), worked out that if the Earth had cooled from a molten ball it would have taken at least 75,000 years. In 1787 he suggested that within its cooling history there had been many periods with many different floras and faunas and that there had been many deluges and catastrophes. Twenty years later, Buffon's disciple, Jean-Baptiste de Monet, Chevalier de Lamark (1744–1829), spoke bravely of 'boundless ages, thousands, indeed millions of centuries.'[6] Lamark became professor of zoology at the Musee Nationale d'Histoire Naturelle in 1794 and in 1801, like Buffon before him, sought to trace all forms of animal life to a common origin. He anticipated Darwin in conceiving of the idea of organic evolution, suggesting that living organisms were always trying to improve themselves. Having suggested that present-day forms had developed out of forms now preserved as fossils, Lamark then looked for a possible mechanism. He suggested that new environmental conditions compelled animals to adjust and that during this process new organs developed and ones that were not used disappeared. Like Darwin, he wrongly believed that characteristics acquired in an individual's lifetime were passed on to its offspring. He stated, 'Whatever characteristic individuals may acquire or lose by consistent use or constant disuse of an organ is transmitted to the next generation . . . provided that the acquired changes are common to both parents.'[7] Lamark included the evolution of human beings in his theory of descent, but he could not substantiate the influence of the environment nor the inheritance of acquired characteristics; his arguments remained more philosophical than biological.

In the early nineteenth century Georges Dagobert, Baron Cuvier (1769–1832), the French naturalist, founded the science of palaeontology. He related the various forms of parts of animals to their particular function; for example, when he found fossil feathers, he stated that this indicated that the animal involved could fly. He pioneered comparative anatomy and zoological classification. While he recognised both evolution and extinction within fossil groups, he maintained that the biblical flood was the last great catastrophe or geological revolution to affect our planet. The theory of evolution continued to be regarded as a crank notion amongst most scientists, who held to the notion that the fauna and flora of the Earth had changed radically between twenty-five and thirty times in the course of its geological history. God, or an unknown natural force, it was argued, had periodically committed mass slaughter of all organisms and then, after total catastrophic destruction, recreated a new set of animals and plants.[8]

The natural sciences, like the physical sciences, were increasingly in conflict with the doctrinal position of the Church, which held to a literal interpretation of the Genesis account of creation. The two main issues of contention were evolution of plant and animal life and the age of the Earth during which such evolution might have taken place. In an attempt to defend a literal biblical chronology, the Irish Archbishop James Usher published *The Annals of the World* (1650), in which he calculated the age of the Earth from the genealogies in the Old Testament. Having traced the descent of human beings back to Adam, he added six days and declared that the Earth was created at 8 A.M. on October 22, 4004 B.C. A very different conclusion was reached in 1862 by William Thomson, Lord Kelvin, through his studies of thermodynamics; he suggested an age of 20-400 million years, the time taken for the Earth to cool from a molten globe. Such a time scale gave room for the process of evolution, and the predictable, mechanical model of the universe presented by Newton gave a basis for the modern interpretation of the rock strata of the Earth's crust.

William Smith (1769–1839), a canal engineer, is recognised as the father of English geology. He used fossils in constructing a set of geological maps of England and Wales, which were published in 1815. James Hutton (1726–97), a Scottish natural philosopher, published his *Theory of the Earth* in 1795, in which he stated that the Earth was older than the 6,000 years suggested by biblical scholars, that the sediment laid down in oceans was the debris of continents, that these sediments could be metamorphosed by subterranean heat, and that only those agents operating today need be invoked to explain the landforms seen in older rocks. This prepared the way for Charles Lyell (1797–1875), a Scottish geologist, who laid the foundations of all modern geology.

Lyell completed the first edition of his three-volume *Principles of Geology* in 1830–1833 and subsequently revised this work twelve times up to his death in 1875. Lyell demolished the catastrophe theory of Cuvier and cited numerous examples of his own view of a step-by-step transformation of landforms in the geological past. He recognised slow, cumulative changes in the surface of the Earth over a long period of time. He demonstrated the operation of agents such as rivers, volcanoes, earthquakes, and the sea in past geological periods and developed the concept of uniformitarianism, whereby the present is the key to the past. The first edition of his work was read by Darwin as he set out on the *Beagle* expedition, and it had a profound effect on his thinking. Up to the ninth edition of his work, however, Lyell clung on to Cuvier's theory that plant and animal species were immutable. His only concession to Lamark was to grant that minor adjustments of species to their environment might take place. Fossils were only important to Lyell as evidence of the living conditions and, therefore, the environment in which the sediments were deposited. He did, however, establish the principle by which changing groups of fossil organisms were the best guide to recognising the sequence of rock strata.

Lyell became a passionate supporter of Darwin after the publication of *The Origin of the Species by Means of Natural Selection* and rewrote the relevant sections of his *Principles* to take account of Darwin's theory. Lyell's studies of palaeontology, of plant and animal morphology, of the geological history of the Earth as preserved in the rock strata, of geological time measured in millions of years, combined with the suggestion of uniformitarianism, laid the basis for the revolutionary work of Darwin.

3. Development through Natural Selection

Charles Darwin (1809–1882) was born in Shrewsbury. He attended Edinburgh University in 1825 to study medicine but, not wanting to follow in his father's footsteps as a doctor, went to Cambridge in 1827 to study classics, with a view to becoming a clergyman. Darwin recalled that Dr. Duncan's *Materia Medica* was replaced by Paley's *Evidences of Christianity,* 'And as I did not then in the least doubt the strict and literal truth of every word of the Bible, I soon persuaded myself that our Creed must be fully accepted.'[9] Throughout this time at university Darwin maintained an interest in geology and botany, being influenced by Adam Sedgwick, professor of geology, and Revd. John Stephen Henslow, professor of botany. Henslow recognised that Darwin's calling was not to the priesthood and persuaded him to accompany Capt. Robert Fitzroy as a naturalist on the *Beagle*. So at the age of twenty-two years Darwin set sail on a five-year voyage of exploration and discovery, which took in the east coast of South America, Terra del Fuego, the Falkland Islands, the west coast of South America, the Galapagos Islands, Tahiti, New Zealand, Australia, the Cape of Good Hope, Bahia, and home. The first materials that Darwin published were the results of his geological studies: *Coral Reefs* (1842), *Volcanic Islands* (1844), and *Geological Observations on South America* (1846).

Darwin took Charles Lyell's uniformitarianism as the basis of his explanation of biological phenomena but radically changed it to include the principle of natural selection, which explained progressive change and indeed made it inevitable. By the end of the Beagle's voyage, Darwin had become convinced that species were not immutable and that they could be transformed into new species. This was his conclusion from observing finches on the Galapagos Islands (volcanic islands 1000 kilometres west of Ecuador, in the Pacific) and the armadillo-like creatures of South America. On the voyage Darwin had noted the mutation of species in changed environments, and also their changing development through the physical isolation of species, which he observed on either side of the Andes and in the Galapagos archipelago. By 1839 he had developed a theory of transmutation by natural selection. He recognised that changed environment could bring about the extinction of a species, but he did not understand why slightly favoured forms might gain the upper hand and form new species. Then in 1838 he read Malthus' essay on population and in a flash of inspiration recognised natural selection: the preservation of favourable and the disappearance of unfavourable variations. Darwin no longer felt able to accept Paley's view in *Evidences of Christianity* that adaptions were evidences of separate creation by Divine design.

By 1844 Darwin had written up his work on the origin of species but shared the conclusions with no one except the biologist Sir Joseph Hooker; for twelve more years he silently added facts in support of his theory. It was not until 1856, encouraged by his friends Hooker and Lyell, that he began to write his definitive work on natural selection. When in 1858 he discovered that the naturalist Alfred Wallace (1823–1913) had reached similar conclusions, he first presented the theory jointly with Wallace to the Linnaen Society and then in 1859 published *The Origin of the Species by Means of Natural Selection or The Preservation of Favoured Races in the Struggle for Life*. The book's first edition was sold out on the day of publication. It was reviewed for *The Times* by a marine biologist and vertebrate palaeontologist, Thomas Henry Huxley (1825–1895), who, when he had read Darwin's theory, exclaimed 'How extremely stupid not to have thought of that!'

The Origin had a notable list of supporters. It included Huxley, the major zoologist of his time; Hooker, the finest botanist; and Lyell, the greatest geologist. Also in support were Herbert Spencer; Sir John Lubbock (later Lord Avebury); Canon Tristram, who had studied the animals recorded in the Bible; Alfred Newton, the ornithologist; and Charles Kingsley, clergyman and novelist. Darwin was opposed by the naturalist Philip Gosse, who was a member of the Plymouth Brethren; by the geologist, Adam Sedgwick; and by the comparative anatomist and palaeontologist Richard Owen. There was a growing opposition from the side of the Church, which had recognised that Darwin's conclusions were incompatible with a doctrine of creation deduced from a literal understanding of Genesis. Owen was the scientific mind behind the religious opposition to Darwin at the Oxford Meeting of the British Association in 1860. But while Owen had briefed Bishop Wilberforce carefully, the Bishop's arguments were largely demolished by Huxley.

In 1863 Huxley published *Evidences of Man's Place in Nature*, and in 1871 Darwin published *The Descent of Man*. These two works laid the basis for the belief that human beings lie at the end of an evolutionary tree that stretches back into the depths of geological history. Darwin deduced that human beings had probably originated in Africa, a conclusion that has found support this century in the work of the Australian anatomist Raymond Dart, who found a hominid skeleton at Taung in southern Africa in 1924 and called it *Australopithecus*. Further confirmation has come from the British archeologist and anthropologist Louis Seymour Bazett Leakey (1903–1972), who found fossil hominids in the region of Olduvai Gorge, Tanzania. This work has been followed up, through the 1970s and 1980s by Richard Leakey's discoveries in Kenya.

Darwin had a passion for the truth, an extraordinary modesty, a hatred of cruelty and injustice, and an essential goodness. He made important discoveries in geology, botany, palaeontology, the inheritance of characteristics in animals and plants, reproduction, behaviour, and general natural history; he virtually created the new sciences of ecology and ethnology; he laid the foundations for a scientific taxonomy and prepared the way for rational anthropology. He was buried in Westminster Abbey side by side with the greatest physical scientist, Isaac Newton. This has led Huxley and Kettlewell to comment:

Newton banished miracles from the physical world and reduced God to
the role of a cosmic designer who on the day of creation brought the
clockwork mechanism of the universe into being to tick away according
to the inevitable laws of nature; and Darwin banished not only miracles
but also creation and design from the world of life, robbed God of his
role as the creator of man, and man of his divine origin. . . Newton
opened the door to a rational understanding of physical nature and to its
technological control; Darwin opened the door to a rational understanding of man and his place and role in nature, and to the possibility
of improving the human condition.[10]

Sadly the fallenness of humanity, which is denied by Darwinian
evolution theory, has prevented such a human-centred possibility and
demonstrates the danger of leaving God out of the equation. At the end
of the nineteenth century Darwin's ideas were used as the basis for what
became known as 'Social Darwinism'. In Germany Darwin's ideas were
picked up by the embryologist Ernst Heinrich Haeckel (1834–1919) and
by Karl Marx (1818–1883), who wanted to dedicate the English translation of *Das Kapital* to Darwin. Marx read *The Origin* in 1860 and
commented, 'Darwin's book is very important and serves me as a basis
in natural science for the struggle in history.'[11] In Germany attempts were
made to apply Darwinian concepts, such as the struggle for existence and
the survival of the fittest, to human affairs. Social Darwinism became a
pseudo-science and led to the glorification of free enterprise, *laissez faire*
economics, justification of war, racism, and eventually to Hitler and Nazi
ideology.

4. Genetic Change

The concept of evolution began with Lamark, but Darwin provided the
theory of a natural mechanism by it which it might be actualised. Yet
neither Lamark nor Darwin were able to show how characteristics of the
favoured species were passed on from one generation to another. The answer was found in the mid-nineteenth century by the Abbot of Brunn, in
Moravia, working with garden peas in a monastery garden but did not
become known until the end of the century. Gregor Johann Mendel
(1822–1884) formulated the laws of heredity through the breeding of garden peas. By crossing pea plants he arrived at the concept of dominant
and recessive genes. His results lay unnoticed until sixteen years after his

death. Mendelian genetics combined with Darwinian natural selection provided the means by which evolution might be understood to progress. Darwin's theory was essentially based on morphology (the outward form of animals, together with the nature of their skeletal parts and internal organs), in the same way as palaeontologists had postulated evolutionary changes; but twentieth-century biochemistry has now demonstrated fundamental similarities at molecular level between all living organisms from bacteria to human beings.

The last thirty years have seen dramatic progress in molecular biology, which is that part of biology that applies the methods of physics and chemistry to living things. Important for our discussion of evolution is the research into macromolecules: the proteins, nucleic acids, and the polysaccharides. These are long-chain polymers composed of linear strings of smaller molecules, and among them it is the nucleic acids that make up the genes. Their principal function is to store and transmit information. There are two kinds of nucleic acid: deoxyribonucleic acid, known by the shorthand DNA, and ribonucleic acid, RNA. In 1953 Francis Crick (b. 1916) and James Watson (b. 1928) discovered the double helix structure of DNA. For this work they shared with M. H. F. Wilkins the Nobel Prize for Physiology or Medicine in 1962. Watson wrote up his personal account of the research in 1968 in a book entitled, *The Double Helix.*

Crick and Watson realised that in the way that the nucleotides in the two strands touched each other there was the possibility of a copying mechanism for the genetic material. In the 1960s it was recognised that double helical DNA unwinds and is copied into complementary strands of RNA. The sequence of nucleotides in the RNA determines the sequence of amino acids in the protein chains. Commenting on this process, Andrew Miller, Professor of Biochemistry at Edinburgh, writes: 'The DNA double helix suggests the mechanism whereby genes are passed on through generations. In order to work adequately the copying mechanism must be of high fidelity.'[12] Errors do creep in, however, altering the amino acid sequence in the proteins. These produce mutations, some of which may bring about a situation whereby the organism cannot survive; others may be neutral; and some give a reproductive advantage. This throws a lot of light on what may be going on in evolution. But it is precisely at this point that a number of questions arise. Miller raises some of them, and he himself finds these questions to be at least suggestive of the grounds for Christian belief. Why do organisms metabolise, reproduce, and evolve? Can life be explained fully in terms of physics and chemistry? Can the apparent self-determination and goal-orientation of organisms be accounted for fully by physics and chemistry? He concludes by stating:

> Molecular biology will always be more than just physics and chemistry, . . . there will be essential boundary conditions. Contingency will be evident.[13]

5. The Search for a Guiding Principle of Change

Although Richard Dawkins begins with an entirely reductionist view, which sees life merely in terms of its chemical and physical components, like Miller he also concludes that there must be some guiding mechanism in the otherwise chance development of complex life forms. Dawkins begins his book *The Blind Watchmaker* with these words:

> This book is written in the conviction that our existence once presented the greatest of all mysteries, but that it is a mystery no longer because it is solved. Darwin and Wallace solved it, though we shall continue to add footnotes to their solution for a while yet.[14]

Dawkins admits that biology is the study of complicated things that give the appearance of having been designed for a purpose, but he is adamant that Darwin's work has dispensed with any notions of purpose. Having considered Paley's argument from design (a watch must have a watchmaker who designed it) he suggests that the analogy between a telescope and an eye, for example, is a false one:

> The only watchmaker in nature is the blind forces of physics, albeit deployed in a special way. . . . Natural selection, the blind, unconscious, automatic process which Darwin discovered . . . has no purpose in mind . . . it does not plan for the future.[15]

Echoing an old argument of David Hume, he points out that we only see life forms with hindsight; we see the end point of a process of evolutionary development and so remark on 'what a good flyer, or swimmer, or climber' an animal is.

Dawkins constantly recognises the complexity of nature and freely acknowledges that the complexity, beauty, and elegance of biological design does need an explanation. He notes, for example, the complexity of the human eye with its three million ganglion cells, which gather data from 125 million photocells. But when faced with the question of how something so complex could evolve, his answer is that it has done so by one small step at a time through the immensity of geological epochs. Dawkins believes that living organisms are the product of cumulative selection and that evolution occurs because there are slight differences in embryonic development from one stage to another. Reproduction from the resulting progeny gives a new generation, and so it is possible that in one hundred generations we can be taken one hundred mutational steps away from the original ancestor. To illustrate this process, Dawkins tells us how he developed a computer programme, entitled 'Evolution', which produced a variety of random shapes. He reports that he did not plan the 'biomorphs' (animal-like line shapes on a computer screen) that 'evolved', and to this extent he was powerless to control the evolution that resulted. This for Dawkins is the powerlessness of any creator; this is the Blind Watchmaker.

Dawkins explains that mutation can take place in 'nine-dimensional genetic space', which is defined by a basic set of nine genes. This is where gradual step-by-step change can take place. Dawkins admits that this process requires there to be a 'target' for change to be aiming at, as he himself actually had a target in mind when selecting successive generations of 'biomorphs' in his computer illustration. But in evolution, the target is not the remote goal of a whole species, but rather the immediate target of 'anything that would improve survival chances.'[16] This is what he claims to be a mechanism of 'non-random survival'. He discusses the possibility of the development of complex organs such as the human eye, and notes that while it would be almost impossible to develop an eye by one step from no eye at all, it would be possible over a great number of intermediate stages through geological time. Each stage would have sufficient momentum to survive and reproduce, and so given infinite time or infinite opportunities, anything would be possible. The immensity of geological time entitles us to postulate what seem on the face of it to be improbable coincidences.

Having shown the steps by which life might have evolved, Dawkins goes on to criticise the religious claim that God was the one who set up the original machinery of DNA and protein that made cumulative selection, and hence evolution, possible. This he dismisses as yet another form of the 'supernatural watchmaker' and a biological version of the 'God of the gaps'. His argument at this point, however, leaves the question of God at least an open one. If the answer is 'God was always there', says Dawkins, then you might just as well say, 'DNA was always there.'[17] He is certainly correct in denying that God's existence can be proved by such arguments, but we ought to note that we cannot in fact say that 'DNA was always there', as we know that DNA was initially formed at some point in the Earth's primal history. Dawkins is an unbeliever, while the biochemist Arthur Peacocke is a Christian believer, but both can maintain that the theory of evolution by cumulative natural selection is the best theory we have to fit the facts and is the only theory that we have that is in principle capable of explaining the evolution of organised complexity. Peacocke, however, sees no mere 'God of the gaps' argument in finding the pattern of evolution (which we can explain) to be part of a universe that bears all the marks of design. He rehearses the evidence that biologists have produced for an anthropic principle, and concludes that for him it is hard to escape the verdict that the actual state of the universe has been chosen or selected; it indicates, for him, a designer or composer.[18]

Dawkins[19] concludes that the essence of life is statistical improbability on a colossal scale. Thus, whatever the explanation for life might be, 'it cannot be chance', by which he means 'pure naked chance.' Cumulative selection, he maintains, is a different form of chance, 'chance at every step'; it is what he calls 'tamed chance.' To 'tame' chance means to break down the very improbable into less improbable small components arranged in series. Then, provided that a large enough series of sufficiently finely-graded intermediates is postulated, we could in theory derive anything from anything without invoking astronomical improbabilities. He also states, however, that there must be a 'mechanism' for guiding each step in the same particular direction, otherwise 'the sequence of steps will career off in an endless random walk.' This guiding mechanism for Dawkins is the urge for survival, and so a 'non-random' aiming at a target of survival exists at every step.

We have every right, however, to question the explanatory power of this theory. Is such small-scale, non-random survival really sufficient to explain the convergence of evolutionary patterns on the separated continents of Eurasia-Africa, North-South America, and Australia whereby similar species have developed in isolation from each other over the last 200 million years? It is significant that Dawkins is looking for an immanent principle by which evolution takes place. He finds it in gradual natural selection alone, but for a Christian believer the guiding mechanism will be expressed as the involvement of the immanent God with his creation. The heart of this issue is not whether natural selection through non-random survival takes place, but whether it is a sufficient mechanism to lead to the development of conscious self-aware human beings.

It is reasonable to suggest that non-random survival on its own might lead to any one of a number of end points to an evolutionary tree, none of which produce human beings. If we take the alternative, theistic viewpoint that an overarching purpose is needed to move evolution through natural selection towards the goal of human life, then of course we are open to the accusation that we are biased by already having arrived at the proposed 'goal.' That is, it may be said that we take this line of argument because we already see the result in ourselves. We are not concerned as Christians, however, to find an irrefutable proof for an overarching purpose; we only want to suggest that such a purpose, working through natural selection and non-random survival, appears to be more reasonable than chance, even if it is a 'tamed' kind of chance.

6. Mere Chance is Not Enough

It is of great interest to modern Christian apologetics that while cosmologists and biologists like Dawkins speak of chance, for none of them is it merely a 'blind' chance. As we have seen, physicists dealing with the movement of atomic particles speak of 'uncertainty' and 'chance'; but they also speak of chaotic systems that are highly sensitive to initial conditions that operate within guiding laws governing the universe as we know it. This Paul Davies describes as the inherent design of the universe. Is not Dawkins wanting to say something similar in the field of biology when he speaks about 'tamed chance' guided by non-random survival?

Dawkins is certainly right in his criticism of William Paley's biological argument, which views each animal and plant species as a special act of God's creative power. Paley could not imagine how plants and animals could have developed without the mechanism of God's particular creation applied to each one; this is in essence a 'God of the gaps' argument. The overall design argument, however, is untouched by evolution theory as it is based on the regularities observed in the whole of the physical sciences. The fundamental question is whether the universe has purpose; Dawkins denies that the evolution of complex life forms indicates purpose, but we must question whether this denial can be sustained with regard to the human mind. Is the human mind merely a computer, part of a mathematical universe? Or does the evolution of conscious human beings indicate the purpose of a supreme and transcendent mind?

In a fascinating study of the mind, Roger Penrose[20] suggests that consciousness is associated with seeing necessary truths and that the hallmark of consciousness is thus a non-algorithmic (i.e. non-computable, not able to be worked out by a specific calculation) forming of judgements. Penrose considers the nature of chaotic systems but discards this as an explanation of the brain. He considers the logic of computers, using a mathematical basis for all computation, but finds consciousness to be something quite different. Consciousness appears to be the element in the brain that allows us to see and appreciate what mathematical truth is, and this in itself demonstrates that the brain is not a computer. We might add to this the perception of aesthetic beauty in art, music, and nature, or the emotions of hope, fear, anxiety, or despair. The brain is distinguished in one further way from mathematical equations in that it operates according to the arrow of time, whereas equations can be run backwards or forwards.

Penrose concludes with these remarks: 'Consciousness seems to me to be such an important phenomenon that I cannot believe that it is something just 'accidently' conjured up by a complicated computation. It is the phenomenon whereby the universe's very existence is made known.'[21] Even though much of what is involved in mental activity might work in the same way as a computer, the conscious mind itself cannot do so. Penrose continues to ask other questions about self-awareness and consciousness, noting for example that children sometimes see things more clearly and ask the questions that adults are too embarrassed to ask. He wonders where our stream of consciousness was before we were born and where it goes when we die.

The whole of the argument about living things in the universe becomes focused when we look at the development of conscious, self-aware human life. A significant feature of this universe is that it is observable by the human mind. While some biologists are moving toward a hard materialism, physicists faced with compelling experimental evidence have been moving away from strictly mechanical models of the universe to a view that sees the mind playing an integral role in all physical events. There is a fascinating irony here in that biologists who ought to be dealing with questions of relationship and community among life forms are moving toward a hard materialistic view of life reduced to chemical reactions and physical equations, while cosmologists, who work with mathematical equations, are increasingly speaking about a 'purpose' that goes beyond equations. In our time, the question thus presses perhaps harder than ever before on the impartial observer as to whether a universe that has seen the evolution of conscious human life requires the presence of a purposeful mind as its origin.

For the scientist, conscious life is the most astonishing phenomenon in nature, distinguished by amazing complexity and organisation. Despite this, notes Paul Davies, there is a tendency among biologists to reduce their study to physics and chemistry and to look at the molecular basis of life in a way that conjures up blind forces devoid of value, meaning and purpose.[22] If we are to resist this tendency and place biological discoveries properly alongside those of modern cosmology, it may be helpful to take a more holistic approach, standing back and taking a look at the whole biological picture. If we do take this kind of viewpoint, we notice something intriguing about order and disorder in the universe.

7. The Phenomenon of Increasing Order

The development of complex biological organisms represents increasing order and therefore contradicts the second law of thermodynamics, which requires disorder to increase in an isolated system. Organisation is necessarily continually breaking down. For example, if we took a container containing a gas in a frozen state and placed it at room temperature, the gas would expand until it reached thermal equilibrium. Without any outside influence this process is not reversible. The movement from a low entropy state to a high entropy state, with a corresponding increase in disorder, is irreversible. We could return the gas to a compact liquid state by means of a vacuum pump, but to run the vacuum pump would require energy to be produced, and in the production of that energy there would be a corresponding increase in entropy.

But while entropy increases in the universe system as a whole, complex life-forms develop in a manner that seems to run counter to this pattern by taking in energy in a low entropy form and discarding it in a high entropy form. The human body, for example, takes in energy in the low entropy form of food and oxygen and discards it in the high entropy form of heat, CO_2, and excreta. In this way, suggests Penrose, we are constantly fighting against the second law of thermodynamics.[23] To keep alive we need to keep lowering the entropy that is within us. Low entropy energy from the Sun is converted through photosynthesis in plants into organised structures, while high entropy radiant heat is given off into space. Such a source of low entropy energy is vital for complex organisms to develop. This phenomenon supplies us with another plank in the argument that the universe shows a remarkable degree of 'fine tuning'. As Penrose remarks, 'For some reason, the universe was created in a very special (low entropy) state.'[24]

If we retrace the expanding universe backwards in time, we come to a space-time singularity about fifteen billion years ago. But how do we fit human life into such a picture? This has been the question addressed by scientists, philosophers, and theologians down through the centuries of the existence of humankind. A depressing materialistic view would see the appearance of human beings as mere blind chance in the otherwise relentless progress of the universe from Big Bang to Big Crunch. The more optimistic view is to see meaning inherent to the universe, with human beings as a part of that meaning. Such a view would find no surprise in the discovery that the universe is tailor-made for human life. But then the objection can always be made that our mere presence as observers would cause us to see things like this. Biologists since the time of Darwin have rejected such meaning and reject the idea of a goal-directed evolution.[25] Even Dawkins, with his modified view of 'tamed chance', takes his stand here as a biologist.

Physicists, however, tend to take a rather different view. The so-called Anthropic Principle puts a different perspective on matters, suggesting that the universe is as it is because if it were different, we would not be here to observe it. Physicists tell us that to produce carbon, hydrogen, nitrogen, oxygen and phosphorus, all vital for life, requires nuclear reactions in the interior of stars, which are dispersed into space during a supernova explosion at the end of a star's life. Almost all the carbon in our bodies will have such an astral history. It is estimated that it would take over ten billion years from the Big Bang of such stellar alchemy to provide the necessary precursors of life.[26] The Anthropic Principle reminds us that if the universe had begun in a different state, we would not be here to know about it. This, again, is suggestive of purpose within the universe and, in particular, in the evolution of human life.

8. Suggestions of Purpose

The time has come to summarise the journey of discovery we have made in this chapter. We have seen that fossil life-forms through time show an increasing complexity, that they demonstrate mutation, change with environmental conditions, and become extinct. Studies of the morphology of different fossil groups suggests evolution, demonstrated by one species appearing to evolve in its outward form into another. The geological record displays a long path of such changes, with the variety and complexity of organisms constantly increasing. We shall consider this evidence in more detail in chapter 4.

Natural selection of favourable mutations in animals was first recognised by Lamark, but it was Darwin's studies that enabled the theory of evolution to be propounded with any security. Mendel, and later Watson and Crick, provided an explanation of the mechanism whereby mutation and natural selection and, therefore, evolution might take place. From the evidence available in the fields of palaeontology, palaeobiology, molecular biology, and genetics it would appear that the theory of evolution provides the best model to explain the diversity and development of living things. But we cannot reduce the process of biological change to blind chance. Dawkins speaks of 'tamed chance', which discerns guidance through natural selection by means of non-random survival at every stage of development, but we might question whether such a guiding mechanism is sufficient to produce human life as an end product rather than any other complex living organism. The theist might with some justice say that we need an overarching purpose that moves evolution toward the goal of conscious human life. It is a guiding mechanism such as this, we can argue, that would be required to find human life at the end of an evolutionary tree of life.

We have also seen that the growing complexity and organisation in living things is contrary to the second law of thermodynamics and is a further indication of a finely tuned universe, as it would require the universe to begin in a special state of low entropy. Increased complexity, especially in the form of conscious human life, suggests purpose, and purpose is suggestive of God. We move a step closer to this conclusion with the discovery that the brain is not simply mathematical, physical, and chemical, but has a non-algorithmic aspect. This again suggests that we are not only looking at the results of the outworking of physical laws. A conscious mind requires explanation, and it is not unreasonable to find this in the conscious mind of a purposeful designer.

In fact, 'purpose' becomes the key issue in the argument. It does not take religious belief to recognise the features of design in the universe. When cosmologists speak of the Anthropic Principle, they are speaking of an inherent design; even Dawkins has to appeal to a guiding principle that prevents evolutionary changes running down so many blind alleys. But design does not of course prove the presence of a Designer, as it may simply be a way of speaking about inherent principles and laws. A step towards a Creator is made when we are brought to speak about purpose, though this too may not necessarily imply a personal giver of purpose; the evolution of human life within the evolution of the whole cosmos is indicative of purpose for many who are not religious believers. The step of faith lies in moving from design and purpose to belief in a Creator, whose mind and purpose are written into the evolution of human life. But the recent evidence of research in the physical and biological sciences would seem to make such a step of faith at least more reasonable.

These researches are also helping us to understand what sort of God is indicated by the world of nature and of living organisms. We see here a picture of the God of purpose, who works through choices at every stage, who works through the world of quantum physics, of physical laws, and of natural selection. The journey of development we have traced in this chapter points us to a God who travels with, and suffers with, his creation. We shall be developing this understanding further in chapter 7, but for the moment we should note briefly that this suffering can be seen clearly exposed on the evolutionary path; it is seen in the mutations that lead to extinction, in the genetic variations that lead to disorder, as well as in those those that lead to an improved life or enhanced reproduction and, therefore, survival of the species. The God who shares this journey with his creation is the God we find in the Scriptures; he is the God of the Cross.

The Anthropic Principle, which is suggestive of purposeful design for the universe, is reinforced by the patterns discovered in evolving life, which culminate with human beings. But does evolution rule out of court the Christian view of a creator in whose purpose the human being is unique? It is to this question that we must now turn our attention.

Notes to Chapter 3

[1]Psalm 8:4 (New Revised Standard Version).

[2]Psalm 8:3-5 (NRSV).

[3]D. N. Adams, *The Hitch-Hiker's Guide to the Galaxy*, 137.

[4]H. Wendt, *Before the Deluge* (London: Palidin, 1970) 31.

[5]Quoted in Wendt, 72, from *Detailed Account of Newly Discovered Zooliths*.

[6]Quoted in Wendt, 81.

[7]Lamark's second law of evolution, included in his *Philosophie Zoologique*, quoted in Wendt, 96-97.

[8]Wendt, 130.

[9]J. Huxley and H. B. D. Kettlewell, *Charles Darwin and His World* (London: Thames & Hudson, 1965).

[10]Ibid., 126-27.

[11]Cited in R. E. D. Clark, *Darwin: Before and After* (Exeter: Paternoster Press, 1948) 112f.

[12]A. Miller, 'Biology and Belief', in *Real Science, Real Faith*, ed. R. J. Berry (Eastbourne: Monarch, 1991) 82.

[13]Ibid., 85-86

[14]R. Dawkins, *The Blind Watchmaker* (London: Longmans, 1986) Preface.

[15]Ibid., 5.

[16]Ibid., 72.

[17]Ibid., 141.

[18]A. Peacocke, *God and the New Biology* (London: Dent, 1986) 33-56, 95-99.

[19]Dawkins, 317-18.

[20]R. Penrose, *The Emperor's New Mind*.

[21]Ibid., 447

[22]P. Davies, *God and the New Physics*, 60-64.

[23]Penrose, 317-22.

[24]Penrose, 339.

[25]See Barrow, *Theories of Everything*, 164.

[26]Ibid., 165.

4

'Through Him all things were made'[1]

The Witness of Geology

Geology has been described, rather romantically perhaps, as 'a science based on observation and experiment [which] brings the student into direct contact with nature, for geology must be studied in the open air.'[2]

Geology is an observational science whose material is collected from quarries, mines, cliffs, boreholes, and road excavations. Such material is measured and analysed and is put under the microscope, often at very high magnifications. To this is added the recording and mapping of rock types and rock structures and also the use of geophysical techniques to study the deeper levels of the crust that are not observable at the surface.

A classical definition of geology was given by Sir Charles Lyell in the opening words of his *Principles of Geology* (1830):

> the science which investigates the successive changes that have taken place in the organic and inorganic kingdoms of nature; it enquires into the causes of these changes, and the influence which they have exerted in modifying the surface and external structure of our planet.

This definition highlights the way that geology explores the process of change in the world around us, and in our quest for an understanding of the evolution of the universe and human life we therefore turn to the geological history of Earth. Geology has a great deal to contribute to the picture of a world that is in movement and development, and this in turn will witness to the nature of a Creator God.

1. The Evolution of the Earth

The new cosmology presents us with a picture of an evolving universe, from a Big Bang singularity some fifteen billion years ago to the huge dimensions of galaxies and space that we see today. Earth has its own place within the evolution of the universe. Our solar system has been evolving for the last 4,500 million years or so, the oldest known rocks on Earth being dated at about 3,800 million years and material from meteorites about 4,600 million years. The fossil record presents us with another picture: one of evolving life forms, from simple algal life in the oceans about 3,200 million years ago to the variety of simple and complex life forms we see in our world today including *Homo sapiens*, which is the only life form on Earth with a consciousness able to perceive the story of the universe. Having looked at the cosmic story, we now turn our attention to Earth. Before we can discuss the creation and evolution of life we need to understand the evolution of the Earth itself, and especially the crust of the planet where that life exists.

The period when I was studying geology, in the 1960s and 1970s, was an extremely exciting time; a revolution was taking place in the earth sciences. This revolution was comparable with that seen in the life sciences following the work of Watson and Crick on genetics in the 1950s, or in the field of cosmology in 1980s following the work of Penrose and Hawking. During this time bold new ideas concerning the fundamental aspects of the structure and evolution of the planet were put forward. These ideas have been tested and confirmed by continuing detailed studies of the Earth's crust. This led Tony Hallam to write in 1973:

> Much of our thinking has had to undergo severe reappraisal, agonising or otherwise, and the application of new concepts to a more accurate and complete interpretation of geological history is still in a youthful phase.[3]

The bold new ideas concerned the structure of the Earth's crust. It was proposed that the entire surface of the Earth comprised a series of rigid, but relatively thin plates, 100-150 kilometres thick. The size of these plates was seen to be variable, but six major plates cover most of the Earth's surface: Eurasian, African, Australian, Pacific, Antarctic, and American plates, as shown in Figure 4:1. These plates are seen to be in continuous motion, moving apart, or towards, or alongside each other at rates of between 1-3 cm/annum. This may seem to be a very small movement, but over a century this would add up to 1-3 metres. If we consider, as an example, that the Pacific Plate has been moving north-westwards relative to the American Plate at some 3 cm/annum for most of this century, along the line of the San Andreas Fault, and that that movement has yet to be seen on the surface of the crust, we can begin to understand its importance to us. The movement is taking place in the more 'plastic' layers below the brittle upper layers of the crust. A minor

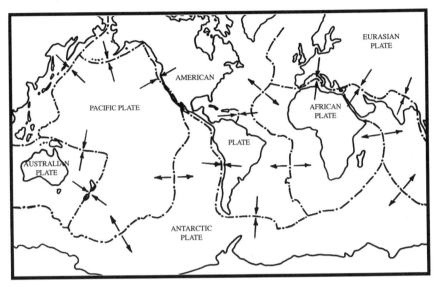

Figure 4:1 The Six Principle Tectonic Plates that make up the
Earth's crust. The arrows indicate the direction of plate movement,
which is in order of 2-3 cm/annum.

movement (a couple of millimetres or less) along a fracture in the Earth's crust will produce a major earthquake. The last major movement along the San Andreas Fault was the great San Francisco earthquake of 1906. From 1906 to 1994 is eighty-eight years, which at 3 cm/year is over two and a half metres. There is a major earthquake waiting to occur!

There is an important theological issue here. In 1755, an earthquake off the coast of Portugal caused a tidal wave that destroyed much of the port of Lisbon, and hundreds of people lost their lives. In the history of thought in the eighteenth century, the Lisbon earthquake became a turning point for many people against belief in a loving, sovereign God. But we now know the structure of the Earth's crust; we can predict where earthquakes are likely to occur; and we know that the evolving structure of the crust is necessary for the development of the rocks and minerals, on which much of our industrial development is based. What will we say when a major earthquake occurs along the San Andreas Fault in California? Using such events as objections to belief in God simplifies a complex matter. We must keep human responsibility in mind (given our present knowledge) and also the creative desire of God, who is intimately involved with his creation, to provide humanity with the materials for an advanced society through such structures in the Earth's crust. But of course these considerations supply no easy answer when we ask, 'Is it worth such a cost being paid in human suffering?' and we shall be returning to this question in a later chapter.[4]

Geologists recognise three types of plate margin: a constructive margin, such as the mid-Atlantic ridge, where the plates are moving apart and new material is added to the crust in the form of volcanic rock; a destructive plate margin, such as the Aleutian arc, where one plate is sliding under another; and a conservative plate margin, such as the San Andreas Fault line, where two plates are sliding past each other, with no material added or lost. These plate margins are the site of almost all the earthquake and volcanic activity seen in the world today.

2. Drifting Continents

The idea that the continents have moved is not a new one. In 1620 Francis Bacon commented on the similarity in the shapes of the coastlines on either side of the southern Atlantic, something that intrigued many scientists in the seventeenth and eighteenth centuries. At this time, however, most geology and palaeontology were explained in terms of catastrophes; the Comte de Buffon's suggestion in 1749, that the Atlantic was formed as the result of the catastrophic sinking of the mythical continent of 'Atlantis', was typical of the views held. By the end of the nineteenth century the geology of the southern continents of Africa, South America, Australia, and India was sufficiently well known for the Austrian geologist Eduard Suess to suggest that they once formed a super continent that he called 'Gondwanaland.' At the beginning of this century Alfred Wegener (1880–1931), a German geologist and meteorologist, suggested that all the continents had once been together and had drifted apart through time. In 1910 Wegener suggested that 200 million years ago the continents of Gondwanaland were united with Eurasia and North America to form a single super continent that he called 'Pangea.' He made his suggestion based on a study of the rocks, the fossils, the indications of past climatic conditions preserved in the rocks (Palaeo-climatology), and the major fault and mountain structures he observed at the edges of these continents. Although he was ridiculed in his life-time, he has been completely vindicated by the research into plate tectonics in the last thirty years.

Wegener put forward his ideas for drifting continents in a lecture in 1912 and a book first published in 1915, which was translated into English in 1924, entitled *The Origin of Continents and Oceans*. The problem for Wegener was just how the continents could drift apart. Before the geophysical discovery of convection currents in the hot plastic interior of the Earth, whose movement toward and away from each other could provide a mechanism for this drift, it was considered that the Earth was a static cooling body. Wegener had a problem, and his mechanism for drifting continents was certainly far fetched. He suggested that the continents were collected together at the North Pole and that their movement away from the pole was the result of gravity. This movement he called 'Pohlflucht', flight from the pole. Lateral movement he envisaged would be the result of tidal forces. It was for this highly doubtful mechanism that he was criticised, and this was the one obstacle to the acceptance of his theory. Palaeontologists seeking to explain the distribution of faunas and floras on the various continents had instead to postulate land bridges, long-since submerged, for which no evidence whatsoever existed. This was also a highly speculative theory, but perhaps the game was given away by T. C. Chamberlin in 1928 who said: 'If we are to believe Wegener's hypothesis we must forget everything which has been learned in the last seventy years and start all over again.'[5] This is always a problem for the scientist or the theologian; conservative prejudice is far more comfortable than having to reach out into the unknown ground of new ideas.

Since the time of Wegener, the amassing of facts by geologists in all parts of the world has only resulted in support for his original suggestions. In the area of geophysics we have not only been able to demonstrate the nature of the upper mantle and crust of the Earth, but also to study palaeomagnetism in the rocks of the continents and oceans. Palaeomagnetism is the preservation of the direction and inclination of the Earth's magnetic field in molten igneous and volcanic rocks as they cooled. These demonstrate that either the continents have moved through time, or that the Earth's magnetic poles have wandered far and wide during time. The discovery of pole reversals in the magnetic field of the Earth has enabled geophysicists to show the way in which the Atlantic Ocean has opened up along the line of the mid-Atlantic ridge, as symmetrical bands of reversed and normal magnetic fields are preserved in the volcanic rocks of the sea floor on either side of the ridge.

3. Changing Environments through Time

This is then, on the large scale of the whole crust of the Earth, a picture of change and development through geological time. If we turn, on a smaller scale, to the rocks exposed along the coastline of Great Britain or inland to the mountains, river valleys, quarries, and mines, we find a similar picture of change and development through time. These rocks show the development of different environments and climates, periods that were quiet and calm, and times of large-scale disruption, when the sea floor was thrown up and folded to form mountains, accompanied by earthquakes and violent volcanic activity. We could go to the Carboniferous limestone rocks of the eastern shoreline of Anglesey and see coral reefs, like those of the Great Barrier Reef of Australia. We could travel eastwards to the North Wales Coalfield and see the remains of a swamp forest, which grew on a large river delta in a tropical climate. All of this is far removed from a typical British summer at Llandudno or Prestatyn! Again if we travelled further east to Cheshire, we would find ourselves in rocks of the Permian and Triassic periods, with evidence of salt lakes and desert sand dunes. Continuing southeastwards we come to the Jurassic limestones of Northamptonshire, which were deposited in a shallow warm sea, not too different from the Bahamas today. There is plenty of evidence that Great Britain has not always been situated so far north of the Equator but has been in both equatorial and tropical latitudes.

The rocks also show the passing of time. Some sediments may accumulate very quickly, with flash flood conditions of a river bringing down great thicknesses of boulders and gravel in a matter of hours; we might think of the Lynmouth disaster in 1953 as an example of this. On the other hand a metre of fine-grained mud on the floor of an ocean may take tens of thousands of years to accumulate. When the 120 kilometres or more of sedimentary rocks laid down in the various geological periods are taken into account, they must represent a very long time of accumulation. To this we must add the periods of great upheaval in the crust, the times when the great mountain chains were being formed: those that today, for example, form the Highlands of Scotland, the Pennines of England, the Appalachians and the Rockies of North America, or the

Alps of Europe. These were times when continents were brought into collision at a destructive plate margin, and the sea floor and all the sediments were buckled and folded and lifted up to form mountain chains. The heat and pressure exerted on the rocks by this process caused some to be changed from sediments into crystalline metamorphic rocks.

Associated with such violent processes was a great deal of volcanic activity and the intrusion of large masses of molten igneous rock into the upper layers of the Earth's crust. As these igneous rocks cooled, they crystallised to form such features as the granite masses of Dartmoor and Bodmin Moor in Cornwall. The heat from such large masses of molten igneous rock affected the sediments into which they were intruded, causing mud to be baked, new minerals to form, and the rocks to be metamorphosed. In South Wales, the mountain-building movements that produced granite masses in Cornwall, produced the more gently folded and fractured rocks of the coalfield. This movement was also accompanied by earthquakes. From my own research[6] I have shown that such earthquakes were experienced while the sediments were still in an unconsolidated condition, and that later, when they had had time to solidify, they were folded and fractured by the earth movements that produced a range of mountains that now underlies northern Europe. In Valis Vale near Frome folded Carboniferous limestone belonging to this mountain range are seen to be cut across by a plane surface and to be overlain by horizontal Jurassic limestone. The Carboniferous limestone has been bored by marine organisms and the minute holes filled in with the Jurassic sediment. This demonstrates a long history of events: the consolidation of the Carboniferous limestone, its folding by earth movements, and its subsequent erosion by the sea that produced a wave cut platform, which itself was submerged to form the floor of a Jurassic limestone sea.

4. The Dimension of Geological Time

These few examples from the geological history of the British Isles are enough to demonstrate the complex development of the rocks that make up the Earth's crust. An overview of the geological history of the crust is shown in Figure 4:2. This account should make clear, in case any are still inclined to doubt an evolution of the Earth, that it makes no sense at all to suggest that all these events could have taken place during a

ERA	TIME PERIOD	MILL. YRS AGO	MAJOR EVENTS (in Europe)	LAT. of U.K.
CENOZOIC	Quaternary	3	glaciation	55°N
CENOZOIC	Neogene	23	Alpine orogenesis	50°N
CENOZOIC	Paleogene	65	volcanic activity	40°N
MESOZOIC	Cretaceous	135		35°N
MESOZOIC	Jurassic	205		
MESOZOIC	Triassic	250		20°N
PALEOZOIC	Permian	290	Hercynian orogenesis	5°N
PALEOZOIC	Carboniferous	355	volcanic activity	5°S
PALEOZOIC	Devonian	410		5°S
PALEOZOIC	Silurian	438	Caledonian orogenesis volcanic activity	
PALEOZOIC	Ordovician	510	volcanic activity	15°S
PALEOZOIC	Cambrian	570		40°S
PROTEROZOIC	Proterozoic	2500		
ARCHAEAN	Archaean	4500		

Figure 4:2 Geological Time Periods, Age, and
Latitude of the Rocks of Europe.

literal six days of creation. Those ('Creationists') who do want to adhere to a literal interpretation of the account of creation found in Genesis 1 suggest that the sedimentary layers and structures of the crust are accounted for in the catastrophe of the biblical flood and that the processes that we see at work in the world today were speeded up during the six days of creation. But why should a God of order and beauty do such a thing, and what sort of picture are we painting of God? The God who is revealed in the Scriptures is faithful, consistent, and reliable. We cannot believe that God, who encourages us to discover his faithfulness and to imitate it, would behave in such an inconsistent way and leave us with so much evidence that would contradict a literal interpretation of Genesis 1—if we were meant to take its truth in a literal way. We shall return to the interpretation of Genesis 1 in chapter 5.

The evidence from the study of the Earth's crust demonstrates, as clearly as is possible, that our planet has had a long history. The twentieth century has seen developments in physics and chemistry that have allowed for the study of the atomic structure of all elements. This led to the discovery of radioactive isotopes of some elements. These radioactive isotopes are unstable and, in time, decay (change by loss of protons and/or neutrons) to stable isotopes of another element. The invention of the mass spectrometer allowed the measurement of the quantities of such isotopes, and this has led to methods of the measurement of geological time known as radiometric dating. Relatively (i.e. relative to the time-scale involved) precise and accurate methods of dating are based on the radioactive decay rates of isotopes of Uranium, Thorium, Potassium, and Rubidium. The rate of decay is expressed in terms of the 'half-life' of the isotope, which is the length of time taken for half the unstable isotopes to decay to their stable equivalents. The following are the main isotopes used in dating the geological history of the Earth:

K^{40}-Ar^{40} (Potassium to Argon), half life 11,900 million years;
U^{238}-Pb^{206} (Uranium to Lead), half life 4,500 million years;
U^{235}-Pb^{207}, half life 713 million years;
Th^{232}-Pb^{208} (Thorium to Lead), half life 13,900 million years;
Rb^{87}-Sr^{87} (Rubidium to Strontium), half life 47-50,000 million years.

Often a variety of these methods will be used to confirm the dating of a particular rock sample. The date that is given will be the time when the individual minerals crystallised in an igneous rock, or during the recrystallisation of a metamorphic rock. Extremes of heat and/or pressure will therefore affect the dating, and the dates will indicate the last time that a rock was subjected to such heat and pressure. The decay rate of potassium to argon has been the most commonly used method, and through it and the decay of isotopes of other elements the geological periods of the Earth's history have all been dated, as shown in Figure 4:2. The oldest dates we have for rocks of the Earth's crust are in the order of 3,400–3,800 million years and for meteorites (planetary debris within our solar system) dates in the order of 4,600 million years.[7] This has led geologists to suggest an age of about 4,500 million years for the formation of Earth.

5. The Origins of Life

We now turn to the evidence of life preserved within the fossil record. Our present views of the evolution of life are based on studies of comparative morphology, physiology, biochemistry, embryology, genetics, population dynamics, biogeography, and other analyses of living things on Earth. The way that the actual order and pattern of evolution can be studied, over any length of time, is, however, only possible by examining the rich and varied remains of past plant and animal life preserved as fossils in sedimentary rocks. So geology is not only a study of rocks, but of the growth and development of life itself.

Only a small proportion of plant and animal life has been preserved because as soon as an animal or plant dies it begins to decay and is at the mercy of various scavingers. It is therefore highly unusual for soft-bodied animals to be preserved as fossils or for the soft parts of other animals to survive. 'Morphology' is the study of the shape and form of an animal, and this is mainly derived from the evidence of skeletons, shells, and other hard parts of animals normally preserved in rocks. Whole insects have, however, been preserved in the resin of Cretaceous trees, and late-Pliestocene mammals, such as the woolly mammoth, have been preserved in the ice. Generally it is the skeletal parts of animals that are preserved, but 'trace fossils' such as animal foot prints, and burrows may sometimes survive when the sand or mud is not disturbed by violent wave action, before being covered by more sediment. Fossils vary in size from the microscopic *foraminifera, ostracods*, and *conodonts,* to the macroscopic *Tyranosaurus rex* and the other large dinosaurs. The succession of life shows a generally increasing variety and complexity, as shown in Figure 4:3. The earliest known fossil life that has been found has been bacterial and algal material, together with the presence of amino acids, in rocks as old as 3,200 million years.

It has been said that one of the most remarkable features of the fossil record is the evidence that at certain times there was rapid morphological diversification of life.[8] There is a sudden appearance of simple marine life at the base of the Cambrian period; in the Silurian period fish appear; in the Devonian period, plants; in the early Cretaceous, the reptiles; in mid-Cretaceous, the angiosperms (flowering plants); and in the early-Tertiary period, the mammals. There is a great deal of variety in the development of animal and plant life. The brachiopod (a marine shell) *Lingula* has remained unchanged from the Cambrian to the present day, over 500 million years, and the modern horse-tail *Equisetum i*s the same as an equivalent plant found in coal measures over 290 million years old. By contrast, the bulk of present-day mammals have developed in the last twenty million years.

What is the origin of this diverse life that is found in the rocks, and in the world today? How did it begin? Why did it develop in the sea first and then on the land and in the air? Life on Earth is carbon-based, and the origin of this has been a puzzle that has intrigued biologists and palaeontologists. Organic compounds—including the key compound DNA —are the very basis of life, and these all include carbon in their molecular structure. How did the organic compounds come about? And where did the carbon come from in the first place?

In the 1930s J. B. S. Haldane suggested that organic compounds were formed in the early atmosphere of the Earth and eventually found their way into the oceans, which formed a hot 'soup' where these compounds could grow.[9] The great leap forward in the study of the origin of life came with the work of S. L. Miller in 1953, who demonstrated in an experiment that the amino acids, purines and pyramidines that are the building blocks of organic compounds, could be produced naturally in such an environment. Miller applied electrical discharges to a mixed 'atmosphere' including methane, ammonia, and water vapour and produced a number of organic compounds. It was claimed that as a result there would be a build-up of organic compounds in the oceans, which would provide a 'nutrient broth' in which the first living organisms developed. This led scientists to believe that carbon was present in the

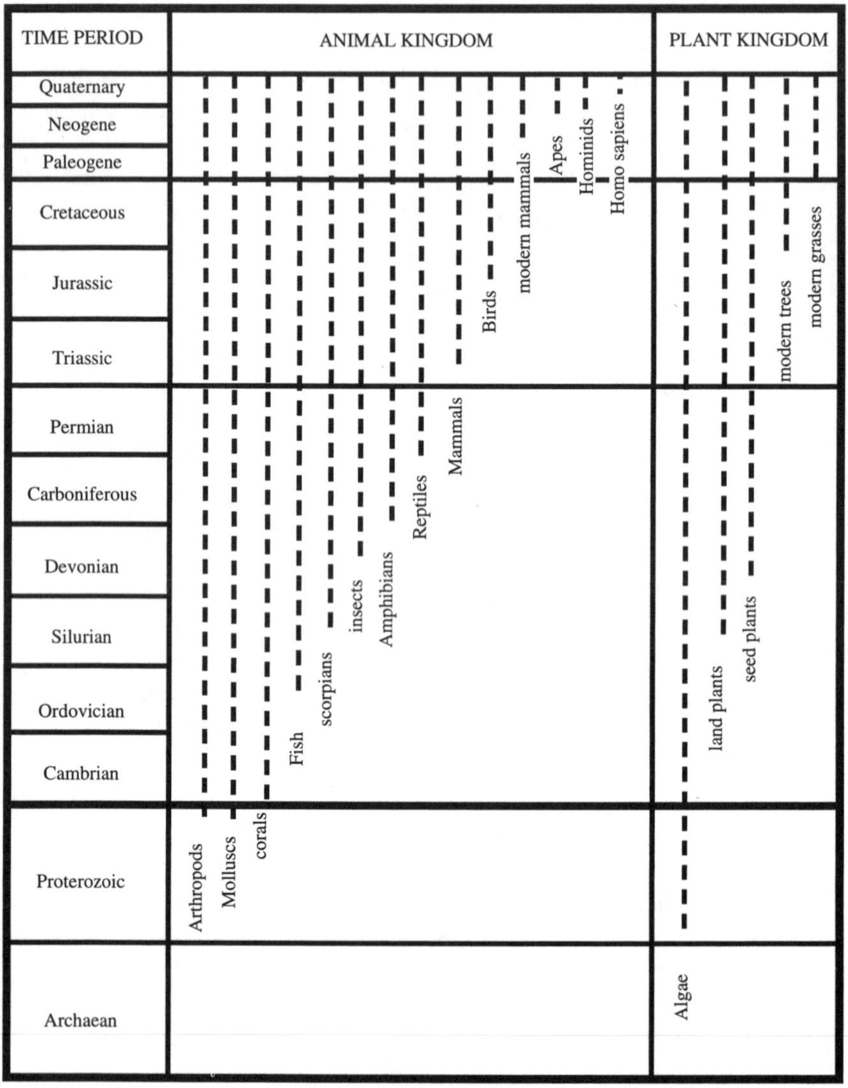

TIME PERIOD	ANIMAL KINGDOM	PLANT KINGDOM
Quaternary		
Neogene		
Paleogene	modern mammals · Apes · Hominids · Homo sapiens	
Cretaceous		modern grasses
Jurassic	Birds	modern trees
Triassic		
Permian	Mammals	
Carboniferous	Reptiles	
Devonian	Amphibians	seed plants
Silurian	insects	land plants
Ordovician	scorpians	
Cambrian	Fish	
Proterozoic	Arthropods · Molluscs · corals	
Archaean		Algae

Figure 4:3 The Fossil Record

Earth's primitive atmosphere in the form of methane. Though today no one doubts the validity of Miller's experiments, there is now considerable doubt, however, over what was assumed to be the composition of the atmosphere. If the primordial atmosphere had been so rich in carbon, then we should see far more evidence than we do of carbon compounds in the Pre-Cambrian sediments.

Carbon does occur in significant amounts in some meteorites, which are products of the evolution of the solar system, if not actually planetary fragments. These 'carbonaceous chondrites' (carbon-rich meteorites) contain compounds of carbon such as methane, paraffins, and amino acids. These, suggests Sylvester-Bradley,[10] are organic aggregates not formed by a biological process ('abiogenically formed') that can be regarded as 'pre-organisms.' Such material would have been insoluble and would have been incorporated into sediments such as mud, sand, and gravel in much the same way as crude oil is present. Today, all forms of life depend for their food on the photosynthetic activity of green plants, which use the energy from the sun to synthesize organic compounds from the carbon dioxide in the atmosphere.[11] Photosynthesis, however, depends on the action of enzymes, which themselves are the product of life-processes. In pre-biological times there were no enzymes, and there could be no photosynthesis. The first life forms would therefore have needed to depend on food produced by non-biological processes, something like crude oil seeping out of the sub-strate. It is possible that some such carbon may initially have been of volcanic origin.

There are a number of suggestions being raised currently about the origin of life, and these were given wide publicity on the BBC-TV Horizon programme called "Life is Impossible," broadcast on 28 June 1993. The programme examined a number of theories, all of which it noted were incomplete, and it gave viewers a good sense of what modern scientific discussion on these issues is like. The programme first dismissed Miller's experiments on the grounds that the early Pre-Cambrian sediments indicate a CO_2 rich rather than methane-rich atmosphere. Donald Lowe of Stanford University, California, demonstrated this fact from evaporite deposits in South Africa, which have been dated at about 3,200 million years B.P. Next, Christopher Chyba, of NASA Goddard Space Flight Center, suggested that organic molecules, which were the basis of life on Earth, came from interstellar debris in the tails of comets. This suggestion was discounted by Jeffrey Bada of Scripps Institute of Oceanography, because his own research had shown the lack of sufficient amounts of amino acids in core samples removed from the Arctic ice. The more far-fetched suggestion of crystal growth, perhaps of pyrite (Iron

Sulphide) around volcanic hot springs, was also considered and dis-missed. It was shown experimentally by Remy Hennet, a consultant Geochemist, that it is possible to produce amino acids in the vicinity of volcanic hot springs on the sea floor, providing that formaldahide and hydrogen cyanide are present. But, even if these chemicals were present in primeval times, which was disputed by Stanley Miller of the Univer-sity of California, then this will always leave the problem of how we develop the nucleic acids, which are the other elements essential for producing life.

This latter point has been made by Paul Davies,[12] who says that even if we can show how amino acids are produced, we are still left with a jump to life. The development from amino acids to the complex mole-cules of DNA that carry the genetic code could not have been left to chance. It is, of course, possible that this was the work of self-organising natural systems, but we need some other concept than mere chance to describe their means of organisation. Here Davies suggests that whether the origin of life is natural or the result of divine intervention, we still have strong evidence of 'purpose' in a universe that produces both amino acids and nucleic acids in some primordial ocean. The precise way in which life originated is an open question yet to be solved by science, although the indications of the experimental work suggest that a natural answer will be found in the end. This answer would not rule out God, but for a Christian believer would rather point to his immanent working within nature, which I intend to discuss in chapters 6 and 7.

From its starting point in the primordial ocean, we now need to consider how and why life developed as it did. Plant life on dry land only existed from about 420 million years B.P. It was only at this stage that the lethal, ultraviolet levels were cut out by the atmosphere, so allowing plant life to develop. Berkner and Marshall[13] suggest that the evolution of life on Earth is related to critical levels of oxygen in the evolving atmosphere. The first level they recognise is one percent of the present abundance of oxygen. At this level sufficient amounts of ultraviolet radiation would be cut out to allow life to develop in the oceans. They consider that this level was reached about 600 million years ago, indicated by the abrupt opening up of the whole oceans to life. Cloud[14] supports this view suggesting that from 3,200 to 1,900 million years ago there was biological production of oxygen in the hydrosphere; and from 1,900 to 600 million years ago there was a build up of oxygen in the atmosphere with a resulting decrease in CO_2. This view is supported by the occurrence of calcareous sediments (rich in calcium carbonate), which incorporated the carbon dioxide.

By 600 million years B.P. the ozone level would have been sufficient to cut out the ultraviolet radiation that inhibits DNA. This would have opened up the oceans to the development and growth of photosynthesizing phytoplankton, which would in turn lead to a large increase in the amount of oxygen in the atmosphere. The increase in oxygen would be accompanied by a parallel decrease in CO_2, which would be bound into carbonate ($CaCO_3$) sediments. A reduction in the CO_2 blanket, which reflected heat radiation back to the Earth's surface, would cause temperatures on the Earth's surface to fall. This is indicated by the first evidence of glaciation in late Pre-Cambrian sediments. By 420 million years B.P. the oxygen content of the atmosphere had reached a level where land plants could survive. Their growth would lead to further, more rapid, increase in oxygen levels. It has been suggested[15] that at this time the oxygen level had reached ten percent of its present-day level. The result gave rise to an immediate evolutionary response with many groups of land plant and animal species developing from their marine counterparts.

6. Evidence of Evolution in the Fossil Record

We have begun to find the answers to the questions of where and when life began and developed on a large scale, but we are left with questions of how and why changes, mutation, and evolution of organisms took place. The basic problem here is how we can detect a new species. Inter-breeding between different species is a necessary part of evolutionary development, and so it is critical to be able to recognise the variations that indicate the production of a new species. But the population of any single species will tend to have variations within it as well as a broad morphological similarity. Distribution may also be controlled by ecological barriers, and variation may reach a level where a geographical sub-species is identified at the very limits of the distribution area. Palaeontologists are limited in the conclusions that they can draw by what (almost entirely) hard parts of animals have been preserved. They may see morphological changes that suggest evolution, but they cannot be dogmatic about the mechanism. Much of the work is subjective, as species can be distributed both spacially at one rock horizon and also temporally through one layer of rock.

One statistical method that seeks to identify species is biometric analysis, which plots one morphological feature against another on a graph. For example, the height of sea shells may be plotted against their width. If the results show a normal distribution curve with one peak, then one can assume that one species is present; a curve with two peaks may suggest the presence of two species. Sometimes the changes from one species to another can be clearly seen in successive rock layers. One example is to be seen in the basal Jurassic (Liassic) rocks of Great Britain, which at a number of localities contain beds of oysters. One locality where I have observed these myself is along the coast of South Glamorgan, between Ogmore and Penarth. At any horizon there is a wide variety in the characters of the oysters present, and this variation incorporates the members of several morphological species. These species were probably capable of inter-breeding, suggests Kirkaldy.[16] The main morphological differences are in the curvature of the left valve and the size of the attachment scar, by which the shell was attached to the substrate. In these rocks we see evolution taking place through a succession of communities, in which several features pass progressively from a state of incipience to that of dominance, as shown in Figure 4:4, which is taken from the work of A. E. Trueman.[17] These changes indicate increasing levels of mud and silt in suspension in the water. While the

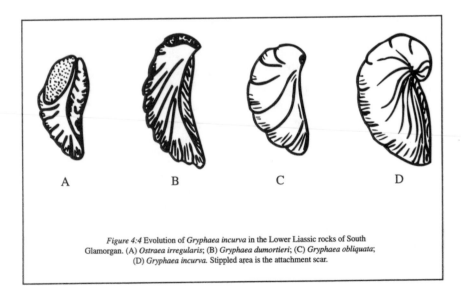

A   B   C   D

Figure 4:4 Evolution of *Gryphaea incurva* in the Lower Liassic rocks of South Glamorgan. (A) *Ostraea irregularis*; (B) *Gryphaea dumortieri*; (C) *Gryphaea obliquata*; (D) *Gryphaea incurva*. Stippled area is the attachment scar.

fossil record is often incomplete and complete evolutionary lineages cannot be shown, there is sufficient evidence of the type described above to demonstrate that mutation in response to environmental change does take place. Such mutation would form the basis of natural selection.

Natural selection may subtract (selecting one adaptation over a number of others), but mutation can add to the number of possibilities, and together over the span of geological time this leads to development of complexity in living things. Dawkins suggests that there are two ways in which adaption takes place. Firstly he proposes that it happens through 'co-evolved genotypes', where genes work together towards survival; genes are selected by virtue of their interactions with their environments, particularly with other genes, which are also evolving. Secondly there are 'arms races', where predator and prey undergo stages of adaption that make them better able to devour or survive, for example improved speed, or eyesight, or hearing.[18]

Fossil evidence is far less clear, because of its incomplete nature. When the available fossil record is studied, it does not demonstrate a smooth curve of developing evolutionary change, but one with gaps and, apparently, sudden bursts of development of species. This has led Stephen Jay Gould, through his work on the Cambrian (530 million years B.P.) Burgess Shale of British Columbia,[19] to suggest periods of stasis, millions of years of no change, and shorter periods of rapid change, possibly in small geographically isolated populations.[20] This so-called 'punctuated evolution' allows for the suggestion of periods of creativity, rather than a steady kind of evolution by natural selection. Dawkins is right to point out that these periods might have been times of rapid evolutionary development (by a geological time scale) and that the sudden appearance of a species at one location may simply indicate that the evolutionary steps to produce it went on elsewhere.[21] Gould, however, draws attention to the wide variety of classes and phyla that are present in the Burgess Shale, leading him to suggest that:

> the maximum range of anatomical possibilities arises with the first rush of diversification. . . . Later history is a tale of restriction, as most of these early experiments succomb and life settles down to generating endless variants upon a few surviving models.[22]

Before considering Gould's hypothesis further we might remember that changes in the environment, such as the levels of oxygen in the atmosphere, will have a marked effect on the development of species. In addition to this we must recognise that the Burgess Shale is noted by palaeontologists for the remarkable state of preservation of the fossils it contains, and also that prior to the Cambrian period it seems likely that few animals had hard skeletons capable of preservation. Therefore we must take care in the conclusions that may be drawn from these rocks. Gould believes that almost the whole variety of possible life-forms have their precursors in the Cambrian period, as demonstrated by the Burgess Shale, and that any slight changes at this stage would have sent evolution cascading into a radically different channel. He admits that the problem with alternative runs of the 'life tape' is that they did not happen, and so we cannot know the details of their plausible occurrence.[23]

He suggests that we consider one 'might-have-been'. When the dinosaurs perished at the end of the Cretaceous period, they left a vacuum in the world of large-bodied carnivores. This leads Gould to ask whether the current dominance of cats and dogs in the sub-human animal kingdom emerged by predictable necessity or contingent fortune. He then notes that in the succeeding Eocene period there was a battle for supremacy between the birds and the mammals. In South America the birds were dominant over the marsupials, but in Europe and North America the placentals (including, of course, cats and dogs) dominated the birds. This leads him to question whether the South American picture is an alternative 'evolutionary tape' for the whole world. This is an unanswerable question as we also have the European 'tape.' Gould says that Darwin saw competition under the terms of natural selection, with the better-adapted species winning, and so for Darwin contingency is the primary support to evolution.[24] Yet Gould maintains that nature was not as smoothly ordered as Darwin suggested, and that large scale catastrophic changes in environment have left their mark. He concludes that the Burgess Shale suggests a pattern of maximum diversity at the bottom, with contingency leading to proliferation along certain lines only—a 'Christmas tree, bottom heavy, evolutionary tree.' This bottom-heavy picture is also suggested by Gould for the mammalian lineages of the Paleocene.[25] There was an initial period of explosive diversification following the demise of the dinosaurs, which was followed by the normal evolutionary progress of the lineages. This leads Gould to the conclusion that early diversification and later decimation, whereby only a tenth of species survive, gives the broadest possible role to contingency; what we see are the few fortunate survivors in a lottery of decimation, rather than the end result of progressive diversification by adaptive improvement.

This alternative view of evolution is not significantly different in terms of the process of development and change through natural selection, except that it draws attention to particular periods of rapid diversification of species. Changes in the oxygen levels in the atmosphere, discussed earlier, might have led us to expect this. Another factor would be the movement of continents into new climatic zones, as the result of plate movements. In terms of Christian apologetics, it is important to emphasise that recent science has not 'overturned' or 'abandoned' theories of evolution, as one sometimes hears over-enthusiastic advocates of divine creation claiming ('no one accepts Darwin any longer' is a typically bold assertion). Recent work like that of Gould has caused scientists to re-think mechanisms of evolution, not the basic idea of evolution itself. But it would be quite proper for a Christian thinker to claim that, while all versions of evolution raise the question of the need for guidance of development, the 'alternative' view raises the question even more acutely, to ensure that only one of a number of possible evolutionary pathways would be followed.

7. Where Does God Fit In?

There has, at least since the time of Darwin, and even before that, been a dispute between those who would see God's hand in the separate creation of each animal and plant and those who see the gradual work of evolution by mutation and natural selection. I have tried in this chapter to set out the evidence in as objective a way as possible. From the record of fossils in the various geological epochs the overall picture is one of evolving life forms, both in variety and complexity. There is clear evidence of adaption and mutation in response to environment, and there are examples of one species evolving into another, on the small scale. The geological record is punctuated by sudden bursts of development of new species, which may reflect the development of beneficial environmental conditions. Finally, however, we must recognise the partial nature of the fossil record, which can only reflect a minute proportion of the life that actually existed at any particular moment in the planet's history. It is, as a result, possible to suggest that we do not have the definitive proof for evolution within the fossil record, and that therefore separate creation of species is still a possibility. From a scientific point of view, evolution is the model that best accords with what we know of the development of life on Earth from both the researches of biology and of palaeontology. From a theological point of view, we must ask a different kind of question: what sort of God is pictured by creationism on the one hand and a view of divinely-guided evolution on the other?

Richard Dawkins speaks of the only 'watchmaker' in nature as being the blind forces of physics, albeit deployed in a very special way. This is his 'tamed chance', the steps of natural selection through non-random survival.[26] But, on the other hand, creationists seem to leave no room for scientific discovery. As Barbour aptly comments, while the 'scientific creationist' makes statements about science that are dictated by religious beliefs, the scientific materialist makes statements about religion as if they were part of science.[27] It stretches credulity to speak of even 'tamed chance' in a universe that has so much evidence of purpose. But, on the other hand, it does not make a lot of sense to consider separate creations for every living thing. What sort of God would this indicate? The biblical picture is of a God continuously involved, in an intimate and patient way, with his creation. The interventionist God who creates trilobites in the Cambrian, trees in the Devonian, and *Tyranosaurus rex* in the Cretaceous (not in a 'Jurassic Park'[28]) period is neither the God of the Bible nor of geology. The God of nineteenth-century natural religion was the 'God of the gaps', and Darwin removed God from one of the gaps that he was filling, namely that of separately creating each individual species. Paradoxically, then, Darwin did faith a service in bringing God back from 'up there' or 'out there' into his own world. It was Cardinal Newman who remarked on having read Darwin's *Origin of the Species:*

> It is strange that monkeys should be so like man with no historical connection between them. . . . I will either go the whole hog with Darwin or, dispensing with time and history altogether, hold not only the theory of sudden creation of distinct species but also of fossil-bearing rocks.[29]

The creationist school of thought is exemplified by *The Genesis Flood*, which was written by H. M. Morris and J. C. Whitcomb in 1967. They contend that the original Earth was created in six days and that it is only since the biblical flood of Noah covered the whole world that the constant physical forces of nature, which we observe today, have operated. They treat the Bible as a textbook and have the tendency to reorganise scientific data to fit in with their views. Their treatment of geological evidence is often selective, and their interpretations are at least as dubious as those with which they disagree. Berry[30] is right in pointing fundamentalists to Galileo, who was condemned by the church for suggesting that the Earth orbits around the Sun, in apparent contradiction of Psalm 93:1 and 1 Chronicles 16:30. But Galileo was right, and they were wrong. We must conclude that the geological picture suggests that both the Earth and the life preserved in the rocks have evolved over a long period of time. As the environmental conditions became more favourable, life blossomed and developed through mutation and natural selection.

8. The Peculiar Case of Human Beings

But what about the origin of human beings? Do all the coincidences, which some scientists recognise as signs of design, simply indicate that we are lucky to be here to observe the universe? Bertrand Russell said that the universe was 'brute fact', no more and no less. But is it all pointless, or was the universe planned with a purpose, and did that purpose include human beings? It is time to consider whether human beings are indeed unique creations of God.

Peacocke points out that there is a clear distinction between the most intelligent primate and human beings, because it is impossible to move a highly domesticated chimpanzee beyond the level of an eighteen-month-old child. We are able to shape our own evolution by shaping our own environment.[31] Jacob Bronowski, in his book *The Ascent of Man*, writes:

> It took at least 2 million years for man to change from the little dark creature with a stone in his hand, *Australopithecus* in central Africa, to the modern form, *Homo sapiens*. That is the pace of biological evolution—even though the biological evolution of man has been faster than that of any other animal. But it has taken much less than 20,000 years for *Homo sapiens* to become the creatures that you and I aspire to be: artists and scientists, city builders and planners for the future, readers and travellers, eager explorers of natural fact and human emotion, immensely richer in experience and bolder in imagination than any of our ancestors. That is the pace of cultural evolution . . . at least 100 times faster than biological evolution.[32]

He notes that the crucial change takes place about 10,000 B.C., when human beings move from being hunters to being farmers. Carlo Cipolla makes a similar point in his book *The Economic History of World Population*, when he writes:

> For thousands and thousands of years, man lived as a predatory animal. Hunting, fishing, gathering wild fruits, and killing and eating other men remained for a very long time the only ways by which man could secure for himself the necessary means of subsistence. As a most ancient Sumerian text put it, 'when the human species appeared, it did not know bread nor cloth.'[33]

Cipolla proposes that ancient farming settlements first appear in the Middle East: at Jerico c.7,000 B.C.; Jarmo in Iraq and Tepe Sarab in Iran c.7,000–6,500 B.C., where people domesticated animals and grew barley and two strains of wheat; and Katal Huyuk in southern Turkey c. 6,600 B.C. If this is correct, then the first agricultural revolution, this 'revolution of first civilization', as Cipolla describes it, took place sometime after 8,000 B.C. In other parts of the world it comes later: c. 5,000 B.C. in China and South East Asia; c. 4,000 B.C. in Egypt and Great Britain; and about 3,000 B.C. in Peru. It appears, claims Cipolla, that civilization spread out from the fertile crescent area to the rest of Eurasia.[34] In my view, this is suggestive of the biblical account in Genesis 3-11 that portrays early humanity as occupying this area of the world.

E. K. V. Pearce, an anthropologist and a Christian priest, has made a case for 'Adam' being a Neolithic farmer, cultivating his patch on the slopes of the Turkish plateau, as the climate improved following the retreat of the last great Pleistocene ice-sheet.[35] This would place 'Adam' about 8,000 B.C. Pearce further differentiates between 'man' as mentioned in Genesis 1:26-27, whom he considers to be Old Stone Age Man, the hunter and fisher, and 'Adam' of Genesis 2:15, whom he considers to be New Stone Age Man, the settled farmer. While not subscribing to these specific identifications, I do consider that there is a general reasonableness about believing that Genesis 3-11 fits into the sort of anthropological and archaeological background uncovered by researchers. While we cannot find an exact history in the Genesis material, it is surely not unreasonable to suppose that the written account in Genesis finally preserves a community memory handed down from generation to generation about the origins of civilization, traces of which also appear in other ancient documents.

The Genesis story bears witness to the emergence of a moral consciousness together with a sense of guilt about transgression; Adam fails to trust the purpose of God for human life and realises that he has failed (Genesis 3). Perhaps the 'critical point' of development that anthropologists mark as the shift into a settled existence coincides with the emergence for the first time of the sense of moral responsibility in relationships, which we discern as a mark of being truly persons; if so, we may see this development as being under the guidance of the Spirit of God who was deeply at work in the creative and evolutionary processes. As Arthur Peacocke notes:

> man constitutes a break in the evolutionary process which had hitherto depended on the continuous operation of natural laws. For man appears to himself to have a free will allowing him to make choices and is free to fail to respond to the challenge presented to him.[36]

R. J. Berry, who is a biologist and a Christian, has sought to consider this issue from the biological perspective and looks to see if he can discern in the biological record something corresponding to a special creation of human beings 'in the image of God.'[37] Berry considers the later stages in the development of hominids. *Homo erectus* was widely distributed in the Upper Pleistocene, about one million years B.P.; they were upright walker, meat eaters, tool makers, belonging to the Acheulian 'Great hand axe' culture. They did not differ greatly from *Homo sapiens* and seems to have overlapped with them. There are a number of well documented intermediary forms, from 300–150,000 years B.P., including, Swanscombe (lower Thames Valley); Vertessozollos (Hungary); Steinheim (Germany); and Montmaurin and Fontechevade (France). Berry points out that the gene pool of any species is the result of the interactions of the past individuals of that species with all their previous environments. If we were to accept the view of the creationist that human beings were instantaneously created, it would follow that all their present behaviour patterns, reactions, and relations would be the consequence of God's intention in his special creation of them, Adam's sin, and the relatively short time that has elapsed since the Garden of Eden. 'Although possible, this is almost certainly untrue' concludes Berry.[38] Moreover, if early *Homo sapiens* had no previous genetic history that equipped them for response to realities outside themselves, God would have had to create genes instantaneously for human beings to respond to him, and this would make human freedom difficult to envisage.

But if it is difficult to conceive biologically of a special creation of *Homo sapiens* in the sense of a separate creation, this does not mean that there is nothing unique about the emergence of man from the evolutionary process. Berry himself goes on to claim that 'no one seriously doubts that the species *Homo sapiens* (as distinct from the races of humankind) has a single origin.'[39] Based on the frequencies of variants of the blood protein, haemoglobin, it appears that *Homo sapiens* has been through a 'bottleneck' in numbers during his recent evolutionary past. This demands, maintains Berry,

> that during the past million years, the human species comprised a single pair for one generation, or an effective population of 10,000 for half a million years, or something in between . . . it is strong circumstantial evidence that humanity has passed through an 'Adam and Eve' situation in comparatively recent times.[40]

It seems to me that Berry's guess at 'something in between' is more likely to be nearer the truth. Moreover, we cannot exclude the possibility that *Homo sapiens* may have developed in a number of places at the same time, each group having its own 'single origin'. For instance, while Gould also argues for a single emergence of *Homo sapiens*, he puts forward as strong an argument for its origin in Africa as Pearce and Cipolla have done for the Middle East. What matters here, I suggest, is that the biblical view of human persons as having a special place in creation and being a unique species is not incompatible with the evolutionary picture and that there comes a critical point in the development of *Homo sapiens* where Christian believers can discern the guiding hand of God, without appealing to a 'gap' that only God could fill.

In his own conclusions about evolution, Gould proposes that circumstances conspired to encourage mentality at the level displayed by human beings. He notes that not all the branches of *Homo erectus* from Africa, Europe, and Asia moved up the evolutionary ladder to *Homo sapiens*. He states that *Homo sapiens* 'arose as an evolutionary item, a definite entity, a small coherent population that split off from a lineage of ancestors in Africa.'[41] While we were emerging in Africa, *Homo erectus* was dying out in Asia, and our collateral cousins, Neanderthal people, were already living in Europe. It does not seem likely to Gould that *Homo erectus* could have taken over as the surviving hominid species as only *Homo sapiens* shows direct evidence for the kind of abstract reasoning, including numerical and aesthetic modes, that we identify as distinctively human. For Gould, biology's most profound insight into human nature, status, and potential lies in the simple phrase, 'the embodiment of potential.'[42] According to Gould, we are here because the earliest ancestor of the chordates, *Pikaia* (found in the Burgess Shale), survived as full of potential and became part of contingent history.

9. The Creative Purpose of God

Homo sapiens is clearly different from the rest of the animal kingdom and also from other hominids. Biology and anthropology have enabled us to recognise the emergence of members of *Homo sapiens* into a self-consciousness, which has enhanced their flexibility for adaption, their power over their environment, and so their ability for biological survival. It is only *Homo sapiens* that asks itself the meaning of its existence. Human beings are more than simply a biological machine. The biblical view is of a psychosomatic unity; the human personality has an outward and inseparable expression in the physical body and a centre that is more than physical and that can be expressed in such terms as 'heart', 'mind', and 'spirit'. From both a biblical and a scientific point of view, human beings are a unity of mind and body, so they are part of nature and at the same time conscious and self-aware.

The paradox of all this is that humanity, which is to be seen as the end point of cosmic purpose and as the climax of the evolution of the universe and of living things, is painfully aware of its weaknesses, failures, and finitude. There is a tension in each of us that longs for completeness, fulfilment, and perfection. We may recognise our freedom to reach out beyond ourselves as the image of God, marking us out as different from other created things. Finally we have the freedom to reach out to God himself (a dimension we may call 'spirit'), but even this is in tension with our finitude and our limits. This paradox accords with a view of a God who has freely chosen to create and who has given that same freedom to his creation.

Have we evolved? Biologically, the sensible answer is yes. Theologically, an affirmative answer accords with the biblical picture of a God who works patiently and intimately in partnership with his creation and is compatible with the biblical account of a special moment within creation when human beings are given life as persons in the image of God. The fundamentalist Christian reaction against evolution does not have a scriptural warrant, and behind a view of the separate creation of humanity there are two fallacies in particular, as Berry rightly identifies.[43] Firstly, it implies that God does not use the whole of his creation for his purpose. Secondly, it requires our relationship with God to be controlled genetically, as genes must be created to enable response to God; but the Bible excludes such a possibility, affirming the freedom of human response and the gift of sonship from God that follows response (John 1:11-12; Hebrews 11:6). With regard to Adam, he is to be seen in biblical perspective as the federal head of humanity, more like a 'clan chief' than a grandparent. The Bible insists on our spiritual unity with Adam, as suggested by passages such as Acts 17:26 and Romans 5:12-14; Adam is envisaged as the head of the old humanity in which we are all entangled with its legacy of sin and rebellion. This does not necessarily imply a genetic unity.

In this chapter we have been exploring the witness of the rocks to the story of an Earth in process of evolution. Studies of the Earth's crustal layers have revealed major structural patterns, tectonic plates, which have been involved in orderly movement through time. These movements have produced the rocks, minerals, ocean basins, mountain chains, earthquakes, and volcanic activity that have been the source of the materials that we need for technology, the soils for agriculture, and indeed the locations where life may have begun. The sediments that make up the uppermost layers of the crust reveal a long and complex history of changing environments, and radiometric dating of the rocks suggests that the Earth is at least 4,500 million years old. The fossil record shows the development of life from simple bacteria to complex mammals, even human beings, and supports an evolutionary model, whether or not this is seen as 'bottom' or 'top' heavy. We have seen that *Homo sapiens* has a special place within the evolutionary process, displaying a uniqueness of consciousness that we might recognise as civilization. All this is consistent with the biblical picture of human beings who are deeply rooted in the natural world that God has created and who are given freedom by God to respond to his love displayed through his self-revelation in creation, in his dealings with his people, and finally in the incarnation of Christ.

The history of the Earth's crust, as traced by geology and palaeontology, shows evidence of the same purpose and design that we have already seen from the witness of physics, cosmology, and biology. Such evidence is not proof but is suggestive of a God who is involved with his creation. We are now in a position to consider the account of creation in Genesis 1 itself, in the light of the witnesses we have so far examined and the theological implications that we have begun to draw.

Notes to Chapter 4

[1]John 1:3 (New International Version).

[2]G. W. Himus and G. S. Sweeting, *The Elements of Field Geology* (London: University Tutorial Press, 1955) 1.

[3]A. Hallam, *A Revolution in the Earth Sciences* (Oxford: Oxford University Press, 1973).

[4]See Chapters 7 and 8.

[5]Hallam, 113.

[6]J. D. Weaver, 'The Structure of the Swansea Valley Disturbance between Clydach and Hay-on-Wye, South Wales', *Geological Journal* 10 (1975): 75-86; and 'Seismically-induced load structures in the basal Coal Measures, South Wales', *Geological Magazine* 113 (1976): 535-43.

[7]S. Moorbath, 'Measuring Geological time' in *Understanding the Earth* ed. I. G. Gass, P. J. Smith, and R. C. L. Wilson (Sussex: Open University, Artemis Press, 1971) 41-51.

[8]M. R. House, 'Evolution of the Fossil Record' in Gass et al., 193-211.

[9]This would have been a 'reducing' or non-oxidizing environment. That is, in such an environment oxygen would not be present in order to turn any carbon present into carbonates, so that the carbon would be available to form hydrocarbons instead.

[10]P. C. Sylvester-Bradley, 'An evolutionary Model for the Origin of Life' in Gass et al., 128.

[11]Sylvester-Bradley, ibid.

[12]P. Davies, *God and the New Physics* (London: Dent, 1983) 68-71.

[13]L. V. Berkner and L. C. Marshall, 'Oxygen and Evolution' in Gass et al., 143-49.

[14]P. Cloud, 'The Primitive Earth' in Gass et al., 151-55.

[15]Berkner and Marshall.

[16]J. F. Kirkaldy, *The Study of Fossils* (London: Hutchinson, 1963) 95-98.

[17]A. E. Trueman, 'The use of Gryphaea in the Correlation of the Lower Lias', *Geological Magazine* 59 (1922): 256-68.

[18]R. Dawkins, *The Blind Watchmaker,* 169ff.

[19]S. J. Gould, *Wonderful Life—The Burgess Shale and the Nature of History.*

[20]S. J. Gould, D. M. Raup, J. J. Sepkoski, T. J. M. Schopf, and D. S. Simberloff, 'The Shape of Evolution: A Comparison of Real and Random clades', *Palaeobiology* 3 (1977): 23-40.

[21]Dawkins, 223ff.

[22]Gould, *Wonderful Life,* 47.

[23]Ibid., 292.

[24]Ibid., 300.

[25]Ibid., 304.

[26]For an exposition of this, see above 64.

[27]I. G. Barbour, *Religion in an Age of Science,* 4.

[28]'Jurassic Park' was the name given to a film directed by Steven Spielberg, which was premiered in London in July, 1993

[29]Quoted in R. J. Berry, *Adam and the Ape* (London: Falcon, 1975).

[30]Ibid., 23.

[31]Peacocke, *God and the New Biology,* (London: Dent, 1986) 51.

[32]J. Bronowski, *The Ascent of Man* (London: BBC Publications, 1973) 59.

[33]C. M. Cipolla, *The Economic History of World Population* (London: Penguin Books, 1965) 18.

[34]Ibid., 20ff.

[35]E. K. V. Pearce, *Who was Adam?* (Exeter: Paternoster Press, 1969) 15-17.

[36]Peacocke, 92.

[37]Berry, *Adam and the Ape.*

[38]Berry, 39.

[39]Ibid.,42.

[40]Ibid.

[41]Gould, *Wonderful Life,* 319.

[42]Ibid., 320.

[43]Ibid., 39f.

5

'In the beginning God created the heavens and the earth'[1]

The Witness of Genesis

In the beginning was the Big Bang. As matter expanded from that initial singularity it cooled. After about three minutes the world was no longer hot enough to sustain universal nuclear interactions. At that moment its gross nuclear structure got fixed at its present proportion of three quarters hydrogen and one quarter helium. Expansion and further cooling continued. Eventually gravity condensed matter into the first generation of galaxies and stars. In the interiors of these first stars nuclear cookery started up again and produced heavy elements like carbon and iron, essential for life, which were scarcely present in the early stages of the universe's history. Some of these first generation stars exploded when they died, spewing out this heavier matter into the environment. As second generation stars and planets condensed in their turn, on at least one of them there were now conditions of chemical composition and temperature and radiation permitting, through the interplay of chance and necessity, the coming into being of replicating molecules and life. Thus evolution began on the planet Earth. Eventually it lead to you and me. We are all made of the ashes of dead stars.[2]

Is this how Genesis Chapter 1 should have been written? Would a biblical account of creation written in these words have saved us from all the arguments between Christians and between Christians and non-believing scientists?

Perhaps for some the answer would be yes, but consider those with no scientific education, or consider people living one hundred, or four hundred, or two thousand years ago—what would they have made of a description of creation written in the language and with the understanding of twentieth century science? In Genesis 1 we have a theological picture of creation; it is dramatic prose, almost poetry; and it carries a strong theological message. As we consider the relationship between the scientific discoveries about creation and the Genesis account, we must first look at the nature of the biblical narrative itself.

The Genesis account of creation is one part of the whole biblical story, which deals with the nature and revelation of God and his relation to his world and to human beings. The biblical story differs from other ancient creation stories in its assertion of the sovereignty and transcendence of God and in the special place it gives to humanity. Creation by a sovereign God is, indeed, an important doctrine throughout the rest of Scripture outside the first chapter of Genesis. In the Psalms Yahweh is celebrated as the creator, over and against other gods (Psalms 19, 47, 65, 67, 93, 99, 104, 121, 148). He is the Lord of the whole created order, as presented in Job 38-41. The prophet Isaiah of Babylon ties the whole of creation together—past, present, future, and new creation (Isaiah 40, 45, 49, 60, and 65). In the New Testament we find Christ defined as the agent of creation (John 1:1-18; Col 1:15-20). When we combine these passages with others that speak of the presence of the Spirit of God in creation, in the individual life, and within the gathered community in re-creation we find a Trinitarian character to creation as witnessed to in the whole scope of the Bible. But, for all this, there is a special contribution made by Genesis 1; it firmly locates human life within cosmic history, as part of God's purpose. This emphasis gives significance to human life both in relation to God and to the world.

1. What Kind of Account Is Genesis 1?

For some people the Genesis account of creation is a stumbling block. According to David Wilkinson,[3] a survey of British teenagers in the early 1990s showed that one third of those who rejected Christianity did so because they thought that Christians believed in a seven-day creation about 6,000 years ago, a picture that was contrary to all that they had learned and understood through science. I have found through leading sessions on apologetics at an annual Christian festival in Britain, 'Spring Harvest', that a similar explanation for rejecting Christianity is given by many adults. Behind this lies a lack of understanding of the creation account in Genesis.

It seems that some Christian leaders will hang on to a literal interpretation of Genesis because they are afraid that to accept the discoveries of science will undermine their faith. Perhaps for others, a rigid, literal interpretation of the Bible is a more comfortable position than having to wrestle with textual problems and meanings. Those who take a literalistic approach to the Bible are often inconsistent, however, being unhappy, for example, to take the dragon motif in Psalm 89:10 literally or some of the more retaliatory laws of the Pentateuch. On the other hand, we must not simply adapt our interpretation of Scripture to fit in with the latest scientific discovery or theory, or to placate people's disbelief.

The Creationist school of thought takes the biblical narrative of creation as a historically accurate account, understanding it to state that the universe was created in six days about 10,000 years ago. This school of thought includes both scientists and theologians,[4] but while its attitude to the Bible, at this point, claims to be a simple acceptance of the written word, its attitude to science is far less straightforward. There are two main ways in which creationists reconcile Genesis 1 and science. The first of these is to suggest that God created the universe as we observe it, with light already travelling from distant galaxies and isotopes at various stages of radioactive decay, so that the universe appears to be much older than it actually is; only the Bible gives the actual age of the universe. The second argument suggests that modern science has got its figures and conclusions wrong. Attention is drawn to the lack of knowledge concerning the Big Bang, problems over the formation of galaxies, inaccuracies in radiometric dating of the Earth's rocks, and isolated pieces of evidence that seem to contradict plate tectonics and evolution. The distribution and form of the sediments that make up the Earth's crust are accounted for by the biblical flood, which is also said to account for the distribution of fossil organisms.

This approach to Genesis 1 raises a number of problems. There are the more 'minor' problems of interpretation, in that Genesis 1 is essentially theological and is a poetic drama, rather than a historical diary. But much more serious are the problems concerning the nature of the God that such an approach suggests. According to the first way that creationism deals with science, if scientists are discovering an apparent age and history of the universe that is not in fact true, then we are presented with a God who has created so as to deceive. This is not the God of Scripture, whom we understand to reveal himself, at least partially, through his creation. This is the testimony of such passages as Psalm 19:1; Acts 14:17, 17:23-28; and Romans 1:19-20. Both creationist arguments also go against any concept that God has gifted all people, including scientists, to enable them to understand, steward, and benefit from creation. The whole enterprise of science rests on the assumption that the world is orderly and that there are patterns to be discovered and categories that can be established. The physicist Paul Davies comments that the miracle of science is that it works.[5] In fact the order and 'contingence' (meaning

things do not have to be the way they are) that Davies seeks to understand is the very nature of God that we discover in Genesis 1. It is
certainly true that human propensity to sin blinds us to God's truth, but
surely not in such a blanket way that all scientists, Christian or non-
Christian, are so blinded.

If Genesis 1 is not to be taken literally, does it therefore fall into the
realm of myths and legends? Ancient stories about creation were all
channels of meaning, to help societies cope with their experiences of the
world in which they were born, lived, and died. They were not essentially
accounts of the observable 'scientific' features of the Earth and sky, but
rather they were vehicles of the hopes, aspirations, and even fears of
people. Barrow writes:

> The primitive belief in order and in the sequence of cause and effect
> displayed by myths is consistent with the belief that it is necessary to
> have some reason for the existence of everything—a reason that pays
> due respect for the natural forces that hold life and death in their hands.[6]

He points out that, whereas the world of experience and observation is
bewilderingly plural and complex, most myths represent a primitive and
simple causation for the world. They portray the victory of light over
dark, the cracking of some cosmic egg, the story of two world parents,
or the defeat of monsters by gods.

Two ancient accounts will illustrate this point. Firstly, according to
a Chinese account of creation there was a huge egg called Chaos.[7] Inside
the egg there slept a god called Pan Ku, who held a hammer in his right
hand and a chisel in his left (the first geologist no doubt!). Pan Ku lived
for 18,000 years and grew nine kilometres in height each day (60 million
kilometres in total). Then he died—a very tall person! After his death, his
body formed the Earth, his head the mountains, his breath the winds, his
voice the thunder, his bones the rocks, his teeth the precious stones, his
blood the seas, his hair the trees, his sweat the rain, and the insects on
his body were human beings. At this point the Emperor of the world sent
time and light into being. He achieved this by standing on the highest
mountain with the Sun in his left hand and the Moon in his right.

A second account comes from Assyria, part of the *Enuma elish* epic,[8]
which may well have influenced the author of Genesis. It represents the
success of the hero-god Marduk. It begins with the earliest generation of

gods who lead up to the hero-god, through whom the forces of evil are overcome and the order of the universe is established. In the beginning there was no Heaven, Earth, land, or sea, only the gods. There were the gods Apsu and Tiamat who had children and grandchildren. Apsu and Tiamat planned the destruction of the other gods, but learning of their plan the water god Ea fought against Apsu, killed him, and made a home from his body. Angered by his death, Tiamat planned revenge. She made poisonous creatures and another god, called Qingu, whom she appointed the commander of her army. Realising the danger, the gods asked who would fight on their behalf. 'Who rushes into battle: Marduk the Hero!' (Tablet II) Marduk struck up a deal for his involvement: 'Whatever I create shall never be altered! Let a decree from my lips never be revoked, never changed!' (Tablet III) Marduk was victorious and killed Tiamat, Qingu, and all the poisonous creatures, and was made king. As part of the ordering of creation Marduk cut Tiamat's body in half, forming the sky from one half and the Earth from the other. Marduk made up his mind to perform miracles, and with Tiamat's blood he made human beings (Tablet VI), who were to be always subservient to the gods. The epic ends with a celebration of praise to Marduk, the Lord of creation: 'With fifty epithets the great gods called his fifty names, making his way supreme.' (Tablet VII)

We might ask whether Genesis presents us with a similar picture of creation or whether it represents a much greater understanding of the nature of the world. I want to maintain in this chapter that Genesis 1 presents us with an account of creation that is not only of theological importance, but which is also perceptive of the observable world in which it was written. In support of this claim we shall first consider Genesis 1 through the eyes of critical scholarship, secondly consider it in the light of modern scientific discovery, and lastly consider the key themes that are presented. It would seem to make sense that if the world, at least in part, reveals the nature of God, that the biblical account of creation, inspired by God, would not only tell us about theological truths, but also something of the observable world.

2. A Creator Who Relates Himself to Human Beings

The writer of the letter to the Hebrews writes, 'By faith we understand that the universe was formed at God's command, so that what is seen was not made out of what was visible.'[9] But the aim of the declarations of Genesis 1-2 is not directly to evoke this kind of faith in an act of creation. The Priestly (P) and the Yahwist (J) documents, parts of which make up Genesis 1:1-2:4a (P) and 2:4b-3:24 (J), are expressing a faith in God's acts of salvation that come through his election, or his free choice to relate himself to people. The faith that is central to these passages is a faith in the God who made a covenant with Abraham, though this God is of course the creator of the world.

G. Von Rad[10] says that Israel looked back in faith from her own election to the creation of the world, and Claus Westermann[11] sees creation faith as the spiritual high point of Israel's understanding of her calling. But Brevard Childs[12] finds that Genesis depicts a wider relationship that God establishes with his creatures; he believes that Von Rad's subordination of universal history to the particular salvation history of Israel runs into serious literary and theological problems, and concludes that 'the canonical role of Genesis 1-11 testifies to the priority of creation. The divine relation to the world stems from God's initial creative purpose for the universe, not for Israel alone.'

Genesis 1 is the dramatic opening chapter to both the Jewish and Christian scriptures. It introduces the creator and his creatures and sets the scene for the relationship of human beings and God. Genesis 1 is unique, but may still be compared with other passages that reflect the mystery of God's creativity, such as Psalms 8 and 148 or Job 38. It goes beyond these passages in the scope and comprehensiveness of its vision, says Wenham,[13] and in its present form it is a careful literary composition that introduces the narratives that follow. The writer does not primarily attempt or want to explain creation; rather he desires to evoke a wonder in creation that will lead to worship, a proper relation between human beings and their creator. Debates that involve a scientific mechanism, such as those concerning a possible time scale, or evolution, or the Big Bang would hardly be high in his thought, as David Atkinson wryly comments.[14] Nevertheless, we must not miss the point that the very function of this narrative as a polemic against other religions inevitably leads the author into some explanation as well.

Genesis 1:1-2:4a is the work of the Priestly Writer and represents a doctrine of creation written from the perspective of the Exile and of the Second Temple in the fifth century B.C. It has been developed from a variety of sources enriched by the experiences of a millennium of living faith. It is, above all else, a carefully worked out statement of faith. It would have been a great encouragement to the faith of those who were suffering the physical and spiritual disruption of exile in Babylonia.

It is written as a narrative that is complete in itself and which stands apart from the narratives that follow it. Wiseman[15] comments that it is a literary form quite unlike any other narrative in the Bible. It is arranged in a unique structure, which Wenham describes as 'highly problematic,'[16] there being eight works of creation, prompted by ten divine commands, which are executed on six days. The third and sixth days correspond to each other with a double announcement of God's word (1:9, 11, 24, 26). This correspondence will be discussed later.

Although there are certainly points of contact between Genesis 1-11 and the Babylonian creation epic, there is a profound difference between the struggles of Marduk with Tiamat and the Genesis 1 narrative. It may not be fair to try to make comparisons as we would not be comparing like with like. Wenham notes that *Enuma elish* is concerned to glorify Marduk; the victory over Tiamat is central, and the creative acts are simply illustrations of his power. He maintains that there is a stronger relationship between Genesis 1 and the Atrahasis epic, but only in as much as creation is the prelude to the flood.[17] The writer was also probably familiar with the Egyptian accounts of creation, but the significance of Genesis 1 is the way in which the Priestly Writer uses other accounts. Rather than comparing the contents of the accounts, it is more illuminating to see the Israelite modifications of other testimonies to creation.

Thus Westermann[18] states that while the Priestly Writer follows the example of presenting creation in a succession of generations—important in Egyptian, Sumerian, and Babylonian accounts—this writer has no genealogy of the gods. He rejects the struggle motif and the births of the gods and instead presents creation as God's act of making, and as the decree of God's word. Wenham[19] concludes from this that Genesis 1 is a deliberate statement of the Hebrew view of creation over against rival views and that it is a 'polemical repudiation of such myths.' Rival cosmologies are attacked in a number of areas: God created all that is out of nothing, in contrast to the idea of matter existing eternally alongside the gods; the dragons that rival the gods in Canaanite mythology are now seen to be merely the creation of God (1:21); the struggle of the gods to divide the waters is replaced by a simple divine decree (1:6-10); the Genesis account avoids naming the Sun, Moon, and stars, which were worshiped in other near eastern cultures. Throughout all this God simply creates, rather than employing mysterious incantations.

In addition, and with particular relevance to our theme, there is the place of human beings; in Babylonian tradition they were an afterthought —they have a walk on part as servants of the gods—but in Genesis they are seen as the climax of creation. This and the other features mentioned above represent a deliberate rejection of other cosmologies. It leads Von Rad to state that Genesis 1 is not myth or saga, but priestly doctrine. It is ancient, sacred knowledge, which has been preserved and reformed, expanded and reflected upon with the experiences of faith. It is both cosmological and theological knowledge; it is theological reflection upon what faith is able to declare objectively. It is a profound passage on beginnings and identity, and as such compares with the opening verses of the Gospels according to Mark (1:1) and according to John (1:1-5).

3. The Ordering of Creation

Westermann records the general recognition among scholars that there are a number of streams of tradition that lie behind the written text of Genesis 1,[20] and that there appear to be two distinct formulae applying to God, which come from different sources: 'let there be . . . and it was so' and 'God made.' Wenham[21] is less convinced of the existence of two such source documents. Westermann maintains that the Priestly Writer's intention is not to interpret but to proclaim, to say something specific about God's action, and in accord with this aim he recognises a framework used by the writer for all the works of creation:

I.	Introduction	And God said
II.	Command	Let it be, let them be granted
III.	Completion	And it was so
IV.	Judgment	And God saw that it was good
V.	Time sequence	And it was evening . . .[22]

These elements spell out the fulfilment of God's command. The works of creation demand the response of praise, but with no one yet available to worship we have God's own declaration that all was good. Westermann suggests that by creating, God enters into time and so time must be taken as an expression of God. Creation is an unbroken sequence of time that leads finally to God's day, the day for worship.[23]

The Priestly Writer is both an innovative theologian and a receiver and transmitter of tradition, and in this he allows voices other than his own to speak. This may be seen in his use of the verbs *yāsar* ('to make') and *bārā'* ('to create'); while for the most part these are interchangeable, this writer can make a theological point by shifting from one to the other. The tradition that the Priestly Writer uses contained the word *yāsar*. Sometimes he places a command of God before this mechanical description of 'making', so that the act is connected with the creative word of God. To prevent the misunderstandings that might arise from the use of *yāsar* (make) the writer introduces *bārā'* (create) into the important passages dealing with the creation of the animal world (1:21) and in the description of the creation of human beings (1:27). The creation of humanity was particularly important to the Priestly Writer, who uses *bārā'* three times in verse 27. Bernhardt[24] draws attention to the use of *bārā'* in the comprehensive introduction and the conclusion of the whole creation account (1:1 and 2:3, 4); all is the creative work of God.

The overall picture is of God creating a world ruled by space and time that provides living space for human beings. In the first three works of creation God 'separated' and 'named' the light (3-5), firmament (6-8), and sea-land (9-10). This separation creates the space where people live out their lives. God names those basic elements as the world of humanity and demonstrates that he is master of the world that he has defined. These three works are followed by 'Let the land produce vegetation, . . .' the Earth being seen here as the mother of all life. After the three works of separation and naming, life can come forth from it, says Westermann, 'but only if the creative word of God is at its origin.'[25] This is followed by works five to eight, in which God gives a destiny to everything that he makes or creates: the heavenly bodies (14-19), beasts of the water and air (20-23), land beasts (24-25), and human beings (26-31). These are created according to their species.

The Priestly Writer relates creation in a way that people in his own culture would understand from their own experience and knowledge. God is seen to bless the animate parts of creation, a blessing that both bestows fertility on them and makes them a part of history. Westermann rightly concludes that Genesis 1 pictures creation as set in space and time, which are first brought into being, and so creation is not brought about by a single, sweeping act of God. There is a distinction in the text between the first three works of creation, which form the inanimate world, and the second five works of creation, which define the animate life placed within the world. There is a clear progression in this arrangement, which Westermann sums up as, 'Everything that God has created has a destiny; this destiny reaches its goal in humanity, which God created as his counterpart; with human beings creation points the way into history'.[26] This sequence between the two groups of works also throws light on the structure of 'days' in the narrative, and this in turn may have a bearing (as we shall see) on the relation between science and the creation story.

Most Old Testament commentators discuss the significance of the seven days that give the structure to this passage. Westermann does not believe that this order was imposed by a tradition that the Priestly Writer inherited but rather that he is seeking to make his own theological statement through the succession of seven days. His use of the seven day structure, however, may well reflect proximity to Mesopotamian traditions, as the seven-day pattern is indigenous to this region. The rest of the seventh day brings creation to its conclusion. Creation then is to be seen as part of history, as being within the kind of time we know and not some distant unapproachable primeval time. The God of creation is the God of history, and the final goal of creation is what is hinted at in the seventh day, namely the celebration of the holy. Creation is depicted in seven days because it ends with the day of worship, the sabbath; worship of God is the ultimate purpose of creation. The Priestly Writer's account is thus to be seen as a chronological unity, ordered and directed toward a God-given goal, beginning with creation and leading to the worship of God that continues throughout history.

There is no need, however, for us to be restricted to the theological meaning that emerges from taking the seven days in their strict chronological order. Taking the week as a whole is a picture of unity, but we may then view it from another perspective; we may see the first three days as setting the broad canvas for creation and the second three days as filling in the finer detail of created things. The Priestly Writer's picture has the quality of a parable. Wiseman and Wenham thus draw attention to the correspondences between days 1 and 4, 2 and 5, and 3 and 6; the events of the last three days being parallel with the first three:[27]

Day 1	Light	Day 4	Luminaries
Day 2	Sky	Day 5	Birds and Fish
Day 3	Land	Day 6	Animals and Man
	(plants)		(plants for food)

Day 7   Sabbath

The first day reveals how light came into existence, and the fourth the sources and purposes of light. The second day explains how the atmosphere came into existence, separating the waters below from those above, and the fifth day details the life in the waters and the life in the atmosphere. The third day relates the emergence of dry land and the establishment of vegetation, while the sixth day deals with the population of the land by animals and human beings, who together depend on the vegetation for their sustenance. For Wiseman[28] the key is found in verse 2: 'without form and void.' He suggests that the first three days detail the formation of heaven and earth, and the second three days reveal the occupation and inhabitation of the void. This is not significantly different from Westermann's own division between the 'separating-naming' of the first three works and the 'making or creating-blessing' of the remaining five. We have then a basic framework for the order and nature of creation.

4. Scientific Discovery and the Genesis Narrative

The important question that we now need to address is whether or not it is possible to relate this understanding of Genesis 1 to our accumulated knowledge of the cosmological, geological, and biological history of the universe and planet Earth. If we place the works of creation in a sequence where days 1-3 are parallel to days 4-6 and then compare them with the cosmological/geological history of the universe, we find that there is a broad degree of agreement, as shown in Figure 5:1. The significant points of development that should be noted are as follows:

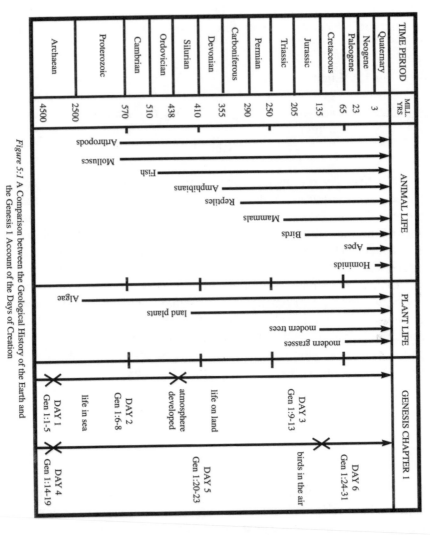

Figure 5:1 A Comparison between the Geological History of the Earth and the Genesis 1 Account of the Days of Creation

Day 1 (1:1-5). This portrays the creation of everything, the initial act of creating the whole universe, which is followed by the ordering of its different parts. God's wisdom is before the whole of creation (Prov 8:22-27 and John 1:1-5). God, in the freedom of his transcendent will, creatively establishes a beginning for everything. It is God's creative activity. Von Rad[29] suggests that 'chaos' in Genesis 1 is a reaching back speculatively behind creation, to make an intermediate state between nothingness (*ex nihilo*) and creation. Theologically we move from chaos to cosmos. Light is the first born, which is a significant theological symbol. But there is also a significance here for scientific cosmology, as there is a parallel between the primal 'light' and the heat and energy in the Big Bang that is the source of life.

Day 2 (1:6-8). The waters of chaos are separated by the formation of the atmosphere. This is significant from a theological point of view, the waters of chaos being held back by the vault of heaven and thus providing the possibility for life to be established; but it is also significant geologically, and for a similar reason. From a palaeontological viewpoint the significance lies in the build up of an oxygen rich atmosphere, which cuts off the harmful ultraviolet radiation, so allowing life to develop first in the sea and then subsequently on the land.

Day 3 (1:9-13). The waters of the Earth are drained into the oceans and we see the fruitful maternal Earth giving rise to plant life. This is in response to God's creative word of command. We might note that the order of plant life recorded in these verses accords with the evolution recorded in the fossil record, namely, the vegetation of two kinds: plants bearing seed and trees bearing fruit.[30]

Day 4 (1:14-19). The lights of heaven are commissioned by their creator's will—the stars, sun, and moon, which are the bearers of light that God created on the first day. They do not themselves create light. Theologically, it is important that there is no sense of the astral powers of rival cosmologies to be found here. We might note the warning in Deuteronomy 4:19 that Israel is not to do its 'science' in the idolatrous ways of other nations. The stars express God's glory and are very much under his control (Ps 19:1; Job 9:7-10; Isa 40:26). From our current understanding of the birth of stars and galaxies in the time following the Big Bang, we see that the cosmological picture mirrors the Priestly Writer's theological proclamation. Taking the fourth day in parallel to the first, as a detailed expansion of it, we find that just as 'light' precedes the 'lights' of heaven, so the energy explosion of the Big Bang precedes the formation of galactic bodies.

Day 5 (1:20-23). The world is now ready for the establishment of living creatures. These are created first of all in the sea, progressing from there to the land and the air, in the same way as the fossil record demonstrates. This could not have occurred until the development of an atmosphere (Day 2) rich enough in oxygen to reduce CO_2 levels (so allowing heat radiation to escape and surface temperatures to fall) and form an Ozone layer to cut out the ultraviolet radiation that would inhibit DNA.

Day 6 (1:24-31). Penultimately we come to the creation of the land animals, and last of all, and in a far more intimate way, human beings. The whole person is created in God's image: physical, mental, emotional, and spiritual, together with sexual distinction. Human beings are seen to have a purpose, to have dominion over and to care for creation. Here we record, as does the fossil record, the culmination of creation in the higher animals and human beings.

5. Consistency with Science, but Not Science

We have thus found in Genesis 1 an accord with modern scientific discovery and understanding of the universe. We might at this point pause to observe how very remarkable it is that a priestly theologian writing some 2,500 years ago was able to present an outline order of creation consistent with that which has been established scientifically only in the last 200 years. Might this be an indication of divine inspiration that lies behind this particular author's work? Perhaps here we have demonstrated the reasonableness of the Genesis account of creation, when it is understood in the light of critical scholarship. It does not lie in some realm of make-believe, far removed from modern scientific experimentation and discovery. This also underlines the need for us to take the scriptures seriously, seeking to understand the context, culture, literary style, and purpose of the writer.

There are, however, dangers of pressing the comparison between scientific discovery and Genesis 1, as Donald Mackay rightly points out.[31] Genesis 1 is primarily a theological counter to rival mythologies; it speaks of the how and why of creation, something that is far deeper than the what and when of cosmology. Furthermore, there is no guarantee that there is not another scientific revolution lurking around the corner.

Genesis 1 is not science, it is a picture, a parable, a hymn, and above all a theological statement. It is a high point of the Jewish faith, and yet it had to fit with the experience and knowledge of the people for whom it was written and to whom it was first proclaimed. As Westermann reminds us:

> All that can be presumed with certainty is that the creation narratives were not originally answers to the question about the origins of the world and of humanity; they arose from the everyday concern about the stability of the present state of human existence.[32]

Genesis 1 takes on the features of a solemn overture; the beginning of events that lead from creation through the Patriarchs, the crossing of the Reed Sea, and the Covenant of Sinai, to the establishment of Israel and the Temple. It is constantly the recognition that Israel's life is lived before God.

The primary purpose of the creation narrative, then, is theological; it is the proclamation of doctrine that belongs to the faith of Israel. Understood in this way it is sensible and reasonable for the reader of the twentieth or any other century. But I should like to go one step further and conclude that it also presents a reasonable account of the history of the universe, as we understand it, and therefore should not be a stumbling block to the modern agnostic. As with our chapters on cosmology, biology, and geology, we have reached the same end point. The Genesis 1 account of creation presents us with a reasonable story of creation including the giving of purpose to the universe, which in the biblical account is clearly seen to be the will of the Judaeo-Christian God. But the step from reasonableness to belief, from the perception of purpose to the giver of purpose, must remain a leap of trustful faith.

6. The Nature of the Creator

So what are the main themes of Genesis 1 that faith must grasp? What is at the heart of the Priestly Writer's proclamation of the doctrine of creation? First of all we recognise that all events of creation are subordinate to God's will and power. God is the sole creator. He creates everything, including the luminaries that were worshiped within some religions and the sea monsters who were the rival deities in others. But God does not stand outside of his creation; he is involved with it, sustaining it by his power (Job 38; Isa 40:18-28, 42:5; John 5:17). God continues with his work; in the imagery of Genesis 1, the seventh day of Genesis 2:1-3 has not brought creation to an end but runs out into history. While Newton placed God 'out there,' somewhere in space, first Darwin and then modern cosmologists and physicists have allowed us to posit an immanent creator, continuously involved with his creation. Westermann is surely right when he says:

> The simple fact that the first page of the Bible speaks about heaven and earth, the sun, moon and stars, about plants and trees, about birds, fish and animals, is a certain sign that the God whom we acknowledge in the Creed as the Father of Jesus Christ, is concerned with all of these creatures, and not merely with humans. A God who is understood only as the god of humankind is no longer the God of the Bible.[33]

The second aspect of God that faith must grasp from the Genesis account of creation is that order is at the heart of God; it is his nature. Theology sees creation as a process, which is an expression of God's creative purpose. Christian theology sees the Creator being free to exercise his will in all that he does, but God's acts are not fickle or arbitrary; his will is constrained by his character. If we recognise a rational universe, then we should not be surprised to find a rational God as its creator. The laws of nature can be seen as evidence of this. When we considered the parallel structure of Genesis 1, that is, days 1-3 in parallel with days 4-6, we saw an ordering of creation that accorded with that of scientific discovery. The Bible affirms order: there is Koheleth's despair that he cannot understand the order that he knows is there (Eccles 1:4-7), God's opening the mystery of creative order to Job (Job 38:31-33), Yahweh's reassurance through Deutero-Isaiah of his power to bring order (Isa 40:25-26), Paul's corrective of the church at Corinth (1 Cor 14:33), and Jesus' affirmation that the signs of nature are dependable (Matt 16:2-3; Luke 12:54-56). The Bible has no place for the 'God of the gaps' nor for Newton's God, who set the machine in operation and then sat back and let it run.

Thirdly we pick up the significant place allotted to human beings within creation. For both the Mesopotamian myths and also for modern biology, human beings are no different from the rest of the animal kingdom, merely a part of ordered creation. But the Bible proclaims a God of love, and love means that freedom in relationship is part of an ordered universe; a loving God does not create automatons or robots. Though this applies in a special way to human beings, it must also be seen on a cosmic scale. Along with Polkinghorne, we can say that 'the world created by the God of love and faithfulness may be expected to be characterised both by the openness of chance and the regularity of necessity,'[34] and leads us to consider more closely the nature of the relationship God enjoys with his creation.

The fourth theme that lies at the heart of the Priestly Writer's doctrine of creation is the relationship between God and his creation, which reaches its maximum fulfilment with human beings, made in the image of God and created with freedom of will. From a Christian point of view the cosmos is seen as a generous expression of God's love. He does not stand outside of his creation, nor does he intervene at specific points, but rather we see the continuing outworking of his creative will and love. God's involvement with creation is personal. This is the difference between mere science and Christian faith. Wilkinson is right when he observes that when science excludes God from his world, the result is war, pollution, exploitation, and the extremes of genetic engineering.[35] A personal creator must have intended the rich variety that we see all around us in creation, and Genesis affirms this intention by portraying God's sense of delight at what he has made (Genesis 1:31).

If we draw out the implications of the Genesis picture of a God who has personal relationship with his creation, we are brought to speak of the risk of the freedom that he has given to it. God, we must conclude, has chosen a 'self-limited' omnipotence and omniscience in order to achieve his purposes. There are areas in which he has chosen not to have sovereign power, for example in the realm of human free will. Peacocke rightly recognises[36] that areas of unpredictability at sub-atomic levels are unpredictable also to God, as this unpredictability is built into creation. The same may be said of the so-called 'chaotic systems.' God's act of self-limitation on behalf of the good, well-being, and existence of his creation is an expression of his love. This leads us to recognise the vulnerable, self-emptying, and self-giving love of God, which is exemplified in the Incarnation and Cross of Christ. God's risk, God's love, in creation is to choose to bring a universe into being, whose crowning glory is the existence of self-conscious, intelligent, self-willed human beings. He looks to and longs for their response in love, and that is the risk of creation for he is vulnerable to being rejected.

The fifth theme of the creation narrative is this response of love it-self, which finds its expression in the worship of God. God is meant to be worshiped, as is clear from the telling of the creation story as a seven-day event that ends on the day of worship. The Genesis 1 account of cre-ation is like a hymn of praise, more majestic even than Psalm 104. It is a hymn in the sense that believers down through some twenty-five cen-turies or more have found it to inspire them to praise of the creator. Creation finds its fulfilment in the restored relationship between humanity and God that is focused in Jesus Christ. This is made clear in New Testa-ment passages that pick up the creation theme (John 1:1-18, Hebrews 1:1-3, and Colossians 1:15-20). We find that all of creation finds its renewal and completion in the final unveiling of the glory of Christ (Romans 8:19-23; Revelation 4-5 and 21-22).

7. The Goal of God's Purposes

We have seen that the biblical account of creation presents or prompts important doctrinal statements concerning God's relationship with his creation. These statements are received by faith, and their reception is ex-pressed in worship. Creation is to be seen in the context of God's being and God's history, his 'becoming'. The God of creation is also celebrated as the God of salvation and the Father of our Lord Jesus Christ. He is the God who is manifest in the world through his Spirit and who will bring the whole universe to its completion. For science the cosmic future is bleak, whether it consists of Heat Death or Big Crunch. What is true of the cosmos is true of humanity, ending in a death that shows the futility of life. This is why Paul tells the Corinthian church that if their hope in Christ is only for this life, it leaves them in a pitiful condition (1 Cor 15:19).

God's purpose in creation must have a goal, and this is where the Christian view of creation differs from that of the cosmologist who mere-ly sees an Anthropic Principle, a design, or even a purpose. Paul Davies can approve the talk of design, while cautioning that to believe in a de-signer is 'a matter of personal taste'.[37] Arthur Peacocke, as a Christian, is able to present a sacramental view of the cosmos, in which one can integrate trinitarian theology with a scientific perspective[38]; the world is sustained by the will of God as 'the will of perfect love', the Word of God is the 'all-sufficient principle and form' of the created order, and the 'continuing creative power' is the Holy Spirit. Every level of the cosmos expresses 'the design inherent in it' and contributes to the 'fulfillment of the common purpose'. We may say that the trinitarian vision of creation offered by the Christian faith takes us beyond *purpose* and fulfillment to *promise* and fulfillment, and so to a personal God. Jesus Christ is not only the agent of creation ('the form of created order' in Peacocke's words); he is also the agent of salvation, fulfilling God's personal promise to heal relationships. Polkinghorne expresses this clearly when he says that the Incarnation of Christ speaks of God's deepest possible involvement with creation; the Resurrection is the hope of a destiny for matter and for humanity; the Ascension is the possibility and promise of being caught up in eternity with God[39]; and we might add that Pentecost marks out God's continuing involvement with his world now, which is also promise of new creation.

There is no conflict between the Big Bang of modern cosmology and the biblical view of creation. But God is the God of creation, which is to be understood as his continuing act, leading towards the goal that he has purposed and promised. If we were to think of God only as the instigator of a creation far back in the past and which is running now according to predictable laws, we would be back with the God of the gaps. Such a tightly deterministic universe might please hyper-calvinistic predestination, says Polkinghorne,[40] but this cannot account for free will as the outworking of the risk-taking love of the creator revealed in scripture.

What do we say about the evolution of humanity in the evolving universe open to scientific discovery? Can we affirm the evolution of self-conscious awareness and also speak of this particular quality of humanity as an indication of our *imago Dei* and the infusing of the breath of God? There is an important hint given to us in the second creation narrative of Genesis 2; the biblical picture of humanity is that of an animated body, dust of the earth to which God has given his life (2:7). We have the ability to observe the universe, to discover its make up, to ponder its beginnings, and to respond to its Creator. This is, as Polkinghorne remarks,[41] the highest and most striking illustration of that potentiality with which the physical world has been endowed. It is this feature that has been recognised by Barrow, Davies, and Penrose, and it is this goal that our studies of cosmology, geology, and palaeobiology have led us to consider.

The two Genesis accounts of creation, in chapters 1-2, lead us to one conclusion about human life: in the first, humanity is seen as the crowning glory of creation, and in the second as its pivot. By contrast, in the Mesopotamian myth humanity is servile and static in its relation to the gods, and there can be no change in their relative positions. Genesis 1 accords humanity a place of privilege, almost in the position of God's peers. The relationship is dynamic and therefore fragile and containing an element of risk. This is further emphasised by the fact that the Genesis account of creation differs from others in relating the entry of evil into the world after it has described the creation of human beings, rather than before. This tells us about the risk taken by a loving creator who creates free-willed, self-conscious human beings, who may or may not recognise their creator and give to him the response of worship that he desires.

We shall now consider how all of this discussion is worked out in our understanding of revelation, of what we can understand of God through the world of which we are a part, and from our very nature as human beings. We turn to the area of natural theology, which has a long history of interaction with the scientific fields that we have so far considered.

Notes to Chapter 5

[1]Genesis 1:1 (New International Version).

[2]J. Polkinghorne, *One World—the Interaction of Science and Theology*, 56.

[3]D. Wilkinson, *God, the Big Bang and Stephen Hawking*, 125.

[4]See J. C. Whitcomb and H. M. Morris, *The Genesis Flood* (New Jersey: Presbyterian and Reformed Pub. Co. Nutley, 1961); and for a full discussion between scientists from both the evolution and creation schools, see D. Burke eds., *Creation and Evolution—When Christians Disagree* (Leicester: I.V.P., 1985).

[5]P. Davies, *The Mind of God*, 20.

[6]J. D. Barrow, *Theories of Everything*, 9.

[7]See W. E. Soothill, *The Three Religions of China* (London: Oxford University Press, 1929) 154f.

[8]S. Dalley, *Myths from Mesopotamia* (London: Oxford University Press, 1989) 228-77.

[9]Hebrews 11:3 (New International Version).

[10]G. Von Rad, *Genesis* (London: SCM, 1961) 33-34.

[11]C. Westermann, *Genesis 1-11* (London: SPCK, 1984) 19ff.

[12]B. S. Childs, *Introduction to the Old Testament* (London: SCM, 1979) 154-55.

[13]G. J. Wenham, *Genesis 1-15*, Word Bible Commentary (Milton Keynes: Word, 1987) 10.

[14]D. Atkinson, *The Message of Genesis 1-11. The Bible Speaks Today* (Leicester: I.V.P., 1990) 17.

[15]P. J. Wiseman, *Clues to Creation in Genesis* (London: Marshall, Morgan & Scott, 1977) 115.

[16]Wenham, 6.

[17]Ibid., 8.

[18]Westermann, 81.

[19]Wenham, 9.

[20]Westermann, 83.

[21]Wenham, 7f.

[22]Westermann, 84.

[23]Ibid., 85.

[24]K. H. Bernhardt, with J. Bergmann, G. J. Botterweck, & H. Ringgren, article *bara'* in *Theological Dictionary of the Old Testament*, Vol. 3, ed. G. J. Botterweck and H. Ringgren (Grand Rapids: Eerdmans, 1978) 242-49.

[25]Westermann, 87.

[26]Ibid., 88.

[27]Table as in Wenham, 7.

[28]Wiseman, 118.

[29]Von Rad, 47, 49.

[30]H. Ringgren, article *deshe'* in *Theological Dictionary of the Old Testament*, Vol. 2 (1977) 307-9.

[31]D. MacKay, "Science and Christian Faith Today," *Real Science, Real Faith*, R. J. Berry, ed. (Eastbourne: Monarch, 1991) 196-217.

[32]Westermann, 92.

[33]Ibid., 176.

[34]J. Polkinghorne, *Science and Creation,* 52.

[35]Wilkinson, 135.

[36]A. Peacocke, *Theology for a Scientific Age—Being and Becoming: Natural and Divine* (London: SCM, 1993) 122f.

[37]P. Davies, *The Mind of God*, 214.

[38]A. Peacocke, *God and the New Biology*, 125.

[39]J. Polkinghorne, *Science and Creation*, 66.

[40]J. Polkinghorne, *One World—the Interaction of Science and Theology*, 70.

[41]Ibid.

6

'God's invisible nature . . . has been clearly seen through the things he has made'[1]

Natural Theology

In his book *The Hitch-Hiker's Guide to the Galaxy*, upon which we have often drawn so far, Douglas Adams presents us with an amusing portrayal of the impossibility inherent in seeking a proof for the existence of God. We are introduced to a useful creature called 'the Babel fish' that, when placed in one's ear canal, takes the brainwave energy from those around and excretes it into the brain of its carrier. The result is that carriers of the fish understand anything that anyone says to them and have an instant translation of every language in the universe. *The Guide* comments:

> Now it is such a bizarrely improbable coincidence that anything so mindbogglingly useful could have evolved purely by chance that some thinkers have chosen to see it as a final and clinching proof of the non-existence of God.
>
> The argument goes something like this: 'I refuse to prove that I exist,' says God, 'for proof denies faith, and without faith I am nothing.'
>
> 'But,' says Man, 'the Babel fish is a dead giveaway isn't it? It could not have evolved by chance. It proves you exist, and so therefore, by your own arguments, you don't. QED.'
>
> 'Oh dear,' says God, 'I hadn't thought of that,' and promptly vanishes in a puff of logic.[2]

Whatever else we might say, cosmology, biology, and geology are no Babel fish. All that science will ever be able to contribute to theology is the demonstration that theistic belief is reasonable. Cosmologists speak of an apparent design within the universe that is suggestive of purpose, and some scientists go as far as to suggest that biological evolution requires a guiding mechanism, beyond the process of natural selection through non-random survival, to enable it to reach its goal in human beings. The geological and palaeontological picture reinforces the conclusions made from the physical and biological sciences, providing an indication of the conditions and time within which evolution might have taken place, and the pattern that evolution followed. The step from purpose or design to belief in a purposeful designer, however, will only be taken as the step of faith to which Adams rightly refers. Science simply provides the indication that such a step may be a reasonable one.

The first chapter of the book of Genesis provides us with an account of creation that can be interpreted as being broadly coherent with the scientific picture and so 'reasonable', but as written from a perspective of faith it discloses the God of purpose behind and within creation. Yet even here there is a further step to be taken by the reader, which goes beyond knowledge and understanding to belief and worship in a personal kind of faith.

1. The Revival of Natural Theology

Modern science has revived the old design argument of natural theology, and has given it new teeth. It presents us with an understanding of the universe that includes a beginning and an end. It also demonstrates a universe that has a 'fine tuning' that is suggestive of purpose. From these two features is developed the 'Anthropic Principle', which proposes that the conditions for human life are written into the very fabric of the universe. Paul Davies has suggested that such an understanding of the universe, uncovered by physicists, provides us with a surer path to God than religion.[3] Albert Einstein earlier expressed the view that the very fact that the universe was comprehensible is a miracle,[4] and such is the apparent order of the universe that Sir James Jeans described God as a mathematician.[5] Though without making an appeal to religious belief, Fred Hoyle urged that 'when by patient enquiry we learn the answer to any problem, we always find, both as a whole and in detail, that the answer thus revealed is finer in concept and design than anything we could ever have arrived at by a random guess.'[6]

These scientific opinions, together with the response of some theologians to them, have led Colin Brown to comment that natural theology 'has something of the irrepressible quality of a yo-yo'; having taken a battering from philosophers on the one hand and theologians like Karl Barth on the other, there is still always someone to bring it back into play.[7] This elastic quality of natural theology, however, depends to a large extent upon the way we define it. It might be defined in a traditional way, as in a recent dictionary article, as 'the attempt to attain an understanding of God and his relationship with the universe by means of rational reflection.'[8] Along the same lines, Lord Gifford, the founder of the Gifford Lectures, which deal exclusively with the subject of natural theology, placed the following definition in his will of 1885:

> Natural Theology is the knowledge of God, the Infinite, the All, the First and Only Cause, the One and the Sole Substance, the Sole Being, the Sole Reality, and the Sole Existence . . . [together with] the knowledge of His Nature and Attributes, the Knowledge of the Relations which men and the whole universe bear to Him, the knowledge of the Nature and Foundations of Ethics or Morals, and of all Obligations and Duties thence arising.[9]

Neil Spurway observes that this definition appears to include the whole of both metaphysical and moral theology, but it offers no mention of Christ, salvation, eternal life, worship, or the Holy Spirit. He concludes that Gifford was influenced by the scientists Maxwell and Kelvin to see the God of the Grand Design and so to exclude an interventionist, miracle-working deity.[10] We may note that equally excluded is a God who is present in the world, free to do new things in partnership with his creatures, and disclosing himself to us from within his creation. Thus we must not assume that a new style of natural theology will confine itself to an understanding of God gained only through 'rational reflection' on the universe, and—as we shall discover—it is this less restrictive approach to natural theology that has given it a new lease of life in recent thought. In my own view, this is the right way ahead in the dialogue between science and faith.

2. Natural Theology in Dialogue with Philosophy: a History

Natural theology has a long history within Christian thought, and one influential point of origin is in Greek philosophy.[11] Plato (427–347 B.C.) had taught that the world that we see with our eyes and touch with our bodies was in reality only a world of shadows, which was a copy of the eternal world of Spiritual Forms to which the pure soul could attain by philosophic contemplation. Plotinus (A.D. 205–269) developed Neo-Platonism in which there was a belief in an Ultimate One, which lies behind all the diversity of experience. In this One all distinction between thought and reality is overcome.

Aristotle (384–322 B.C.) was a member of Plato's Academy. He recognised four causes that produced all things: the full explanation of anything should say what it is made of (material cause), what it essentially is (formal cause), what brought it into being (efficient cause), and what its function or purpose is (final cause). J. Urmson makes the interesting point that the notion of explanation by the four causes is derived from reflection on the process of production (natural or artificial), and this implies a kind of universal teleology or a purposeful direction in which all things are moving.[12] Aristotle's *Physics* sets out a good deal of theory about the workings of the universe and includes an argument for a Prime Mover, starting from his conception of change and causation. There could be no first moment of change, he argues, as change implies existing matter. There must therefore be an Unmoved Mover. This Prime Mover, eternal, changeless, and containing no element of matter or unrealised potentiality keeps the heavenly bodies moving and maintains the eternal life of the universe.

Aristotle's concepts within the fields of science and philosophy were the basis of the thinking of many who followed, including the Christian theologians Anselm and Aquinas. In his *Monologion* Anselm (1033–1109) begins with the experience we have of differences in degrees of value, of goodness, and of being in objects around us. From this he argues for the necessary existence of an absolute standard, an absolute good, an absolute being in which the relative participates. This absolute we call God. This argument was to be more fully developed by Aquinas. In his *Proslogion,* however, Anselm is the first to set out an argument for the existence of God relying upon rational concepts alone, rather than on observation of the world around. This is the so-called 'Ontological Argument.' He began with what he considered to be a commonly accepted idea, that the term God means a being 'that than which no greater can be thought'. Such a being can be said to exist in the mind since we think of him. But we can go a stage further and say that in the case of everything we know, to exist in actuality is always more perfect than to exist only in the mind. If he were presenting his case today, Anselm might urge for example that a real five pound note was greater than one that was simply a thought in our minds. Even more so then goes the argument, to deny the actual existence of God is to fall into foolish contradiction. If God is truly 'that than which nothing greater can be thought', he must exist in reality as well as in the mind.

This was an attempt at natural theology, seeking to establish the existence of God without appealing to any particular revelation that comes through Christian faith. We should notice, however, that Anselm insisted on a reasoned presentation of Christian belief because he taught that faith must lead to the right use of reason. He said, 'I believe, in order that I may understand'. This has led Karl Barth to deny that Anselm was doing natural theology at all, but was rather drawing out the philosophical implications of an existing Christian faith.[13] The truth, however, is probably more complex; I suggest that in Anselm we can see the kind of interplay between reasoned reflection, faith, and revelation that we can develop in new forms in a natural theology of today.

Thomas Aquinas (1225–1274) continued the search for a rational proof for the existence of God. In line with Aristotle he saw the world as being composed of real things that act as true causes; they are principles and goals of activity and not merely instruments or occasions for what happens. They are complete as far as they go, but must be seen in the light of the 'First Cause.' So Aquinas believed that we can arrive at the conclusion that God exists from a deeply considered acceptance of the world about us. His celebrated five ways of thinking about God's existence take up five general observations about the universe, namely its change, dependence, contingency, limited perfection, and utility. He infers a changeless changer, an uncaused cause, a necessary being, a completely perfect one, and an ultimate end; all this combines to form a definition of God.

Aquinas' five ways include what later became known as the 'cosmological' argument (God as the ultimate cause of the cosmos) and the 'teleological' argument (God as the ultimate designer).[14] In all five ways he was following the principle of analogy. He argued that a dynamic world in motion must have causes; God is the single original cause. Within the world one can observe cause and effect; the sequence of cause and effect can be traced back to God as the original cause—the First Cause, Aristotle's Unmoved Mover. The existence of human beings needs the explanation of another order of Being; we are contingent (we do not necessarily need to be here), and so we must owe our existence to a necessary Being (who owes his existence to nothing outside himself). Moreover, human attributes such as truth, goodness, and nobility must have their origin in a being who has these attributes perfectly. Finally, the universe shows evidence of design; there must be a designer, for how else have things come into existence at all?

While Aquinas presents his five ways as if they are proofs of the existence of God, Alister McGrath argues that they were not intended to prove the existence of God from rational argument, but were designed to provide a rational defence of an already existing faith in God. In a similar way to Barth's view of Anselm, McGrath maintains that Aquinas was offering supports and not proofs.[15] Aquinas' two most important works were the *Summa Theologiae* and the *Summa contra Gentiles*. Together they represent an encyclopedic summary of Christian thought, the first based on revelation and the second designed to support Christian belief with human reason. Both works, it may be suggested, use Aristotelian logic in unfolding the connections and implications of revealed truth.

We may certainly agree that Aquinas wanted to hold reason and faith together, and again this will be our concern in thinking about natural theology today. Aquinas (and to some extent Anselm), however, was responsible for a style of theology in the Middle Ages that worked in two stages. First there was a natural theology that established certain basic truths about God from rational reflection on the nature of things (for example God is one, good, eternal, and creator), and then this was 'topped up' by a revealed theology, which offered particular truths disclosed to people by God through the scriptures (for example, God is Trinity and is incarnate in Jesus Christ). From the time of Aquinas onwards natural theology provided the intellectual basis of the Christian faith, although at the time of the Reformation this was challenged. Reformation theologians saw God essentially revealed in Christ through scripture; the world was simply to be appreciated for its own sake. Calvin (1509–1564), however, while emphasising faith and salvation in Christ alone, does affirm general knowledge of God through his creation—in humanity, natural order, and in historical process. He states that while natural knowledge of God through his creation is imperfect and confused, it nonetheless leaves people with no excuse for ignoring God.[16]

3. Natural Theology in Dialogue with Science: a History

The rooting of natural theology in philosophy has often been traced. The influence of the emerging disciplines of science upon the philosophers who developed or supported a natural theology, however, has not been noted as it should. Alongside the great scientific discoveries of the seventeenth and eighteenth centuries there was the flourishing of rational philosophy, which was focused on the world rather than on God. Rene Descartes (1596–1650), who was a contemporary of the scientists Kepler and Galileo, saw rational argument as the only source of truth. He believed that the essence of a natural science was the discovery of relationships that could be mathematically expressed, and so he attempted to find certain knowledge. He recognised that he could doubt many things (maybe he was dreaming), but one thing that was immune was the fact that he was doubting. From this it followed that he could not doubt that he was thinking, for doubting was only a form of thinking. This led him to conclude; 'I am thinking (or more accurately doubting), therefore I exist.' Among other ideas is the idea of a Perfect Being or God, and reflection on this idea led him to conclude that there must be something outside himself corresponding to this idea; that God must exist in reality and not merely in his own thoughts. Two lines of reflection led Descartes to this conclusion: firstly he was impressed by Anselm's ontological argument, and secondly he held that since the idea of a perfect being could not be brought into being by an imperfect agency, there must therefore be a perfect being. While Descartes considered that we might be deceived by objects (we might imagine or dream about them), he argues that a perfect being would not allow us to be deceived. Urmson[17] and Brown[18] rightly see the strong suspicion of a circular argument here.

During the same period Benedictus de Spinoza (1632–1677) took the view that God did not exist outside nature but within it. He thus held a rational pantheism, conceiving God as One, infinite, necessarily existing, containing all being, and the sole cause of every existing thing. The British equivalent of the continental rationalism was empiricism, whereby statements were seen to be true or false by testing them against experience.

John Locke (1632–1704) was a member of this school of thought. He was brought into close contact with the current work in physics and chemistry through his friendship with Sir Robert Boyle, while at Oxford. He himself took a degree in medicine following his degree in philosophy. Influenced by Descartes, he believed that the world is really and fundamentally what the physicist says it is; the answers to questions about the nature of the world are those that the physicist would give. This shows at least a half-conscious acceptance of the scientific worldview. He considered that our senses (stimulated mechanically) produced ideas. These ideas are derived from experience, and we can have knowledge no farther than we have ideas. Material bodies are known by the ideas (qualities and sensations) that they produce in the human observer. Locke concluded that God must exist as a reality beyond our idea of him and saw miracles as evidence for the Christian faith.

George Berkeley (1685–1753) sought to press Locke's views further, being concerned that we could be deceived by our senses. He was also concerned that if the material universe were eternal, one could deny the existence of God altogether. He therefore resolved the problem by denying the existence of matter. He held on to Locke's 'ideas', stating that these were caused by God. The result was a remarkable doctrine of a theocentric, non-material universe, which existed because it was perceived and in which human beings were conceived of as conversing directly with the mind of God. In his reasoning things only exist in so far as they are perceived, but when people are not present, they are always perceived by the infinite mind of God. Perhaps the best account of this is not to be found in philosophy text-books, but in a limerick by Ronald Knox:

> There was a young man who said, 'God
> Must think it exceedingly odd
> If he finds that this tree
> Continues to be
> When there's no-one about in the Quad.'

> 'Dear Sir:
> Your astonishment's odd,
> I am always about in the Quad.
> And that's why the tree
> will continue to be,
> Since observed by
> Yours faithfully
> GOD.'[19]

At the same time Isaac Newton was claiming that God could be perceived through reason in the workings of nature. For Newton reflection on the phenomena of the natural world led to the conclusion that the universe was the rational design of God. God was on the outside holding the whole dynamic system within a timeless and motionless framework.

William Paley, as we have already seen,[20] followed Newton in believing that the scientific discoveries of nature pointed to a creative mind as the author.

David Hume (1711–1776), however, had already mounted powerful rebuttals to Paley's kind of argument. He suggested that while one could accept the common sense view of causation (the cosmological argument), it could not be used as a rational proof for God. He believed that truth or falsehood could only be learned from experience and that the only field of demonstrative reasoning was mathematics. In his *Treatise of Human Nature* (Book I, Part IV) he discusses the fallibility of both reason and the senses, expressing the doubt that any cause could be known simply from its effect, much less that God as a supposed supreme cause could be known in this way. In his *Dialogues concerning Natural Religion* he acknowledged that the argument from design was the strongest of the traditional 'proofs', but then proceeded to undermine it by some devastating arguments. First, he observed that the universe was more like a living organism than an artifact that had been made, so that order could be said to be immanent in nature itself, rather than being derived from a designer. It was as if the universe was just 'growing' by itself according to its own internal guidelines. Second, he pointed out that for any universe to exist it must be ordered, and so it will be bound to look as if it were designed. Third, we know that a watch is designed because we have other mechanisms to compare it with; but the universe is unique and incomparable. Fourth, we cannot deduce from a finite, imperfect world that there is an infinite, perfect creator; the design argument can only indicate a creator who is one degree different and more clever than we. While the discovery of random mutations and natural selection in the living world seems to confirm Hume's argument, especially the appearance of the world as a 'great animal' rather than a piece of machinery,[21] we must not forget that modern cosmology is presenting us with a new kind of model of design, in the form of a finely tuned universe.

Hume's criticisms of natural theology were taken further by Immanuel Kant (1724–1804), who studied mathematics and physics as well as philosophy. In an early essay he describes what later became known as the 'Kant-Laplace theory' for the origin of the Solar System, suggesting that the Sun and the planets condensed from a cloud of hot gas. He was influenced by the rationalism of Leibniz and the empiricism of Hume. Kant was convinced, states Urmson,[22] that the mathematics of his day,

Newtonian physics, and Aristotelian logic were complete to the extent that their analysis by the methods of critical philosophy would yield all those fundamental propositions from which others may be deduced by ordinary reasoning. In his work *Critique of Pure Reason* (1781) Kant thus deals critically with the three speculative proofs of God's existence: the Ontological, Cosmological, and Teleological Arguments, arguing that all three types are fallacious.[23] In fact, Kant argued that the Cosmological and Teleological Arguments presuppose the Ontological Argument by identifying a 'first cause' or 'final designer' with God, and so cannot succeed if it fails.

In criticism of the Ontological Argument, which maintains that the very idea of God is such that God could not not exist, Kant says that existence cannot be included as a quality, attribute, or predicate of an object; so it makes no sense to say that someone (God) is greater if he does have existence than if he does not. Hick[24] helpfully explicates Kant's argument along the lines that to speak of something 'existing' is not to add a further predicate (existence) to a definition, but to assert that the definition does apply to something in the world. So, to say that cows exist means that the concept of a cow has instances and to say that a unicorn does not exist means that there are no instances of unicorns. As well as presupposing the validity of the Ontological argument, the Cosmological argument fails because it assumes that there is not an infinite causal series. Kant considered that the Teleological Argument, or argument from design, was acceptable, but not logically compulsive. Following Hume he pointed out that it only proves the existence of an architect of the universe whose powers may be remarkable, but not necessarily infinite.

4. The Ambiguous Witness of Science

In the story we have been tracing, scientific perceptions of the world were appealed to in order to discount natural theology as it had traditionally been done. But at the same time, many scientists believed that they were uncovering the works of God in nature; Newton could speak of 'thinking God's thought after him'. Darwin was also a religious man; as he recorded morphological changes in the animal kingdom in his *Origin of the Species* (1859) and proposed natural selection as the mechanism of evolution, he believed that he was showing how God worked. Huxley, the most ardent supporter of Darwin, described his own position as atheistic; but Charles Kingsley wrote in a very different vein to thank Darwin for his work, enthusing that 'Now that they have got rid of an interfering God, a master magician as I call it—they have to choose between the absolute empire of accident and a living immanent, ever-working God.'[25] There was no doubt how Kingsley the clergyman would choose, but Karl Marx chose to take the alternative possibility. Marx read *The Origin of the Species* in 1860 and commented that 'Darwin's book is very important and serves me as a basis in natural science for the struggle in history.'[26] The struggle in Marx's view was the class war, in which state and society invent religion as a way of maintaining the *status quo*, keeping working people in their place as the producers of wealth for the elite. Colin Brown may therefore be right to conclude that evolution came to fulfil the role in communist doctrine that Marx cast for it.[27]

Here then is the problem for the arguments for the existence of God based upon scientific discovery of the natural world; they are equally capable of leading toward a position of no belief, precisely because they are not proofs. Realising this, from Calvin to Barth there have been Christian thinkers who have stressed the need for revelation, as opposed to reason. Their criticism is not just that rational arguments do not work; they make the theological point that our knowledge of a God who is other than us must come from God's own initiative, whereas with natural theology the movement seems to be from us to God.

But 'natural theology' takes on a different aspect if we begin from the initiative God takes in coming to meet us in the world. Can we not believe that God encounters us where we are, through nature and daily experience, in the same way as he encountered the Magi through their study of the stars? (Matt 2) Does not God also encounter the agnostic scientist or the hesitating enquirer through their discoveries or their enquiries? From a Christian perspective, the quest of science for meaning is not a proof of God, but it is always the result of a meeting with God who indwells his creation; as Paul Fiddes puts it, response to this encounter 'might take a wide variety of forms in human life',[28] so that we are not surprised when there is an ambiguous witness, or even a negative one. Macquarrie is surely right to conclude that the old-style natural theology was at least a bridge between experience of the ordinary everyday world and the faith made explicit by theology.[29] Barth's stress that knowledge of God can be found only in the witness of scripture to Christ would seem to be denied by scripture itself, in such passages as Psalm 19, Acts 14:17, 17:22-31, Romans 1:19, 32 and 2:12-16.

The questions that are posed by modern scientists, whether Christian or non-Christian, therefore have a great deal to offer us in a natural theology based upon encounter and experience. Macquarrie suggests[30] that when we see theistic proofs being developed by a person who has religious convictions, we see that they have exposed those convictions to confrontation with the observable facts of our world, and have shown that they are at least not incompatible with them. But then, he says, we are pushed back to ask where the convictions came from. We need to begin with the experience of encounter with God, including both general experience through nature and specific revelation through the witness of scripture; from here we can move towards the doctrine that the theologian tries to articulate. For the remainder of this chapter we shall follow this track, but not only looking through the eyes of cosmologists and natural scientists who begin from a position of personal religious faith. The ambiguous—and even the agnostic or atheist—witness of science is also of interest for a natural theology, for it bears witness (albeit unawares) to the presence of God in his world, whose initiative in being present prompts the questions as much as the answers.

John Barrow, who professes no specific beliefs, describes how science has always looked for a theory that would explain the whole of our knowledge of the universe. He notes[31] that the early Greeks, with a teleological perspective on the world of living things, saw the world as a great organism. But for those who developed geometry, the universe was seen as a geometric harmony. When clockwork, the pendulum, and Newton's mathematics were the basis of science, a cosmic clockmaker was sought. With the industrial revolution and thermodynamics, the universe was pictured as a giant heat engine. Today some scientists liken the universe to a computer. Barrow enquires, 'What will the next paradigm be?'[32] These successive models show that for many hundreds (if not thousands) of years scientists have been impressed by the intelligibility and comprehensibility of the natural world, together with its apparently rational nature.

This scientific witness to comprehensibility is, however, ambiguous. While scientists may use theistic language as a means of denoting this basic character of the universe, we must not assume that they are inferring a personal God who is intimately involved with his creation and is looking for a response from it. Scientists and theologians may use similar words but give them different value and meaning. This is seen in the writings of Paul Davies and Stephen Hawking, who both use 'God' language in describing the origin and evolution of the universe.

Paul Davies begins his book *God and the New Physics*[33] with a quotation from Albert Einstein, who said: 'Religion without science is blind. Science without religion is lame.' Davies believes that the new physics, based on the theory of relativity and quantum theory, is leading physicists closer to mysticism than materialism, with questions like: How did the universe begin? How will it end? What is life? and What is mind? While Davies believes that science usually leads in the direction of reliable knowledge, the breathtaking answers of science still leave the question why.[34] The universe may well show astonishing ingenuity in its construction, and human beings certainly appear to be part of the scheme of things, but we are left with the question of whether the chain of explanation ends with God or some super law.

Physicists see the universe either governed by the laws of nature, which are the bedrock of logic, or as an abstract computation, where logic governs something discrete rather than continuous. Stephen Hawking remarks that 'we find ourselves in a bewildering world. We want to make sense of what we see around us and to ask: what is the nature of the universe? what is our place in it and where did it and we come from? why is it the way it is?'[35] He then proceeds to note that in the last 300 years more and more regularities and laws have been discovered within our universe. From the scientific determinism of the seventeeth, eighteenth and nineteenth centuries we have developed more precise mathematical understandings of the beginning and possible end of the world. Hawking is concerned above all else to find one law that will ultimately explain the origin and nature of the universe, and so unveil 'the mind of God'.

5. New Forms of the Design Argument

From a Christian standpoint, scientists like Peacocke[36] and Polkinghorne[37] take the arguments down a more distinctly theological track. They believe that in a search for an explanation of the cosmos and for meaning to human existence, we are now more closely bound to the scientific discoveries, exemplified in the 'Anthropic Principle.' While it at one time appeared that natural theology died with Darwin, modern cosmologists are throwing up questions that point beyond the universe of scientific discovery and transcend its power to give answers. They see a structure inherent in the world that is tightly knit and interlocking in character, which led Davies to believe that it provided a surer way to God than did religion. Keith Ward[38] suggests that science joins hands with theology in making God the best explanation of how the world actually is. The theological view of the world is a holistic (physical and spiritual) view, and so there must be an agreement between science and theology, if both pictures of the universe are correct. Understanding the world in which we live is a quest that unites science and theology, and such a quest will require an openness to God, scripture, and scientific research. The world is not a neutral place and if it is the creation of God we should expect it to be a starting point in recognising him.

This was certainly the ground of eighteenth- and nineteenth-century thinking. William Paley's argument from design in 1802 stated that a mechanism must be designed by an intelligent person for a purpose; it was then a simple step from the watchmaker to the cosmic designer. Associated with the design argument was the view that the universe was programmed to develop towards some final goal. The major problem with these arguments is that complex order can be explained as the end result of ordinary natural processes. Darwin demonstrated that biological order could be produced through mutation and natural selection. Genetics has demonstrated that random alterations, chance selection, together with disaster and extinction occurs regularly, and so we can conclude that order can and does occur spontaneously.

According to the second law of thermodynamics, however, disorder always increases, which means that the universe that we observe must have been created in an orderly condition. This state of initial order is the first aspect we may identify within a modern version of the argument from design. According to Paul Davies, the odds against randomly generated initial order are staggering:

> If the universe is simply an accident, the odds against it containing any appreciable order are ludicrously small. If the Big Bang was just a random event, then the probability seems overwhelming that the emerging cosmic material would be in thermodynamic equilibrium at maximum entropy with zero order. As this was clearly not the case, it appears hard to escape the conclusion that the actual state of the universe has been chosen or selected.[39]

He therefore suggests a selector or a designer for our universe.

This same point is made by Penrose, who says that for some reason, the universe was created in a very special (low entropy) state.[40] If there was enough time, stars, galaxies, and even human life might form accidently in a universe, but the time factor is estimated to be in excess of 10^{800} years (10 followed by 800 zeros!). Our observation of this universe is only possible because we exist, and our existence is either a miracle or an incredible accident. This leads cosmologists to discuss the Anthropic Principle.

A second aspect of the modern design argument is the nature of the universe as an inter-related organism. From a scientific perspective we see that under the diversity and complexity of the universe there is an underlying unity, an interconnectedness in its fundamental forces and principles. This would suggest one unifying source of creativity or origin. In an attempt to picture this, John Wheeler gives a symbolic representation of a 'participatory universe' (see Figure 6:1), presenting the universe as a self-observing system.[41]

It should be added immediately that Wheeler himself sees this interconnected system as having brought itself into existence. For us to see the universe we might reasonably suggest, however, that it must have developed with us in mind. This brings us to the third and perhaps the key aspect of a modern design argument, the *Anthropic Principle*. Our universe has to take account of our presence. The universe is bigger and older than we ever imagined, and we seem to be an almost totally insignificant part of the whole, and yet physicists tell us that the universe had to be the size and age that it is to make our existence possible. We have seen the necessity of a low entropy state; to this is added the nature of the Big Bang, where expansion must be sufficient to overcome gravity, but not so large as to inhibit the development of stars and galaxies; the nature of the temperatures involved had to be sufficient for the chemical reactions in the first formed stars that would ultimately lead through super-novae to the distribution of life-forming carbon in that part of the universe, where the Earth formed.

Such factors as these have led Barrow to conclude[42] that the influence of the Anthropic Principle has grown as cosmologists have probed closer and closer to the initial state in their attempts to reconstruct the past history of the universe. As an extension of the Anthropic Principle, we may also observe that there is a remarkable congruence between the way our minds work and the way the universe is, which leads to the suggestion that behind the universe is a mind like ours.

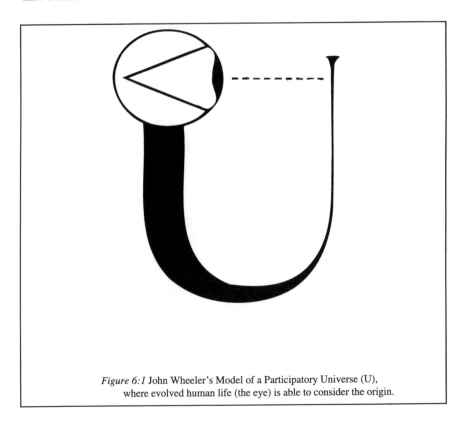

Figure 6:1 John Wheeler's Model of a Participatory Universe (U), where evolved human life (the eye) is able to consider the origin.

Amazingly, tiny changes in many of the fundamental constants of nature in the initial state of the universe would have prevented the existence of atom-based life of any sort. It is this fine tuning that has been one of the most fascinating discoveries of modern science, and which provides a fourth aspect of a modern design argument. With regard to this feature, there are two possible interpretations that we can put forward. On the one hand we can conclude that this is the only possible universe, and that it has been designed with the purpose of bringing conscious observers into existence. On the other hand it might be argued that this universe is one of many universes, so that although our position is special, we are here by accident. An alternative suggestion that has been made is that the order of the universe is imposed upon it by human minds. Such a natural illusion is not probable, as the theories and laws with regard to the universe have arisen as a response to our discernment of what actually is. Polkinghorne states that 'the anthropic arguments of natural theology, based on law and circumstance, seem to survive the discussion of the problems associated with them.'[43] We must always remember, however, that such arguments are based on our present knowledge of cosmology, and the nature of science is that it is always open to change its opinions in the light of new evidence.

A fifth aspect of the modern design argument is the mystery of personality. Even for biologists the appearance of *Homo sapiens* is a surprise. There is a distinctiveness in personhood. Peacocke[44] finds that the subjectiveness of our self-conscious personhood is quite unpredictable from even our present state of sophisticated science; here mechanism ends in mystery. Penrose[45] says much the same in concluding that some of the mind's functions are not computable. So we have to ask: what kind of universe can be the context for the evolution of beings such as us? The Anthropic Principle, together with our distinctive personhood would lead us to raise the possibility of God who is both transcendent as the purposeful creator and immanent as the God of personhood. Yet these scientific arguments have the same fundamental problems as the philosophical arguments of Anselm and Aquinas. They can be pointers to, but not proofs of, the existence of God.

6. 'It Ain't Necessarily So!'—Scientific Problems with Design

There are scientific arguments that oppose the conclusions of the Anthropic Principle. Richard Dawkins would take a quite different view from Paul Davies, drawing attention to the nature of chance and uncertainty in the universe in general, and in the the evolution of life in particular. While he does not suggest brute chance, his 'tamed chance' is blind. It is the process of natural selection, through non-random survival, that leads to the variety and complexity of life as we know it, including ourselves. So for Dawkins, Paley's watchmaker is not the careful creative designer, but the 'Blind Watchmaker' of Darwin's natural selection.[46]

Dawkins is right in recognising chance and novelty in the universe. The factor of chance is the first major challenge to any argument for design (let alone for a Designer); any natural theology has to address the extinctions, malfunctions, and suffering that are seen within the physical world we experience. At sub-atomic levels the quantum theory reveals random happenings, although these cancel each other out at macroscopic levels to reveal an observance of physical laws. Dynamic systems often show a surprisingly unstable response to minor variations, which limits our ability to predict or control them and which has led to the description 'chaos.' As with quantum events, however, many acts of chaos add together to give predictable order. Gould[47] takes a similar line to Dawkins, when he says that the 'divine tape player' holds a million scenarios, each perfectly sensible. Slight changes in selection of the favoured species at the outset cause a very different evolutionary pathway to be followed.

If we wish to recognise human beings as the goal of creation, then we must believe that the pathway that nature did follow was guided. Rather than denying chance, we might then try to incorporate it into the design. Polkinghorne[48] attempts to do this, arguing that chance and necessity give a world with ragged edges, where order and disorder interlace with each other; chance then leads both to systems of increasing complexity and new possibilities, and also to imperfectly formed, malfunctioning systems. 'Natural evil' is thus seen as a kind of untidiness and disorder. The large question then arises, however, as to whether such a world could be one created in love by a good creator. This is a point we must return to in the next chapter, when I want to suggest that as well as chance there is a freedom deeper than chance, at least in animate nature. We note that for Jaques Monod[49] the role of chance simply becomes evidence of meaninglessness in the process of the world and, consequently, moves us away from the possibility of a God of purpose.

A further problem with the design argument appears to be the opposite to the challenge of chance. There is a difficulty of keeping freedom really in view the more that design is stressed; consequently there is a problem with the kind of God that scientific arguments seem to lead to. Scientists have a variety of beliefs, which will be based, at least in part, on the models that they derive from observation and experience of the universe. Science is not necessarily concerned with ultimate truth and is always ready to accommodate change in the light of new discoveries. The basis of the Christian faith, by contrast, lies in God's revelation of himself and the truths that are formulated in reflection upon this revelation. Cosmologists can look for one super-law, a theory of everything, without reference to God, because all their talk about design is merely an expression of how they observe the universe. Most scientists are certainly not looking to prove or to disprove the existence of God, but simply to understand the universe scientifically. So religious believers (including some scientists) can build a picture of 'God' on scientific models and present him as a divine 'mathematician' or an infinite 'computer programmer'; the resulting defect, from a truly theological point of view, is that a logically consistent universe that is the creation of a supreme mathematician or programmer seems to leave no room for freedom.

No freedom means no relationship and, therefore, no personal involvement of a personal God. Certainly Stephen Hawking is not looking for God at the centre of the universe. For him 'God' is a shorthand expression for the ultimate mathematical solution to the Big Bang, getting behind the Big Bang singularity and explaining how the universe came into being. Hawking is looking for the triumph of human reason, a unified theory that would explain why we and the universe exist; and so he concludes: 'If we find the answer to that, it would be the ultimate triumph of human reason—for then we would know the mind of God.'[50]

Davies wrestles more rigorously than Hawking with the tension between the apparent design of the universe and its apparent contingence or openness to a whole range of possibilities. Like Hawking, he asks whether 'God' (the ultimate solution) had a 'choice' and whether the world could have been otherwise. Different initial conditions for the universe would have produced a different universe, but not one in which human life would have evolved. Davies therefore poses a number of questions.[51] Is 'God' constrained by logic? Is this the best of all worlds or would a world free of suffering be better? Are the physical laws the optimum regulating of the universe? If this world reflects 'God's' nature, then does his nature becomes a necessity for the universe? Is 'God' actually necessary? Does the universe require something outside of itself? He is inclined toward a necessary reality or being, but sees difficulties in relating such a reality to the changing, contingent universe.

In his later work where he poses these questions, Davies also questions whether there is any difference between God and a Theory of Everything as the ultimate origin of the universe. In so doing he demonstrates that this is not the surer path to God that he suggested nine years earlier,[52] but by making this equation he also forecloses the nature of the God we are thinking about. As a scientist he is impressed by the beauty of law, but seems to have lost the sense of freedom that belongs to being a person. He recognises the rationality of nature, governed by physical laws, but then cannot resolve the paradox of the changing and eternal, or becoming and being. He recognises the complexity of the organised variety of an evolving universe, both in the fine tuning of the physical universe and in the development of humanity. It all leads him to conclude that the world is a marvellous and ingenious mathematical scheme, which, if God were invoked as a matter of 'personal taste', would mean that we would be central to his plan. But would we then be truly free persons with real options and choices? I suggest that any Christian use of the design argument must meet the challenge of showing that belief in a personal God can bring together transcendence (the eternal) and immanence (commitment to change and openness), and I aim to attempt this in the next chapter.

Science throws up the matching problems of chance and freedom with relation to design in general. But beyond these there is the problem that a religious attempt to prove God through design presupposes the very thing that it is meant to establish—meaning in the mind of a creator. Certainly, there are signs of meaning behind the reality we know. Many people have pointed to the complex nature of the universe, its intelligibility, the nature of human conscious life, and the natural sense of morality. John Hick sums up the position of one such author, F. R. Tennant, as

> when the human mind surveys the universe in which it finds itself, its conviction that this indefinitely complex cosmos could not have come into being in a completely random and unplanned way is a reasonable even though not logically compelling conviction, reflecting . . . an improbability in the chance hypothesis.[53]

But this can be seen as a personal judgement, where our own beliefs and feelings affect the way that we think. As well as sign-posts to meaning, there are also signs that throw doubt upon the presence of meaning in the universe. The world is full of events and experiences that speak for or against theism, for example, miracle or suffering, evil, religious experience, moral choices and their consequences. These, as Hick rightly observes,[54] cannot be weighed against each other to produce a sum as they have no common currency.

The design argument neither proves the existence of a creative mind behind the universe, nor does it in an objective sense even show it to be probable; so why, asks Hick, does the design argument continue? His answer is that: 'Cosmic evolution constitutes a transcendent-suggesting mystery to which religion is the natural response.'[55] The argument from design does not establish the existence of God, but it does pose the question, to which one answer can reasonably be, God. As John Houghton puts it, there is no proof but a matter of 'perspective'[56]; the question can rightly be urged as to whether the features of the universe that we observe fit into the perspective of a belief in God, or not.

7. A New Form of the Cosmological Argument

Just as support may be found in modern science for a new version of the teleological argument (from design), so there are features of modern cosmology that appear to be working in the same direction as the older cosmological argument, i.e. from cause. The quest for a 'theory of everything' may be understood as a search for the cause behind the Big Bang. There is a wistful belief that if only one could find the equation that brought all the factors together, the law by which the other laws work, one would be able to explain how the Big Bang happened. If time and space ('real time') began with the primal explosion, then one might with Stephen Hawking conceive of a continual oscillation between 'imaginary time' (before creation) and 'real time' until the conditions were right for the Big Bang to occur. Finding the equation that expresses these conditions would be finding the First Cause, so that a modern design argument would be based on the manifestation of purpose 'from the Big Bang forwards', and a modern cosmological argument would be based on the detection of causation 'from the Big Bang backwards'.

There is some point, then, in supporting the older argument that God is the first and necessary cause of all reality by appeal to the modern search for a first cause. Indeed, some scientists seem to be interested in seeing how the parallel might work, without necessarily having faith themselves. John Barrow, for example, considers the three basic factors of God, the universe, and the laws of nature, and then draws up three groups of parallel propositions. (1) Either the laws of nature existed before the universe (a 'first cause'); or the laws are dependent on the universe; or the laws are to be equated with the universe. (2) A similar set of propositions can be made with regard to God: either the universe is part of God ('panentheism'—everything in God); or God is part of the universe (a creation of the human mind); or God is the same as the universe ('pantheism'). (3) Again, a third set of propositions might be: either the laws of nature are part of God; or God is part of the laws of nature; or the laws of nature are the same as God.[57]

There is, of course, no logical necessity for coming to the conclusion that the universe points to the God of the Christian scriptures, but there is an interesting affinity between the first of these propositions in each set, and a potential here for a 'suggestive' natural theology. We should recognise a defect immediately in this form of argument, however, which should lead us to handle it cautiously. Even with the first propositions in each case, what results from this analogy is a God in whom law is the dominant characteristic, rather than the high profile of personal relatedness that emerges from the story of Israelite and Christian experience of God. Indeed Barrow, like Penrose, recognises that there are features of the universe that do not compute according to a scheme of laws—namely beauty, simplicity, truth, or personal opinions. He concludes that: 'there is no formula that can deliver all truth, all harmony, all simplicity. No theory of everything can ever provide total insight. For, to see through everything, would leave us seeing nothing at all.'[58] Penrose, in speaking of the human brain, says that mere computation is unable to evoke pleasure or pain; nor can it appreciate beauty in nature, or poetry, or music; and it cannot hope, love, or despair. Consciousness is, he says, 'the phenomenon whereby the universe's very existence is made known. One can argue that a universe governed by laws that do not allow consciousness is no universe at all.'[59]

Nevertheless, at the same time as highlighting the defect of an analogy with law, these comments by Barrow and Penrose can also be seen as a reasonable basis for moving from a merely scientific first cause to God as first cause. A God of personal relationships could be argued to be a more convincing explanation for all the features of the universe, including consciousness, than a super-law or mere 'theory of everything' would be. Here we are rehearsing the cosmological arguments of Aquinas: from the fact of change we consider the ultimate source of change, which does not require to be moved by something else; from the ordered series of causes in the universe one is forced to suppose a first cause, or else have an infinite sequence of causes; and the existence of things in the world are contingent and are only explicable by reference beyond themselves, the universe being explained in terms of a self-explanatory or necessary being.

But we must underline once again that we are not dealing with a proof here. John Hick is right to complain that advocates of a cosmological argument too easily suppose that any reasonable person must agree that the existence of an eternal creative Mind would be self-explanatory in a way in which the existence of the physical universe, exhibiting the fundamental laws that it does exhibit, would not.[60] In this respect Paul Davies is right to point out that the design of the universe is a fact, but that belief in a designer is 'a matter of personal taste'; this would apply equally to an argument from cause. Because of the rational way in which our minds operate we see the universe as needing explanation. This need grows stronger when we picture a universe that begins in a Big Bang explosion, as this means that we are able to conceive of a universe that might have been different; that is, it is 'contingent'. It makes sense then, as we consider the 'fine tuning' of the universe, to think of a creative divine Mind behind the universe. Yet having reached such a point in the argument, Bertrand Russell's conclusion is still open to us as a logical possibility; namely, there is the explanation of brute fact, that the universe is just there and that is all. The cosmological argument, like the argument from design, points to the possibility of God, but does not provide a proof of his existence.

8. The Limitations of Natural Theology

The failure of a natural theology, as developed from recent scientific research, to prove the existence of God has been amply demonstrated throughout this chapter. With regard to the central issues of the 'Anthropic Principle' and 'fine tuning', it can always be argued that human life only appears to be woven into the very fabric of the universe because we actually exist to observe this particular universe. We cannot, on grounds of pure logic, rule out the possibility of many universes that remain unobserved, and so the possibility that the existence of this one, and our place in it, is merely accidental. We see that the new cosmological and teleological arguments suffer from the same weaknesses as those of the last three centuries; they are not proof for the existence of God, but remain as pointers to that possibility and support for such a belief. The modern scientific discoveries have up-dated the cosmological and teleological arguments; they have given them a firmer grounding in the character of the universe as we understand it; and it is the scientists who are asking the questions and forming the arguments, rather than the theologians. For our own day and age the questions and possible answers of modern cosmology do provide us with a reasonable basis for our belief in a creator who is intimately involved with his creation. Yet, even with all this support from the scientific community, it is only through faith that we believe in a purposeful creator, who created a world with human beings in mind; brute chance remains an alternative.

Beyond this basic limitation, we may, however, notice several others. In the first place, we have seen that in modern versions of natural theology the key issue is the special place of human beings in the evolution of the universe. Among the aspects of an argument from design, the Anthropic Principle is prominent, and arguments from ultimate causes have to take account of human consciousness with its emotions, apprehensiveness, appreciation, and aspirations. Scientists have presented us with a universe that has a biography, a beginning in the past and a predictable end in the future. They have demonstrated that this universe must have been finely tuned if conscious, self-aware human life is the end-point of the whole process of evolution. If this is the case—although we must remember that it is only because we are here to observe it that we can suggest it is—then the universe has a clear sense of shaping, ordering, and design. But for all this stress upon the significance of humanity and the development of intelligent life on earth, no answer is given to the basic question, 'What are we here for?' or even, 'Why is there anything at all?' Likewise, success in finding one simple, unifying mathematical equation to explain the universe would still leave the question of the 'why?' unanswered.

Thus a natural theology based on these scientific factors will suffer from the same limits when it comes to questions of meaning. The material is just not there to take us any further. We are dependent upon the witness of scripture to what its writers believed had been revealed to them. God's self-disclosure is seen most clearly in Jesus Christ, but Genesis 1 already presents us with a picture of God who is intimately involved with his creation, and whose final aim is fellowship with created persons. This does not mean that we are left with a two-level approach of natural and revealed theology; rather, each dimension of knowledge illuminates the other. The universe, with its order, intelligibility, and potential, fits together with the picture of a creator who is patient, open, and content to achieve his purposes through the slow outworking of physical laws and natural processes.

Such a universe contains freedom and the resultant risk of evil, pain, and suffering. This will point us towards the creator's purpose in making persons with a destiny beyond this world. Angela Tilby is thus surely right in noting that when God gives his answer to Job, his answer comes out of the whirlwind, out of the heat of a chaotic system.[61] God did not engage with Job's questions, but showed him how little he knew of the structure of the universe: its ebb and flow, darkness and light, chaos and order. The new cosmology, likewise calls us to recover something of the mystery of God's wholeness; God is the one author of the whole of creation. But our ultimate hope cannot be formed without the revelation of God through scriptures such as Revelation 21:1-4, where God is portrayed as finally coming to dwell fully among his creatures in a new heaven and a new earth.

If natural theology on its own is limited in what it says about the nature and destiny of human beings, it is even more limited in what it can tell us about God. We notice that the Bible takes the existence of God for granted; it never seeks to demonstrate it. Hick accurately sums this up, when he comments that the biblical writers 'did not think of God as an inferred entity but as an experienced reality.'[62] The God who is inferred simply as the end-point of a philosophical argument is but a shadow of the living God of biblical faith. We have already raised this point when thinking of God as equivalent to the object of the search of cosmologists for a final cause; we end with an ultimate law or theory and not a personal God who gives himself away in love. With regard to the teleological argument, David Hume has a point when he states in his *Dialogues concerning Natural Religion*[63] that the notion of a divine Designer in itself does not tell us anything about a personal and holy God. A Designer superior to human beings may still be finite or infinite, perfect or imperfect, omniscient or fallible, the One or a member of a pantheon. He may, as Hume puts in mocking parody, be a retired deity in the last stages of dotage, an apprentice deity just embarking on his career of making worlds, or even a clever devil. We need not follow Hume all the way here, for with the help of modern science we have been developing an idea of a creator who 'fits in' with the world as we know it, and so one for whom patience and self-sacrifice are appropriate attributes. But in arriving at this idea of God we are not dependent upon natural theology alone, but an interaction of reason and revelation.

A final limitation of natural theology we should note is the one with which we began this chapter, with the help of Douglas Adams. A logical proof of God's existence would be incompatible with God's desire for a free response from people, as the fictitious story of the 'Babel fish' in *The Hitch-Hiker's Guide to the Galaxy* makes clear. If God were to provide such an undeniable proof, we would be coerced into belief and there would be no room for the response of trust that is the basis of the loving relationship that he desires. But then we need to remember that it was unlikely that Anselm and Aquinas were setting out to prove the existence of God without any reference to faith at all. Whatever they actually intended to do, their arguments for the existence of God were helpful in giving reasonable support to a belief that was already there.

The recent scientific research into the origin, nature, and evolution of the universe—and of the nature and place of *Homo sapiens* within it— add a great deal of support to the reasonableness of belief, and as such provide a place to encounter those who have no belief. We will consider the areas of apologetics and proclamation in Chapter 8. For the moment we need to note that the reasonableness of belief will depend on understanding and experience. A perfect proof of God's existence would not necessarily produce anything more than mental assent; in fact Hick[64] is right to conclude that for many people such a proof would have little effect. Our beliefs are affected by our experiences and change in the light of these. The awareness of God for a Paul of Tarsus or a Jeremiah was as vivid as their experience of the material world around them, but most people do not have such experiences, and even Jeremiah's awareness was tested by adverse experiences. If we were to argue from human experience, we might suggest that for Christians the step of faith has resulted in a describable experience of God, which confirms their faith. This is God's self-revelation to the individual believer.

Cosmology is concerned to extrapolate backwards in time on the presumption of continuity and to picture the initial situation to which the present state of affairs would form a natural sequel. The Bible, on the other hand, claims to be the clue to the origin of the world in a quite different sense; not its origin in time but its origin in the purpose of God. We must discuss the place of natural theology within the whole theology of revelation, and it is to this that we must turn our attention in the next chapter. Archbishop William Temple said: 'Natural theology ends with a hunger for that Divine Revelation, which it began by excluding from its purview.'[65] Or to take a quotation from one of the modern cosmologists: 'The theologians think they know the questions but cannot understand the answers. The physicists think they know the answers but don't know the questions.'[66] Perhaps William Paley was right to say:

> My opinion of astronomy has always been that it is not the best medium through which to prove the agency of an intelligent Creator; but that, this being proved, it shows, beyond all other sciences, the magnificence of his operations.[67]

Notes to Chapter 6

[1]Romans 1:20 (translation based on New Revised Standard Version).

[2]D. Adams, *The Hitch-Hiker's Guide to the Galaxy*, 49-50.

[3]P. Davies, *God and the New Physics*, ix.

[4]Quoted in P. Davies, *The Mind of God*, 148 and A. Tilby, *Science and the Soul*, 72.

[5]Quoted in Davies, *The Mind of God*, 140.

[6]F. Hoyle, *The Nature of the Universe* (New York: Blackwell, Oxford, 1960) 103

[7]C. Brown, *Philosophy and the Christian Faith* (Leicester: Tyndale, 1969) 271.

[8]C. Brown, article 'Natural Theology' in *New Dictionary of Theology* (Leicester: I.V.P., 1988) 452; italics are mine.

[9]Quoted by Neil Spurway in '100 Years (and More) of Natural Theology' in N. Spurway (ed.) *Humanity, Environment and God* (Oxford: Blackwell, 1993) 9.

[10]Ibid. 10f.

[11]It is held by many that this is the only point of origin, but as I argue in chapter 7, natural theology also has origins in the Jewish and Christian scriptures.

[12]J. O. Urmson, *The Concise Encyclopedia of Western Philosophy and Philosophers* (London: Hutchinson, 1960) 28-51.

[13]K. Barth, *Anselm: Fides Quaerens Intellectum. Anselm's Proof of the Existence of God in the Context of his Theological Scheme*, English translation I.W. Richardson (London: SCM, 1960) 59-72.

[14]Brown, *Philosophy and the Christian Faith*, 26.

[15]A. E. McGrath, *Bridge-building: Effective Christian Apologetics* (Leicester: I.V.P., 1992) 60.

[16]F. Wendel, *Calvin* (London: Fontana Library of Theology and Philosophy, Collins, 1965) 169-77 and McGrath, 33-34.

[17]Urmson, 94.

[18]Brown, *Philosophy and the Christian Faith*, 51.

[19]Included in K. Amis (ed.) *The New Oxford Book of Light Verse* (Oxford: Oxford University Press, 1987) 222f.

[20]See chapters 2 and 3 above.

[21]David Hume, *Dialogues Concerning Natural Religion (1779)*, Part VII; ed. N. K. Smith, *Hume's Dialogues Concerning Natural Religion* (London: Nelson, 1947).

[22]Urmson, 201-208.

[23]Immanuel Kant, *Critique of Pure Reason*, trans. and ed. N. K. Smith (London: Macmillan, 1933) Second Division, Book II, chapter III, Sections 4-6 (500-25).

[24]J. Hick, *Arguments for the Existence of God* (London: Macmillan, 1971), 82-3.

[25]Quoted in Spurway, 11ff.

[26]Quoted in R. E. D. Clark, *Darwin: Before and After*, 112f.

[27]Brown, *Philosophy and the Christian Faith*, 149.

[28]Paul S. Fiddes, *Freedom and Limit* (Basingstoke: Macmillan, 1991) 32.

[29]J. Macquarrie, *Principles of Christian Theology*, 2d ed. (London: SCM, 1977) 54.

[30]Ibid.

[31]J. D. Barrow, *Theories of Everything*, 204.

[32]Ibid.

[33]P. Davies, *God and the New Physics* (1983) frontpiece.

[34]P. Davies, *The Mind of God*, 13.

[35]S. W. Hawking, *A Brief History of Time*, 171.

[36]E. g. A. Peacocke, *God and the New Biology* and *Theology for a Scientific Age—Being and Becoming*; *Natural and Divine*.

[37]E.g. J. Polkinghorne, *One World—the Interaction of Science* and *Theology and Science and Creation*.

[38]K. Ward, *The Turn of the Tide* (London: BBC Publications, 1986) 67.

[39]Davies, *God and the New Physics*, 167-68.

[40]R. Penrose, *The Emperor's New Mind*, 339.

[41]J. Wheeler, 'Information, Physics, Quantum: the Search for Links,' W. H. Zureck, ed., *Complexity, Entropy and the Physics of Information* (Redwood City CA: Addison-Wesley, 1990) 8. Cited in Davies, *The Mind of God*, 224-25.

[42]J. Barrow, 'Inner Space and Outer Space' in N. Spurway (ed.) *Humanity, Environment and God*, 48-103.

[43]Polkinghorne, *Science and Creation*, 30.

[44]Peacocke, *Theology for a Scientific Age*, 106ff.

[45]Penrose, 447f.

[46]R. Dawkins, *The Blind Watchmaker*, passim., but see 21ff, 37ff.

[47]S. J. Gould, *Wonderful Life: The Burgess Shale and the Nature of History*, 321.

[48]Polkinghorne, *Science and Creation*, 47f.

[49]J. Monod, *Chance and Necessity* (London: Collins, 1972).

[50]Hawking, 175.

[51]Davies, *The Mind of God*, 161-93.

[52]Davies, *God and the New Physics*, ix.

[53]Hick, 29.

[54]Ibid.

[55]Ibid., 33-36.

[56]John Houghton in his Templeton lecture, given at Rewley House, Oxford, on 5 November 1992.

[57]J. D. Barrow, *Theories of Everything*, 23-29.

[58]Ibid., 210.

[59]Penrose, 447-48.

[60]Hick, 46.

[61]A. Tilby, *Science and the Soul*, 184.

[62]Hick, 102.

[63]D. Hume, *Dialogues Concerning Natural Religion (1779)* Part V; ed. N. K. Smith, *Hume's Dialogues Concerning Natural Religion*, 165-69.

[64]Hick, 106.

[65]William Temple, *Nature, Man and God* (London: Macmillan, 1935) 520.

[66]Barrow, 1.

[67]W. Paley, *Natural Theology* (1802) repr. in R. Lyman (ed.) *The Works of William Paley* (London, 1925) 8f.

7

'In him we live and move and exist'[1]

The Mutual Witness of Science and Faith

Some years ago, a former colleague of mine in a department of Geology was rejoicing over the birth of his first child. He spoke with a great deal of emotion about the actual birth and of the enormous privilege (for a man) of being present to witness the event. He then went on to speak of the wonder and miraculous nature of human life. He told me that he had recently been reading an article about conception, gestation, and birth, in which it said that one microscopic male sperm carries the total 'blue-print' for the new life. The article had said that if such a 'blue-print' were to be drawn out by a draughtsman, it would fill a space of about 2000 cubic metres. This led my colleague to conclude, 'I could almost believe in God!' Yet this emotional experience and intellectual discovery did no more than develop a sense of amazement; no faith resulted.

The problem is that, since the Enlightenment, most scientific people have seen religion as belonging to an ignorant and superstitious past, while religious people have lost interest in the attempt to interpret science and have limited the relevance of religion to the world of values and feelings. Both sides are having to take stock of their respective positions when famous scientists speak of 'knowing the mind of God.' What are scientists up to? asks Angela Tilby; 'Have they found God at the end of the cosmic rainbow?'[2] Like the legendary pot of gold, answers to the universe and everything through scientific research are just as illusory. Scientists push our knowledge of the beginning of the universe back to the Big Bang, but are left with the unknowable. John Barrow recognises that while we can produce mathematical formulae to explain stars and planets, gravity and thermodynamics, science meets a brick wall when it comes to the nature of human personhood.[3] He notes that not every feature of the world is either listable, computable, or encompassed by a finite collection of laws; beauty, simplicity, and truth are properties that are prospective. At this point we have to turn to an understanding of the world and humanity's place, which is beyond the reach of scientific research, belonging instead to the realm of metaphysics and theology. Yet while faith goes beyond science, it ought not to leave its insights behind.

1. Holding Science and Faith Together

As a physicist and a Christian priest, John Polkinghorne believes that there must be no compartmentalisation; theology and science must both be held together in the creator, who is the single ground of all there is.[4] We need to avoid a dualism that separates scientific 'fact' from religious 'belief' and recognise that our apprehension of the real world is both mental and material. There is an openness about human life that includes intuition and inspiration, as well as observation and measurement. The fact that we are made of the same basic material as the cosmos does not explain how we can understand the universe, which is a fact that Roger Penrose underlines in his book *The Emperor's New Mind*. Conversely, however, our newly acquired scientific knowledge about the cosmos does allow us to see the ways in which God is related to his world and, in this, may help us toward a more complete doctrine of creation. The quantum world of sub-atomic particles is a world of uncertainty and should lead believers to be open to the unexpected in our pursuit of the divine.

Natural Theology reaches its limit when it has brought us to the Mathematical Designer or Cosmic Architect. As John Macquarrie remarks, 'Who ever addressed a prayer to necessary being?'[5] The God and Father of our Lord Jesus Christ must be sought through other means, involving faith and commitment. Religious experience involves a greater degree of personal commitment than science, dealing with human experiences that are not open to experimental verification in the same way as many scientific propositions might be. Religious beliefs involve a community of faith, and it is within this community that religious experiences can be validated. The Bible itself is a book that belongs to the religious community, and it is within this community that its revelations are tested and interpreted. In this way faith transcends scientific discovery. On the other hand, however, all of our religious experiences and our faith itself must accord with our total experience of the world, otherwise we could not continue to hold onto such beliefs. Polkinghorne is correct when he says: 'Religion without science is confined; it fails to be completely open to reality.' But also: 'Science without religion is incomplete; it fails to attain the deepest possible understanding.'[6]

Faith is bound to challenge a world-view based on mere experiment and deduction, because its object is both transcendent and immanent. While our belief is anchored in historical events and personal experience that can be examined, we do not have words capable of encompassing the transcendence of God, and so we are driven to use analogy and metaphor. Religious belief will therefore appeal to a whole range of sources, and three in particular: tradition, or the experience of the Church; scripture, which is largely the account of events that were experienced by people like ourselves; and reason, which includes natural theology.

The conclusions of scientists like Paul Davies who take no account of revelation or religious experience will take us no further than some power or force, a kind of demiurge, behind the universe. Scientists are likely to avoid the theological implications of their conclusions and so will not recognise the ways in which human sinfulness will prejudice their views. Basing a religious belief mainly on science can therefore lead to an anthropocentric view of God who, having been discovered as the author of life, is reduced to a being or mind just like us. There can also emerge a deist view that sees God as the distant origin of nature or natural laws, rather than God who is intimately involved with his creation. Nor should we forget that scientific views change and rapidly become out of date. Cosmology can only be a pointer toward a deeper theological inquiry and understanding, which must be based on the present and historical experience of the community of faith.

We need not, however, share the deep suspicion of Karl Barth that an understanding of God gathered from nature will be merely a God in the image of ourselves. The Bible presents us with many instances of God encountering people where they are, and in this way our understanding of God through our contemplation of the natural world can be seen as a part of the way in which he reveals himself to us. Knowledge of God and awareness of him is a natural part of our humanity, and may even provide a point of contact for God's special revelation. The apostle Paul was certainly ready to concede this point, as evidenced by his address to the Athenians in the Areopagus (Acts 17) and his statements in Romans 1:18-20 ('God's nature has been visible in the things he has made') and 2:14 ('Gentiles . . . do by nature what the law requires'). Indeed, in his recent Gifford Lectures James Barr surveys a whole range of material in Old and New Testament that looks like a sort of natural theology.[7]

Barr begins his book by pointing out that natural theology often appears to support a general theism, to which the special content of the Christian faith is added by special revelation.[8] Though he does not find this an attractive way of thinking, he notes that it does at least have an apologetic function in providing a reasonable justification for belief, and a critical function in causing Christians to consider what passages like Genesis 1 might telling us about God; Moltmann similarly refers in his own Gifford Lectures to a hermeneutical function,[9] helping people to understand what they believe. In what follows in his study, however, Barr develops a much more interactive view of natural theology and revelation than the traditional two-stage view, and we shall return to this in a moment.

2. The God of the Universe We Know

Jürgen Moltmann asks whether nature actually discloses itself as God's creation or whether it is only experienced as creation in the light of the self-revelation of the creative God.[10] This is another way of stating the useful distinction between 'natural theology' and 'theology of nature'. Moltmann himself believes that it is not what nature can contribute to our knowledge of God that matters, but rather what our concept of God contributes to our knowledge of nature. The answer to his question, however, is surely both/and rather than either/or, for in the realm of the new cosmology science is posing some questions for which theology is able to provide answers.

Wolfhart Pannenberg has recognised that many scientists, in a variety of fields, are facing questions, often of a moral nature, that they do not have the resources to deal with. Here he believes that there should be a dialogue between science and the churches. He recognises that the past history of relations between church and science has not been good, but he urges the need for a real integration of faith and science:

> If the God of the Bible is the creator of the universe, then it is not possible to understand fully, or even appropriately, the processes of nature without reference to that God. If, on the contrary, nature can be appropriately understood without reference to the God of the Bible, then that God cannot be the creator of the universe, and consequently he could not be truly God and could not be trusted as the source of moral teaching either.[11]

Pannenberg himself suggests various ways in which it can be demonstrated that the biblical God can be conceived as the creator of the actual universe that we know.[12] For instance, he notes that the laws governing matter in a higher level of organisation can never be entirely deduced from the properties of lower levels.[13] We might illustrate this (though Pannenberg does not) by noting that the laws that govern electricity cannot be deduced from the laws that govern clockwork. So, although regular sequences of events take place within the frame of natural laws, the sequences are contingent or 'open' to new possibilities of evolutionary development. There is an irreversibility in these processes that is based on the irreversibility of time. The God of the Bible can be recognised as the God of this universe, because the Bible describes his continuous creation as showing the same blend of contingency and regularity. On the one hand, the future acts of God in history cannot be merely deduced from past events; he is free to do new things. On the other hand, there are regularities in the history of creation because of the faithfulness of God and his maintaining of his identity. He is faithful in keeping promises, but promises are open to different kinds of fulfilment.

To take another example, the Bible presents the Spirit of God as the origin of life, transcending physical organisms (Genesis 2:7; John 3:8; 1 Corinthians 15:42ff). The Spirit comes from beyond humanity into our midst. In biology there is a similar sense of dependence beyond the living organism, as it is not a closed system but is open to its environment, and in its inner drives it relates to a future in a way that transforms its present form of life. In a moment we shall consider how this drive might be understood as the immanent activity of God.

3. A Biblical Kind of Natural Theology

The biblical picture is of God's continuous involvement with his creation described in terms of the 'covenant' agreement he initiates and offers. Israel understood the world as God's good creation in the light of her experience of the exodus from Egypt, the Covenant made at Sinai, and entry into the Promised Land. It was from its experience of the life, crucifixion, and resurrection of Christ, and the establishment of the new covenantal community in the power of the Holy Spirit, that the New Testament Church understood God's intention to perfect and complete his creation. Thus the natural world is given a place in the whole story of

God's purpose to make covenantal fellowship, a process with an eschato-
logical goal. All biblical witness to the creation in which God acts begins
from these insights of faith, made in response to what people found to be
a revelation of God's purposes.

A natural theology that builds a concept of God totally outside the
experience of revelation and the community of faith thus belongs to
Greek philosophy rather than to Hebrew concepts of the world. But, as
James Barr has recently argued, this does not mean that the Bible only
presents a 'theology of nature'. He argues that the Bible contains 'principles akin to natural theology',[14] in that appeal is constantly made to
knowledge of the world that is universally available, or to ideas about
creation by God that are anterior to the instances of revelation that were
so critical for the life of Israel and the early Church. But this appeal to
a wider awareness of the world and God is woven into insights of revelation and cannot be separated from them. Psalm 104, for example, begins
from a perspective of faith in God as creator that is rooted in Israel's
historic experience, but it then develops the content of God's creative
work in a way that draws upon traditional mythology (draining off the
waters of chaos) or publicly available knowledge (the springs give water
to the wild asses). Psalm 119 begins from the distinctive revelational experience of a law (*torah*) given to Israel; it then goes on to develop the
concept of law without mentioning Moses or the written commandments,
but rather the experience of a divine 'word set up in the heavens'. It is
as if the commandments celebrated by the Psalm are a kind of 'revealed
natural law'. All this Barr suggests shows that natural theology is 'an in-
terpretative stage through which revelational material passes'.[15]

Another way of perceiving this, Barr suggests, is that material derived from common experience is 'recast' in the light of revelation. The
accusations against the nations in Amos 1-2, for example, assume a kind
of international morality that is not in doubt, but this takes a new form
in the revelation that God is standing in judgement over them.[16] Images
of God such as 'Shepherd', and even the very idea of covenant itself,
were familiar to people all over the ancient world as a way in which they
ordered reality around them.[17] The actual languages and cultures within
which the Bible was written express the way in which the world was
perceived and understood. But all this universal awareness is re-shaped
through the particular experience of the great moments of revelation within the community of faith. The parables of Jesus especially transcend any

contrast between natural and revealed theology.[18] While they do not express a totally 'scientific' picture of the world, as has sometimes been suggested, they are still grounded in public experience of nature (the lilies of the field, the birds of the air, the growing of crops, the relation between parents and children) and use that experience to open up a little more knowledge of the creator who is already known through revelation. I agree then with Barr that we are wrong to draw hard and fast distinctions between natural theology and revealed theology. But I suggest that Barr's careful exegesis of scripture shows us that 'natural theology' is not just an element of experience woven into revelation, but is actually part of the whole scope of God's revelation of himself through all the variety of human experience.

The world of modern science with its discoveries and beliefs is a part of the world that we experience in our time. In the same way as the biblical writers developed their understanding of revealed truths in constant interaction with the beliefs and principles of both their own people and those of neighbouring cultures, it should not be surprising if modern Christian thought does the same. We bring our understanding of theology to the discoveries of science and allow each to inform the other. As John Habgood rightly remarks,[19] however, religions are not closed immutable systems; they can lose their plausibility, die, be defeated, or be radically transformed—'Who now believes in Baal?' he asks, although once this god ranked with Yahweh. What is true of religions is true of scientific theories; they remain provisional until they have stood the test of time. So our understanding of the God whom we worship through Christ will be primarily shaped through the revelation we receive by means of scripture and tested both through the interpretation of scripture in the believing community and through scientific investigation of the world. Science has made theologians look more carefully at their interpretation of scriptures, and science has learned to be more careful in distinguishing between fact and interpretation.

Modern Old Testament scholars, according to Barr, have broken away from the assumption (developed under the powerful influence of Karl Barth) that biblical theology has nothing to do with natural theology, and they now increasingly see world 'order' as a central idea. He remarks that this idea

is evident especially in the Wisdom literature and in its relations with
ancient Near Eastern culture; and through these it spills o er into many
aspects of Old Testament thought, especially the idea of creation, which
on the one hand takes the form of separation and ordering, and on the
other hand . . . develops into the central base for natural theology.[20]

We must not fail, however, to mark the major difference between the biblical view of God and the theist position. In a theist picture based solely
on natural theology God is transcendent, omnipotent, omniscient, complete in every way without others, incorporeal, and cannot suffer or
change. But biblical natural theology looks to a biblical God, the God of
Israel, the Father of Jesus Christ who is personal and opens himself to all
the hazards of love for others; it places God in an immanent, intimate
relationship with his creation.

4. A Biblical View of the Immanence of God

The Priestly writer of Genesis 1 invites us to reflect on God's transcendent freedom in creation. It is his choice to bring form out of
formlessness and order out of chaos. It is God who gives shape, pattern,
and beauty to his creation. But the universe that is created is not static,
but open and dynamic, filled with the life of the Spirit, and in such life
there is liberty. I agree with David Atkinson,[21] who points out that the
immanence of God indwelling his world must affect the way in which we
think of space. Space is not a receptacle into which God comes; this is
Newton's God, outside of his creation. Rather, the Bible indicates a more
'relational' notion of space. 'God's relationship with his world is one of
dynamic and creative interaction.'[22]

It is the incarnation of God in Christ that supremely points to God's
dynamic and intimate relationship with his world; this is the fullest expression of his immanence. We need to hold on to this self-revelation of
God, for otherwise we may be left with a deism that emphasises God's
transcendent power, purpose, and mind, but which, in so doing, places
him outside of the world and outside of our lives. Such a God is ineffec-
tual once he has set creation in progress. God is not remote to Christians;
prayer is part of an intimate relationship with God who has expressed his
love for humanity. Creation is seen by Christians as an act of free love.
But the question we must try to answer is how does God continues to act

in love. In the mutual witness of science and faith, how can we understand the immanent involvement of God with his creation?

(a) One answer might be that God acts in the chance events of quantum physics or of biological mutation. Chance offers a space where God can manipulate sub-atomic particles. Science has recognised unpredictability at a microscopic level, and also an unpredictability in some macrosystems, which can then be described as 'chaotic'. There are real gaps in our ability to predict certain events, but the danger of suggesting that this is where God works is to make God the 'God of the unpredictable gaps.' Increasing human ability to predict would gradually push God out of the picture. A picture that limits God's freedom to the area of micro-events does not fit with our own human freedom of choice that we believe to be God-given. Further, we are left with a God who sometimes acted in this way, but at other times did not. So in some people cancer cells might begin to reduce in number, leading to healing, while in many more they would multiply, leading to death.

(b) This problem of the apparently selective activity of God applies even more strongly to a second answer to the question of immanence; that is, we may understand God's involvement as interventions, or occasional 'forays' of God into creation in miracle. While some people may not take all the supposedly miraculous accounts in the Bible as literal, the resurrection of Jesus stands for most Christians as the supreme miracle, as our experience is that dead people stay dead. Polkinghorne is right when he says that, once we accept a personal God and resurrection, the question is not 'How can these things happen?' but 'Why don't they happen more often?' namely in the case of avoiding tragedies.[23] If God can intervene, why does he not intervene more often? Why does he not prevent the suffering of the innocent? Intervention is not a word that we can easily use to describe the God of steadfast love. Moreover, from a scientific viewpoint the laws of physics give a broadly predictable universe, which is reliable in the unfolding of events. If God 'intervenes', it means setting aside his own laws, and I have been arguing that these display his faithfulness in creation.

This is not the place for an extended discussion about miracles. I simply want to register here that they cannot be a way of expressing God's continuous creative activity. I suggest that they must be seen in the context of revelation; it is not so outrageous to propose that God may interrupt his own laws if this is in order to disclose some special insight into his wider purposes. The moral problem of 'selectivity' is reduced if the point of miracles, and especially those associated with the incarnation of God in Christ, is to reveal God's nature and purpose rather than to assist created beings to achieve something good or avoid something bad. So John presents miracles in his account of the gospel as being 'signs' of a deeper meaning, which may not immediately be understood.[24] Miracle will be ambiguous, as God's self-unveiling will always have an element of hiddenness to finite minds. Miracle is a sign that does not coerce consent.

(c) A third notion of immanence is that found in 'process theology': God is depicted as a creative participant, persuading and inspiring the community of beings towards new possibilities of a richer life together.[25] Such a picture can helpfully be developed through an understanding of the fatherhood of God. The universe is seen as God's unfinished work, with human beings given freedom to cooperate with God and persuaded to love, freedom and justice. Evil is then the product of such freedom misused, and suffering results from the struggle of conflicting goals; yet God seeks to redeem suffering by working with us. The world is seen as evolving, dynamic, in the process of becoming, always changing and developing. The ecological interdependence of the world of nature is recognised, and evolution is seen as a creative process, whose outcome is not predictable.

One objection often brought against this model of God's relationship to creation is that his transcendent power appears to be reduced. I do not find this a convincing objection, as there is a real power of persuasive love, a creative power, that is not irresistible but is inexhaustible. Such love is seen in the Cross of Christ; human beings may respond to or ignore this love, for God's grace cannot be irresistible when we understand this not as an impersonal force but in terms of personal relationship. There remains, however, the problem that the extent of God's power over nature is strictly limited, unless one can accept the process view that subatomic particles can 'enjoy' experience, make choices in some sense, and respond or fail to respond to God. This seems to require a view of the existence of mind at every level of nature. I take the view of most scientists that inanimate nature is largely 'mechanical', under the control of physical laws; it is only with human beings, and possibly with all other living organisms, that we can speak meaningfully of God's influencing and persuading the world.

Process thought has a great deal to offer to our understanding of both the Bible and the world of science. It does direct us to consider both the realm of sub-atomic physics and the love of God in the cross of Christ. We can learn much from it about the power of persuasive love as the mode of God's involvement in the world, yet there is one fundamental modification I would want to make to such a picture; that is, we need to introduce the basic idea of the self-limitation of God.

(d) The Bible speaks of God's self-limitation (e.g. Phil 2:7) rather than a limitation imposed upon him from outside. Barbour suggests that like the artist with his work of art, God has chosen a medium that imposes restraints.[26] The very nature of the evolving universe, with human beings able to exercise free will, is one that gives God limited control; it is one in which he is able to redeem but not prevent imperfections. God is seen as the parent who loves, persuades, and suffers with failure. Real love is always vulnerable and risks suffering, a point we will consider further below.

If we place humanity as the climax of creation, as both the Bible (Gen 2:4b ff.; 1:1-2:4a) and some modern scientists do, and if we recognise, as science and scripture do, that human beings have self-awareness and self-will, there are consequences for the doctrine of God. We must conclude that God is limited in his power over creation and is affected by creation. This does not mean that there is no dependent relationship between the creature and creator, as Being that 'lets be' must be transcendent and prior to creation, as Macquarrie rightly observes.[27] Human beings are seen in scripture as the stewards of creation and not lords, and creation is not a ready made world, but one to be attained as people work in cooperation with the creator. Yet herein lies the risk, that the potential may not be attained, because free-will leads to the possibility of selfish exploitation, with the resultant suffering.

Process theism has refused to root God's persuasive love in an initial act of self-limitation in creation, as this in itself would be a unilateral decision rather than an event of cooperation; it therefore regards God's limitations as just part of the process, required by the ultimate value of 'creativity'. Correspondingly, it cannot accept a unilateral and coercive divine act of creation *ex nihilo* as the beginning of a process of partnership; it argues that if God now works persuasively in the universe then God and universe must always have co-existed as elements in the whole process. I prefer, however, to follow Moltmann in making a distinction between the beginning of the universe as an original act of God alone (*creatio originalis*) and the working out of that creation in the evolutionary development of systems of life (*creatio continua*). When we look at evolution, Moltmann is correct in saying that, 'theologically we have to describe the forms through which God preserves, suffers, transforms and advances creation in its open-ended history.'[28] Creation is not finished, it has not reached its end; the biblical doctrine of creation does not present us with a static, closed cosmos, but one moving toward fulfilment and consummation. Humanity, observes Moltmann, for all its significance is not actually the centre of creation; the crown of creation is the 'feast of creation which praises the eternal and inexhaustible God' and in which human beings participate.[29] This is the picture that the Genesis 1 account presents, moving as it does toward the sabbath of worship (*creatio nova*).

The distinction between original and continuing creation is an important context, then, for a belief in an original act of self-limitation by God. Moreover it fits in well, argues Moltmann, with a cosmos in evolution. The scientific view of creation, as demonstrated in the Big Bang theories, has replaced the stable cosmos with an expanding universe, travelling along an irreversible, forward moving time arrow. Moltmann suggests that a cosmos in which systems of matter and life evolve is one in which possibilities are never diminished. As they are actualized, even more complex structures come into being, which, in their turn, open up new ranges of possibility. The possibilities are further increased as systems, which are developing separately, open communication with each other. The whole cosmos, and not just its individual systems, must then be viewed as an open system in totality, open to the future and transcending itself. The question naturally arises, then, as to what kind of transcendence it is open into. The Christian answers that it is open to God, who is 'the encompassing milieu, from which and in which it lives'. In an original transcendent act of creation, God therefore gives the whole system a contingency or openness, simultaneously with the creation of time. In his continuing creation God is immanent in the system in the power of his Spirit, always opening up new possibilities so that the cosmos moves towards its future consummation in the transcendent glory of God.

Thus we cannot think of God's world transcendence without his immanence; and we cannot think of God's evolutive immanence in the world without his world transcendence.[30] Evolution urges us to consider *creatio continua*, in which God is present to endure breaches of communication between systems, and to find new ways through his suffering to open up communication again when it has broken down. As Moltmann puts it, 'It is not through miraculous interventions that God guides creation to its goal and drives forward evolution; it is through passion, and the opening of new possibilities out of his suffering.'[31] The prophetic theology of God's creative acts in history (e.g. Isa 43:18-19) pushes us to understand this immanent activity as anticipating the *creatio nova* and the consummation of time. We can conclude that God is guiding an evolutionary process that includes not only law but chance and the emergence of novelty.

(e) There is a final aspect under which we should understand the immanence of God, and it is a Trinitarian one. John Macquarrie notes that Christian theology has used two models of creation: 'making' and 'emanation.'[32] While 'making' points to the transcendence of God, emanation —like that of the sun's rays from the Sun—suggests something of the immanence and closeness of the relationship between God and the world. Making refers to a transcendent letting-be, and emanation has God putting himself into creation. The Christian faith finds the balance between these two most fully expressed in the incarnation of God in Christ. As the 'expressive Being' of God, the eternal Son is the agent through whom creation is brought into being (John 1:3; Col 1:15f; Heb 1:2); he is generated or 'emanates' from the Father (as 'primordial Being'), and while creation itself is certainly not generated from God, the 'expressive Being' of God really enters into creation. Thus already in creation the transcendent God is intimately involved with his creation, and this is the basis for Creator and creature becoming truly one in the incarnation. The Spirit is then to be seen as 'unitive Being', uniting God with himself in his triune being, and lifting the whole creation toward God in reconciliation (Rom 8:19, 22-23). The risk of creation is overcome and the potentiality is fulfilled as creatures participate in the life of God.[33]

5. The Scope of Creativity

As we have tried to hold science and a scriptural faith together, we have had to hold the transcendence and immanence of God in tension. Genesis 1 works through this tension, painting a picture of a transcendent creator God who makes human beings in his own image; in immanent involvement he breathes his life into them and gives to them the control of the rest of creation. As the later of the two creation narratives, Genesis 1:1-2:4a was written after the Hebrew prophets had revealed God's nature and guidance in history, and the priestly writers now extended this experience back into the event of creation. The kind of God they had encountered was one who allowed human beings to share in his own creativity or letting-be of others (Gen 1:31). The risk-taking, creative love of God is reflected for example in the risky love of human parenthood. Macquarrie aptly concludes,

> Living beings which reproduce themselves participate in 'letting be' more than do inanimate things; but on a far higher level is man who, with his capacity—however limited—for creativity and love brings the 'imitation' of God onto an altogether new level, that of free cooperation in letting be.[34]

Another aspect of human creativity is the psychological factor of striving for fulfilment. Humanity does not find satisfaction with merely existing, but is driven on to quest for Being itself, often wrongly expressed in the form of some lost 'Golden Age.' This will mean that either human beings are doomed to frustration in the pursuit of an illusion or that there is indeed a destiny for which they were created. Science expresses this in terms of the fine-tuning of creation and the fact that we are observer participants of the universe, able to ask questions about beginnings, endings, and meanings. Roger Penrose in his study of the human mind, which we discussed in Chapter 3, states that human consciousness is an important element in the brain. This allows us to see and appreciate mathematical truth and in itself demonstrates that the brain is not a computer.[35] Macquarrie expresses this theologically by stating that God goes out into creation, where Being confers itself, gives itself, entrusts itself to the beings that have been called out of nothing to participation in and cooperation with Being itself.[36] God's self-giving is thus the basis of the sense of 'quest' that all beings have.

Such a self-limitation in creation on God's part longs for response, but risks rebellion. It is a creativity that is limitless in self-giving, and this again coheres with a scientific evolutionary view of the cosmos. The universe exhibits chance, unpredictability, and an evolution that—while leading to human beings—leaves a liberal scattering of corpses of extinct living things in its wake. What kind of God fits such a universe? It will not be the timeless impersonal God of Aristotle; nor the machine minding God of Newton; nor the secret intelligence of nature seen by Einstein; nor yet the designer of Davies. The God of this kind of universe accompanies creation through its evolution, a dynamic God, closer to the God revealed in scripture, rather than the mathematical formula of Hawking. This God is an artist rather than an engineer, who tolerates diversity and freedom that leaves us with a universe with ragged edges. The limitless love of God means constancy, but not predictability. Love is risky; it risks the outcome of the freedom that it allows.

In his book *Love's Endeavour, Love's Expense,* Vanstone considers the sef-emptying of God, stating that Christianity should have no hesitation in attributing to God that authenticity of love that it recognises in Jesus Christ.[37] The love of God is not only in redemption but is the totality of divine activity, which is the ground and source of all that is. God's activity in creation can then be correctly described as limitless creativity, there being no limit on God's self-giving. The immense size and nature of the universe is seen as an expression of this. Limitless self-giving love includes within it the potential for tragedy as well as for triumph, and our faith is in the creator who accompanies his creation and does not abandon the object of his love. Vanstone is surely right to conclude that 'the creation is safe not because it moves by programme towards a predetermined goal but because the same loving creativity is ever exercised upon it.'[38]

Limitless love is not incompatible with the existence of evil and suffering in the world, since this is the consequence of the freedom that is given by such loving creativity. Vanstone dares to take as a paradigm the tragedy at Aberfan in South Wales in 1967, when a coal tip slid down onto a school and caused the deaths of more than a hundred children. Here God's step of creative risk was a step of disaster. Science and technology enabled the coal to be mined; human greed seen in the demand for profit led to the siting of the spoil heaps where they were; and the result following freak weather conditions was the suffering of the innocent. But our faith, affirms Vanstone, is not in a creator who permits disaster from the top of the mountain, but rather in one who is at the foot of the mountain receiving the impact. His limitless love is evidenced in not abandoning people in their suffering but suffering with them.[39] It is this vulnerability that results from creation as an act of love, freely choosing to give freedom to created beings. Several thousand years earlier Isaiah of Babylon writing to the captive Israelites, reveals the God who shares the deep waters and fires of life with his people (Isaiah 43:1-5). This is the God of the Cross, revealed by Isaiah as the Suffering Servant.

6. Progress and Disorder in Nature

In the eighteenth and nineteenth centuries the current scientific thought saw a universe that was infinite and progressing to a better future. In response, theologians of the same period were able to speak of creation moving smoothly toward a future divine event that would be the consummation of all the higher developments in life. Modern cosmology, however, does not confirm this simple progressive view. It envisages an increasing entropy and so an increasing disorder, with a hostile end in a 'Big Crunch' or 'Heat Death'. How this relates to the nature of the universe as an 'open system' (as discussed above) is a complex matter I shall consider shortly. For the moment we should observe that the state of increasing entropy at least makes it possible for human beings, through their freedom of choice, to disturb the balance of nature with its finely tuned laws so that tragedy results. According to one dimension of evil we can see the self-centred free-will of people leading to immoral acts and the suffering of innocent and guilty alike.

The movement of the cosmos into turmoil and suffering, however, does not all stem from moral evil. A great deal of it results from natural events themselves. On the large scale there are floods, storms, volcanic eruptions, and earthquakes; and on the small scale there are the abnormal cells that produce cancer, the altered or missing chromasomes that cause handicap, and the intrusion of microbes that lead to disease and illness. Science is able, through its discovery of the ways in which the Earth's crust moves, how weather systems develop, and how oceans and rivers react to various weather conditions, to predict when and where most natural disasters will take place. We can further complicate our discussion of this issue with the recognition that scientific discovery has shown that the very processes within the Earth's crust that bring about earthquakes and volcanic activity are the ones that produce many of the minerals and rocks, which are the raw materials for industry and medicine. Furthermore the weather systems of the world that result in violent storms and flooding are the source of the varied global climates that enable the growth of the food that we need for life. While prediction means the possibility of protection, it is often the poor of the world who cannot move their homes who suffer as a result of most natural disasters.

This process of disorder raises a question against a God who is claimed to be immanent within the processes of nature, always opening up new possibilities and drawing creation onwards towards the goal of his purpose. Vanstone seeks to deal with the challenge by drawing attention to the new flora and fauna that become established, as the equilibrium of nature is restored after a natural disaster.[40] The balance of nature may be disturbed, but the creativity of nature is not destroyed. We might also say that disaster will bring out the best qualities in many human beings, as may be evidenced by the tireless activity of the rescue agencies after a flood or earthquake, or the selfless sarifice of many during a time of war or famine. Yet we cannot clutch this straw too firmly either, as the reverse is also true; some environments are completely destroyed, for example permanently submerged beneath the ocean, and some human beings are completely broken by suffering or take advantage of disasters for selfish gain.

To cope with the whole problem of evil and suffering, Paul Fiddes suggests that freedom must be allowed in the whole of the natural world from which human beings have evolved. One aspect of this freedom is chance among the world of sub-atomic particles, but freedom must be understood more profoundly than mere chance, namely as the freedom to respond to God's creative spirit or to reject his persuasion.[41] In a similar way to process thought, Fiddes argues that if human beings have emerged from the context of nature, there must be something at least analogous to human freedom at all levels of nature. Creative evolution requires some characteristic of resistance and response to God.[42] While this may be true when considering a guiding mechanism in the evolution of life, is it always necessarily the case in every instance of apparent disorder? For example, the natural 'evil' of an earthquake that causes destruction to animal and human life results from the pattern of stresses that make up the structure of a dynamic Earth. It is surely implausible to think of its arising from some lack of response to God at sub-atomic levels of nature.

I conclude that much suffering resulting from natural causes must remain a mystery, being part of a creation that groans as it awaits redemption (Rom 8). There can be no neat and rational answer to the problem of evil and suffering, but we can place the problem in the wider context of the dual process of progress and disorder in nature. John Hick has suggested that the risk God takes in creation can be understood as his creating human persons at a 'distance' from himself, to give room for genuine response rather than being overwhelmed by his glory.[43] Paul Fiddes takes up this idea, extending it to all levels of nature, and suggesting that God thereby freely exposes himself to whatever new things, alien to his purposes, might emerge from the choices of an unresponsive creation.[44] He further proposes that this risk can be pictured in the symbol of 'non-being'. The making of creatures 'from nothing' *(ex nihilo)* means that as finite beings they will always be limited by non-being, as a boundary to life that is typified by death. While this 'non-being' is neutral in itself, the freedom that God has granted to creation leads to an environment in which a lapsing toward hostile non-being is practically inevitable. That is, the human 'no' to God (sin) results in an aggressive and alienating power that wants to reduce personal life and relationships to nothingness.[45]

In creation 'from nothing', therefore, God exposes himself to a 'non-being' that begins as a natural boundary to life and becomes increasingly hostile and alien to him. It is possible to represent this diagramatically, as shown in Figure 7:1. Alongside this theological statement, and interacting with it, we can place the Big Bang of cosmology through which God creates our universe with its fine-tuning, and through whose evolution we see the development of self-conscious human beings. We have a whole series of arrows, all of which are pointing in the direction of the space-time arrow, but which represent the contrasting movements of progress and disorder. There is the arrow of evolution, giving an increasing complexity and variety of life forms within an 'open system'; but paired with this arrow of progress is that of disorder as entropy increases and the cosmos heads towards the Big Crunch or Heat Death. Parallel to these cosmic movements is the arrow of sin leading towards hostile non-being, paired with the arrow of redemption as God continuously participates in his creation to seek to draw it back to himself.

We should notice that the 'theological' and 'scientific' beginnings are not exactly simultaneous, as we cannot know whether God's initial act of creation is identical with the creation of this universe. So also the endpoints are not coterminous, as God's consummation of the universe is at his initiative and not a matter of scientific prediction. I have represented this on the diagram (7:1) by the broken centres of the vertical lines marking beginning and end.

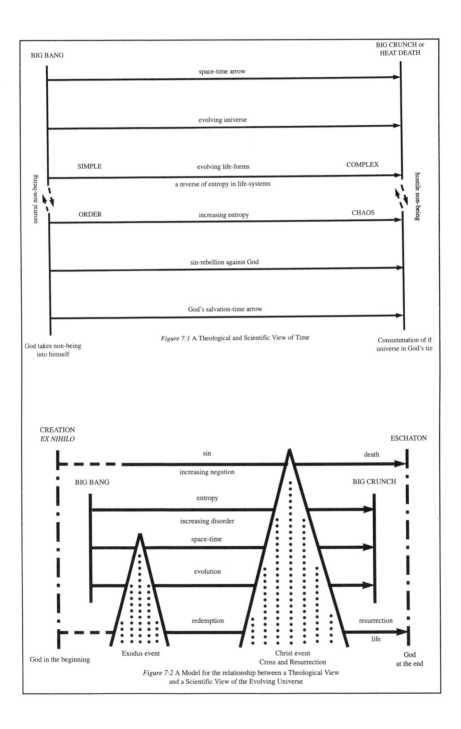

Figure 7:1 A Theological and Scientific View of Time

Figure 7:2 A Model for the relationship between a Theological View
and a Scientific View of the Evolving Universe

The fact that there is no exact identity between the beginnings and ends of the story of the universe, as calculated by science, and of the story that God gives to the universe is mapped in a different way in Figure 7:2. Here I have also tried to express the theological conviction that all the arrow-lines of both stories are transfigured by one defining moment, when God participates in his creation in the deepest possible way through his incarnation in Christ. As Jüngel says, "In the death of Jesus Christ God's 'Yes' which constitutes all being, exposed itself to the 'No' of the nothing . . . and in the Resurrection, this 'Yes' prevailed over the 'No'."[46] So there is the possibility of humans being taken out of the descent to hostile non-being and being caught up in the Being of God who is on his way to his goal of new creation. Through Cross and Resurrection the arrow of redemption ends in resurrection and renewal for the whole cosmos. Though the event of Christ is the supreme moment of God's involvement in the world, it is foreshadowed and followed by other moments when the God who is continuously at work in the world acts and saves in a particular, defining way. Prominent among these in the Judaeo-Christian tradition is the Exodus of the Israelites from Egypt, and so I have marked this on the diagram; however, a whole series of lesser peaks should also be envisaged linking the beginning and the end.

These two diagrams (7:1 and 7:2) put in picture form the mutual witness of science and faith that I have been exploring in this chapter. They also express the complex relation between evolutionary progress and entropic increase of disorder in a scientific cosmology, which parallels the complex relation between fallenness and redemption in a Christian view of the world. As I have already indicated, it is not possible in a scientific perspective to make the neat distinction that Moltmann does[47] between entropy at a level of individual systems and openness at the level of the whole system of the universe. Nor are the arrow-lines of movement according to science and theology simply analogous; there is a real interaction between them that we have only begun to explore in this study.

Another feature of complexity here belongs to God's goal in creation and redemption. On the one hand, according to the New Testament God is sure to bring about a perfected creation, which celebrates his glory and brings forth joy and thanksgiving and praise from every living thing. This is seen as the ultimate deliverance of creation from frustration and suffering into the freedom and bliss of God (Rev 21). It is the final working out of the goal of creation set out in Genesis 2:1-3 and can be seen as the fulfilment of the Anthropic Principle suggested by modern cosmology. But at the same time, the arrow-line of human development allows for real freedom in making choices and selecting possibilities; so we must ask whether the end is fixed or a risk.

Here I think that Fiddes is right to draw our attention to the nature of God's project in making persons. He suggests that when we are dealing with persons, we cannot separate the road from the destination.[48] He proposes then that the risk upon which God has embarked is real and serious, though not a total one. God has a certain hope in the fact of the end, which shifts creation onto an altogether new level of existence; but there is a genuine openness about the route and therefore the content of the end, which is the nature of the persons who are being reconciled. So there is room for tragedy as well as for triumph in God's victory over suffering. In the final vision of God the worshippers will not be disappointed, but God knows that they may not have reached their full potential.

At the heart of this view of the world is the immanent suffering of God, feeling pain in his relationship with his creation, which is in the mixed condition of progress and decline. Fiddes suggests that this suffering inflicts change upon God,[49] but here I beg to differ from him. That God suffers is undeniable, and that God is fulfilled (in some way) through creation must also be true, but this does not imply that God is changed in his inner being by creation. Fiddes argues that the nature of love means that all participants in a relationship are changed in their experience by the contribution of the others and that such a movement in experience must touch their very being. But I would point here to another analogy that Fiddes himself employs, that between God and a creative artist, who sets out with the desire to paint a picture.[50] The artist has the possibility of the finished work in his mind, but the actual painting has new elements within it, which come about as he plays with the materials at his disposal—the variety of brushes, textures, and paints. So God uses the materials of free personalities, from whom he looks for a response in achieving his purposes. Fiddes himself uses this analogy to stress that God can have no detailed plan for the future, but a purpose to which his creatures themselves contribute. With this I agree, but surely the analogy also shows that while the picture may change, the divine Artist himself remains essentially unchanged, with the exception of the pain that comes with disappointment in those who fail to respond to his love.

7. General and Special Revelation

The created order, I have been arguing, is a part of God's self-disclosure. In so far as it brings us a new understanding of ourselves and of the wider existence within which we have our being, it may be considered to be a means of general revelation. Science studies the ordered rationality of the created universe, and its findings can be used by Christians to support the view that the universe originated in the transcendent, rational mind of God. Science investigates the contingent ordering of the world, and Christians see this contingency or openness as derived from God and dependent on him. It is our human minds that allow us to study and interpret the universe, and Christians and theistic scientists suggest that this marks human beings out as unique and indicates the possibility of a Mind behind creation. All this is a part of God's revelation, but can only be understood in this way by the eye of faith.

Thus general revelation is bound up with special revelation and cannot be separated from it. In the first place, the moment of creation itself does not come within the field of science; cosmology investigates the history of the universe from its beginning, but not its final origin. It is through moments of particular revelation, witnessed to in the account of Genesis 1, that we are brought into contact with the wonder and mystery of the act of God, who creates out of nothing as a choice of his free will. Faith moves beyond the field of empirical knowledge and understands creation as God's creation. Such faith provided an anchor for the Israelite captives in Babylon, in whose community the Genesis 1 account of creation probably took shape.

Special revelation is not a short cut to answer our problems of understanding. We can conclude from previous chapters that the revelation of God's purpose and its outworking in creation has gradually unfolded through the centuries of scientific research. Yet at the same time we must affirm that faith is primarily an existential attitude, and the convictions of faith cannot be tested and formulated in an empirical fashion.

There are further moments of special definition within the experience of God's people, which were and are looked back upon as exceptional. It is a reasonable historical claim that some events happened at the time of Israel's leaving slavery in Egypt that were understood as exceptional by those who participated in them. Faith can perceive God's special revelation of himself occurring in the normal events of the physical world; for example, there was the strong wind blowing back the waters of the Sea of Reeds (Exod 14), and the resulting destruction as the tide swept back in, creating the kind of tragedy that frequently occurs on coastal mud-flats such as Morecombe Bay, though on a massive scale. The miracle is seen with the eye of faith; it is belief and faith in God who acts for deliverance. It is possible that here we have an instance of divine intervention, in the sense I have defined it above,[51] bringing about a combination of tides and winds at just the right time in a way that may have broken through the regularity of natural laws; but the point of the event is revelation—through it the people discover who God is, and they also discover who they are in his creation. God is the God who saves; and they are the people whom he saves. For Christians, our supreme moment of definition and revelation is found on a cross on a hillside outside Jerusalem and an empty tomb a couple of days later. Here we discover the God who saves and that we are people whom he saves.

But these events are not proof; they must be apprehended by faith. This salvation is a process, and as such includes our vulnerability as well as God's risk. In Exodus 14:8 we find the vulnerability of the 'cloud', where God places himself between the Israelites and the Egyptians, which is followed by the power of the parting of the sea. In the Passion narratives we see the vulnerability of the Cross, where God places himself between us and hostile non-being, which is followed by the power of the resurrection.

God reveals his transcendence and his immanence in his creation. The Bible presents this clearly in both God's utterances through his prophets and his actions on behalf of his people and his creation. We have seen that science has gradually made discoveries that can be seen as supporting the same conclusion; they suggest a God who is both transcendent in bringing the universe into existence and immanent in his involvement with the evolution of that creation. Cosmology is helping us to understand the magnitude, majesty, and careful purpose that is to be found in the universe and so helps us to understand more about the power and care of God. Geology and biology are helping us to see the evolutionary path that has culminated in the presence of conscious human beings, and they help us to recognise the God who has journeyed with his creation. In the 'disasters' of exploding stars, earthquakes, volcanoes, storms, and mutated plants and animals we have seen something of the suffering that is involved. We have recognised that the suffering of the world is a demonstration of God's self-giving love that takes risks in giving freedom to creation.

Our discoveries in the field of science have driven us back to the scriptures and forced us to study these more seriously, seeking to understand what God is seeking to reveal to us there. Science is a corrective to a literal interpretation of scripture, and like the Priestly writer of Genesis 1, we too seek to understand the nature of our God from our experiences in the world and through faith. We recognise that we are created in the image of God; we have been called into a relationship with the creator, with a task to be undertaken and a destiny within his purpose. I warm to the way in which David Atkinson describes this: 'While it is proper to speak of Jesus Christ as the true Human Being, we should speak of ourselves as Human Becomings.'[52]

We may say, though daringly, that our task is to represent God on earth. Moltmann describes our role in this way:

> As God's image and appearance on earth, human beings are involved in three fundamental relationships: they rule over other earthly creatures as God's representatives and in his name; they are God's counterpart on earth, the counterpart to whom he wants to talk; and they are the appearance of God's slendour, and his glory on earth.[53]

Part of this representation is also witness to the God of creation and reconciliation. We live in a world where there is anxiety over human finitude and death, where there is a recognition of choices, possibility and responsibility, and where for many there is a quest for meaning. There is a growing interest in the history and future of the universe by scientists, and through their books by the wider public. All this means that there are new opportunities for witness, in the form of 'apologetics' or reasonable argument, to the Good News of God's reconciling acts. It is to a consideration of this opportunity that we must finally turn.

Notes to Chapter 7

[1]Acts 17:28 (New International Version).
[2]A. Tilby, *Science and the Soul*, 3.
[3]J. D. Barrow, *Theories of Everything*, 210.
[4]J. Polkinghorne, *Science and Creation*, 69.
[5]J. Macquarrie, *In Search of Deity* (London: SCM, 1984) 23.

[6]Polkinghorne, *Science and Creation*, 97.

[7]J. Barr, *Biblical Faith and Natural Theology*. The Gifford Lectures 1991 (Oxford: Oxford University Press, 1993) 81-101.

[8]Ibid., 3f.

[9]J. Moltmann, *God in Creation. An Ecological Doctrine of Creation*. The Gifford Lectures 1984-1985. Transl. M. Kohl (London: SCM, 1985) 57f.

[10]Ibid., 53.

[11]W. Pannenberg, 'Theological Questions to Scientists' in A. R. Peacocke, ed., *The Sciences and Theology in the Twentieth Century* (London: Oriel Press, 1981) 4.

[12]Ibid., 3-6.

[13]Ibid., 9.

[14]Barr, 199.

[15]Barr, 151.

[16]See J. Barton, *Amos' Oracles against the Nations* (Cambridge University Press, Cambridge, 1980).

[17]Barr, 183, 187.

[18]Barr, 190-92.

[19]J. Habgood, 'Is there Reliable Knowledge about God?' in N. Spurway, ed., *Humanity, Environment and God*, 214-25.

[20]Barr, 173.

[21]D. Atkinson, *The Message of Genesis 1-11*, 27.

[22]Ibid.

[23]J. Polkinghorn, *One World—the interaction of Science and Theology*, 74ff.

[24]John 2:1-11, 23; 4:43-54; 5:1-15; 6:1-15, 30; 9:1-41; 11:1-44, 47; 20:1-30.

[25]See J. B. Cobb & D. R. Griffin, *Process Theology: An Introductory Exposition* (Belfast: Christian Journals, 1976), chapter 3. Classic works in process thought are: A. N. Whitehead, *Process and Reality: An Essay in Cosmology* (Macmillan, New York, 1929) esp. Part V; Charles Hartshorne, *The Divine Relativity. A Social Conception of God* (New Haven and London: Yale University Press, 1948).

[26]I. G. Barbour, *Religion in an Age of Science*, 251.

[27]J. Macquarrie, *Principles of Christian Theology*, 211-17.

[28]Moltmann, 196.

[29]Ibid., 197.

[30]Ibid., 206.

[31]Ibid., 211.

[32]Ibid., 217-22.

[33]Ibid.

[34]Ibid., 225.

[35]R. Penrose, *The Emperor's New Mind*, 233.

[36]Macquarrie, *Principles of Christian Theology*, 233.

[37]W. H. Vanstone, *Love's Endeavour, Love's Expense* (London: Darton, Longman, & Todd, 1977) 59.

[38]Ibid., 63.

[39]Ibid., 65.

[40]Ibid., 83.

[41]P. S. Fiddes, *The Creative Suffering of God*, 227.

[42]Ibid., 228.

[43]John Hick, *Evil and the God of Love* (Glasgow: Collins, 1979) 317.

[44]Fiddes, 45.

[45]Fiddes, 210ff.

[46]Quoted in Fiddes, 263.

[47]Moltmann, 204; cf. my discussion of entropy in chapter 3.

[48]Fiddes, 105f.

[49]Fiddes, 63.

[50]Fiddes, 94ff.

[51]See above, ???.

[52]Atkinson, 39.

[53]Moltmann, 221.

8

'Have you not heard? The Lord is the everlasting God, the creator of the ends of the earth'[1]

Apologetics and Preaching

As the discoveries of science have gradually revealed a universe of incomprehensible proportions, and of an equally incomprehensible age, the importance of planet Earth and of the short history of humankind has become minimal in many people's minds. The human population of this planet has seemed increasingly to dwindle into total insignificance, from the discovery of Copernicus in the middle of the sixteenth century that the Sun and not the Earth was the centre of the solar system, to modern cosmology's revelation of a universe that is 10-20 billion years old, 10-15 billion light years across, and composed of over a billion galaxies the size of the Milky Way, each containing some 100 billion stars the size of our Sun. The often drawn conclusion that the Earth must be extremely insignificant is portrayed vividly in a scene in Douglas Adams' *Hitch-Hiker's Guide to the Galaxy*. Arthur Dent enquires from his extra-terrestrial companion, Ford Prefect, what entry for the Earth has been made in the galactic guidebook, especially after Ford's own fact finding mission to the planet. First, Arthur cannot find the entry at all; then . . .

> Arthur followed Ford's finger, and saw where it was pointing. For a moment it still didn't register, then his mind nearly blew up.
>
> 'What? Harmless? Is that all it's got to say? Harmless! One word!'
>
> Ford shrugged.
>
> 'Well, there are a hundred billion stars in the Galaxy, and only a limited amount of space in the book's microprocessors,' he said, 'and no one knew much about the Earth of course.'
>
> 'Well for God's sake I hope you managed to rectify that a bit.'
>
> 'Oh yes, well I managed to transmit a new entry off to the editor. He had to trim it a bit, but it's still an improvement.'
>
> 'And what does it say now?' asked Arthur.
>
> 'Mostly harmless,' admitted Ford with a slightly embarrassed cough.[2]

The growing chorus of voices from the fields of cosmology and physics have pointed us away from the view of the Earth as a very minor entry in a cosmic list. The more recent proposals of a 'Big Bang' beginning to the universe, the Anthropic Principle that appears to be woven into its fabric, and the non-algorithmic nature of the the human mind that suggests the special nature of *Homo sapiens* have all sought to give planet Earth a central place in the apparently purposeful evolution of the universe. This must lead inevitably to a paradigm shift in the scientific and secular world-views held by many people outside the Church. It will, in turn, open up the possibility of a new apologetic: a new opportunity for the gospel to encounter the world outside the Church.

1. Finding Purpose in the Universe

A universe without hope would be a desperate place in which to exist. Steven Weinberg, who is Professor of Theoretical Physics at the University of Austin, Texas, and a Nobel Prize winner with Abdus Salam on the symmetry of forces in the early universe, declared in his book, *The First Three Minutes*, that the more the universe seems comprehensible, the more it also seems pointless.[3] Weinberg believes that doing science gives human beings some sense of grace in the midst of the tragedy of being trapped in a hostile world. From his perspective it would appear that doing science gives point to living, but the discoveries thus made present existence as pointless. Such a state of affairs would seem to be a recipe for utter despair.

We have discovered that other cosmologists present a more hopeful picture, finding that the dimensions, nature, and age of the universe demonstrate an inbuilt purpose. The fundamental constants of nature appear to be carefully set. John Barrow and Frank Tipler make this point in *The Anthropic Cosmological Principle*,[4] and John Barrow draws out the conclusions of the Anthropic Principle in *Theories of Everything*.[5] In his earlier book *Superforce*,[6] Paul Davies records the amazing delicate balance between gravity and the electromagnetic forces within stars. He goes further to suggest that changes of as little as $1:10^{40}$ would spell catastrophic destruction for a star like our own Sun. In his later work, *The Mind of God*, he emphasises the design that appears to him to be a fundamental aspect of the universe. He says that when it comes to the laws and the initial conditions of the universe we need a fine-tuned high precision that leaves design as a compelling suggestion.[7] He believes that we have uncovered a fine-tuned universe that is uniquely suitable for life forms such as ourselves.

This more hopeful picture is also developed when it comes to the place of human beings. While Richard Dawkins in *The Blind Watchmaker* is at pains to point to the natural processes at work in evolution that require no help from God, he does at least recognise that a mechanism is needed to produce *Homo sapiens* at the end of the evolutionary tree of life. This process, in his view, is non-random survival through natural selection. Roger Penrose (in *The Emperor's New Mind*) moves from the universe to the human mind and points to the unique features of our minds, which are not computable; like Paul Davies, he also recognises that there were very special initial conditions in the creation of the universe to enable conscious self-aware human beings to evolve. But for all this talk of design and purpose, these scientists would all agree that to speak of design is a scientific conclusion, while to speak of a Designer would be a matter of belief.

It is not surprising, then, to find that scientists who are Christians will take the talk of design and purpose a lot further. For John Houghton,[8] Roy Peacock,[9] Arthur Peacocke,[10] John Polkinghorne,[11] and David Wilkinson,[12] their own research together with the recent discoveries of physicists and cosmologists leads them to see support for a purposeful Creator in the pattern of the universe. R. J. (Sam) Berry, who is Professor of Genetics at University College, London, and a Christian, has drawn attention to the unique nature of *Homo sapiens* within the evolutionary history of life,[13] and E. K. Victor Pearce, who is an anthropologist and a Christian priest, has drawn attention to both the unique biological nature of *Homo sapiens* and to the archaeological support for the arrival of civilized human beings in the Fertile Crescent around 8,000–10,000 B.C.[14]

Christian believers would agree with Roy Peacock[15] that it is difficult to imagine such a delicately balanced universe that was not the act of God who intended to create beings like us. The question 'How?' of science directs our rational minds to ask 'Why?', a question that belongs to philosophy and theology. Yet we must take care as we begin to answer this question. Stephen Hawking suggests that all scientific theories about the universe are only mathematical models existing in the human mind, and as he seeks an answer to the origin of the universe, his 'god' is a super-law of mathematics, the finding of which would be the greatest human achievement.[16] So we have to ask what sort of God is being implied by our scientific discoveries. We are in danger of positing a rational God who has designed a universe with precision and laws, but who cannot bring about changes in the design of his creation. The creation of such a God would be perfect and rational, with no possibility of choice within it. This is not the God revealed in Scripture. It is difficult to arrive at a picture of the eternal, loving, and self-giving God from the ever-changing theories of science. However rational in our perception these theories may be, they do not offer a proof for the existence of God, nor do they point to the God and Father of our Lord Jesus Christ.

There are two fundamental problems with the argument for God's existence from the apparent design of the universe. Firstly, it is possible to accept the design as a brute fact, with the rider that this universe that we are able to observe is just one of many, and just happens to be the one that by chance has the characteristics needed for our evolution. Secondly, a God who is the originator or designer of the universe need in no way have the character of the Christian God of love. Although the modern arguments for design are far stronger than those of Anselm and Aquinas, they still have the same inherent problems. John Hick[17] is right to draw a number of conclusions. First, the argument from design does not establish divine existence, but poses the question to which one answer can be God. Second, one cannot suggest that the existence of an eternal creative Mind is self-explanatory, while a universe that exhibits the fundamental laws it does exhibit, is not. Lastly, while we all perceive the physical world around us, our beliefs about that world will depend on the information and experience available to us. For a Christian, belief in a purposeful creator is seen to be completely reasonable in the light of scientific research, but for a non-Christian there may be other explanations for the nature of the universe. We will have to bear this in mind as we consider the ways in which we present the God revealed in creation to those outside the Church of Christ.

2. A Paradigm Shift in World-view

One thing is certain: the developing views of the new cosmology imply a new scientific world-view, and in turn this will imply a new secular world-view. No longer do we have the view of an infinite cosmos that is in a continual state of progress. Instead we are presented with a cosmos that has a beginning, whose level of entropy (disorder) is steadily increasing, and whose story will either end in rapid contraction ('the Big Crunch' as a mirror image of the 'Big Bang') or in the elimination of all energy (the so called 'Heat Death').

The Enlightenment of the eighteenth century had its roots in Aristotelian philosophy and presented a scientific explanation of the way things are. Newton began from observation, rather than revelation and formulated laws. Objective reality replaced belief, and nature replaced God, whose position became that of the deist's Prime Mover. With the recognition that every human being possessed reason and conscience, people were seen as autonomous, able to discern truth from error, subject only to the laws of nature. Science was seen as understanding and controlling events, and people had equality and rights, especially the right to happiness. During the last 300 years of what might well be termed the Age of Reason, that which could be scientifically 'proved' was said to be truth and all else was seen to be a matter of personal opinion.

In recent years, however, science, technology, and industrial advances have had an increasingly bad press, and materialism has for many people been found to be an empty dream. The result has been a turning to a galaxy of religions and ideas, many of which come under the umbrella term, 'New Age'. There is a desire for a source of knowledge and power that lies outside of science and a 'spirituality' that lies outside of traditional Christianity. The evidence for this is seen in the numerous shops selling crystals, runes, tarot cards, herbal potions and perfumes for aromatherapy, together with a wide variety of occult material. It is also not accidental that large amounts of space are given to astrology in newspapers and magazines.

We may also be seeing a parallel situation in schools in Great Britain, with the increasing unpopularity of science and technology and the attraction of the majority of students to the arts. Could it be that science is perceived as coldly analytical and dead, separated from emotion, values, and ideals? There is surely, in such a climate of opinion, a great opportunity for the gospel of Christ, which speaks of value and purpose that encompasses the whole of life—science and arts, the material and the spiritual. The secular world-view is cracking at the seams, but a new world-view has not yet emerged, so that we find ourselves in a period of flux. Before looking at the nature of the paradigm shift in world-view that modern cosmology is presenting, it will be helpful to consider the characteristics of the secular world-view that has held centre stage for the last few hundred years.

Secularism originated in the seventeenth century with Newtonian physics in the field of science and Cartesian dualism (a separation between object and observer, matter and mind) in the field of philosophy. John Locke took this a stage further, with the view that knowledge is only obtained through our physical senses. A world-view developed in which materialism, hedonism, Marxism, and secular humanism were all logical options. The view of the cosmos here is strictly materialistic. The universe is a closed, orderly and predictable system, which is not open to influence from outside. No miracles are possible, and God is excluded or relegated to the deist position of first cause. Human beings are complex machines, which respond to environmental stimulae and are influenced by their culture. Their chemical makeup is disrupted by illness, and all the chemical and physical processes come to an end at death. Knowledge is seen to be obtained by rational processes, and whatever cannot be determined by the physical senses is not real. Human beings are in control of this rational world, and progress is not only possible, but is the goal. Time is seen as linear, each second is unique, and so there is the optimistic view of always 'new' and 'better.' With the emphasis on individual human reason, there is a tendency towards individualism rather than family or society. Values, as a result, become a matter of expediency, what is best for people in a particular situation. Ethics become essentially 'situation ethics', which have a tendency to be relative.

This world-view, with its base in empiricism, has seen the flowering of science; but, ironically, it is from the rational discoveries of science that this world-view is now being challenged. In contrast to secularism, science is looking for ultimate answers, though preferably without recourse to the transcendent. This is underlined by Stephen Hawkin's desire to know the 'mind of God'[18] and Paul Davies' intention to trace the logic of scientific rationality back as far as it will go in the search for ultimate answers to the mystery of existence.[19] He says that 'maybe mystical experiences provide the only route beyond the limits to which science and philosophy can take us, the only possible path to the Ultimate.' He sums up the modern view of the cosmos with its Anthropic Principle in words that I quoted earlier:

What is man that we might be party to such a privilege? I cannot believe that our existence in this universe is a mere quirk of fate, an accident of history, an incidental blip in the great cosmic drama. Our involvement is too intimate. . . . We are truly meant to be here.[20]

A universe with a beginning and an end, and design and purpose recognised in the Anthropic Principle, must entail a change in world-view. Add to this the unpredictability within physical processes and the guiding mechanism that is required in the evolution of life, and we recognise a universe that is contingent and not necessary. We have a paradigm shift in our view of the world. The universe is not infinite, nor closed, nor entirely predictable. It has purpose, it is open to change, and so there is a place for faith to find God's immanence as well as his transcendence. Human beings cannot be viewed as machines, as science has recognised the non-algorithmic nature of the mind and of personhood; there are perceptions that are not computable; and the universe seems to have evolved with humankind having a central place. We must therefore question how we obtain information and knowledge, and we cannot see our own individualistic rights and needs as an end in themselves, because we appear to be a part of a cosmic plan. In short, in the modern scientific view of the world there is a place for the mystical, for a God who accompanies creation.

3. Towards Serious Theology—The World-view in the Bible

Despite its variety of writings, the Bible offers a coherent world-view in which God is not only allowed a place, but which is explicitly orientated around him, and we need to understand how this world-view came about. We have already recognised that the writers of the biblical accounts of creation were influenced both by their understanding of the world that they experienced and also by their religious experiences that included the revelation of God. These revelations were within their own particular culture and understanding of the world. Thus their perception of the world is both objective and subjective. The cultural influences on various world-views is well dealt with by David Burnett in his book *Clash of Worlds*,[21] and the reader is directed to consider the points that he has made, when considering the understanding of biblical passages within western society. There is the fact to be reckoned with that the Old Testament arose within a nomadic, agrarian culture, while the New Testament is influenced by both Greek and Roman culture in addition to its Jewish milieu.

From a biblical perspective, God is identified with power, holiness and love. The Creator is distinguished from his creation. He is transcendent, beyond human intellect, and yet is not outside of his creation. The personhood of God is understood as love, which is further explored in the form of triune relationships within God by the early Church as it reflected on the biblical witness; in the biblical account, it is in this love that God is involved in creation and communicates with it. Creation is seen as good, but evil emerges within creation as a result of the freedom with which God, in self-limiting love, endowed the world. This is expressed in the account of the Fall in Genesis 2-3. Time is seen to be part of God's creation and progresses toward fulfilment, which is God's purpose and is our hope. God is seen to be involved in time, and, in the Incarnation, to enter time. From a human perspective, time is our opportunity to respond to God's love.

Human beings are affirmed as being in the image of God (Gen 1:27) and, as such, are able to think, reason, discover, and exercise control over their surroundings; nevertheless, full understanding lies beyond this world (1 Cor 13:12). Human life is God-breathed life (Gen 2:7); while humanity has a solidarity with the rest of creation, it is seen to be distinct from it and in the image of God to have an exceptional freedom to make choices and to love. Choices include ethical decision-makings, which is guided by the moral standard of the Creator's revealed character. While God, in love, gives the freedom of choice to all human beings, all such choices are subject to his judgement and open to his forgiveness. It is the self-limiting love of God, in giving freedom to his creation, that is the source of God's suffering with his creation. I suggest that it is the character of this immanent relationship of the Creator with his creation that distinguishes the biblical world-view from all other world-views.

When seeking to address the people outside the Church as well as inside it, we will need to treat the biblical accounts seriously, as we have sought to do in dealing with Genesis 1 in chapter 5. The Bible should be critically evaluated and the cultural influences understood, but at the same time we recognise that we are dealing with literature of a particular kind. We are dealing with written witness to God's self-revelation within the experiences of people over a period of at least 1,500 years, and then a process of interpretation by the Christian Church in the light of a further 2,000 years experience; all of this, Christians find, has been under the guidance and inspiration of the Holy Spirit.

In its view of the Bible, the Church has reacted in a variety of ways to the Enlightenment's emphasis on reason and verifiable facts, as Leslie Newbigin has noted.[22] Some have sought to defend the Bible's factual accuracy, which is a concept that is foreign to the Bible itself. Others have sought to hold on to a 'religious' meaning of Scripture, while recognising the writers in all other respects as people of their time; there is a danger here, however, of creating an unbridgeable gap between those writers' experience and our own. Another route has been to suggest that the Bible presents us with basic concepts and principles that can then be applied in more detail to modern life, but this leads us to ask how we find these authoritative principles without using tools of interpretation. Another way is to see the Bible as a record of experiences, not so much presenting historical facts, but the 'salvation history' that lies behind the recorded events. While it is important to recognise the dimensions that cannot be tested by historical enquiry, it runs the danger of leaving the experience without any objective reality. Such a view becomes more clearly focused in an existentialist position, where faith belongs to the private world and has little chance of interaction with scientific fact or with history. It leaves open the conclusion that faith is a psychological condition with no cognitive element. Newbigin is right to conclude[23] that if the Bible is to influence us, it must address us in our own language as part of the real world that we inhabit.

While there is a continuity between the life experiences of the people we read about in the Bible and ourselves, there is also a discontinuity. The Bible records the struggle of people to understand the world they lived in and the events they experienced in the light of faith in the God who had revealed himself to them. We cannot divide history or scientific research into secular and sacred, but it is possible to understand either atheistically or theistically, as we have already seen in the conclusions of different scientists. So all Christian readers come to study the Bible with the spectacles provided by the tradition that is alive within their believing community, and that tradition is being constantly modified as each new generation of believers endeavors to be faithful in understanding and living out Scripture. 'This,' says Newbigin[24] 'is the hermeneutical circle operating within the believing community.' The Bible is itself the result of such a process, as we discovered in considering Genesis 1, and biblical texts are understood in the dialogue of living out the Christian faith in the community of the church.

So in our consideration of the creation narratives of Genesis, and other passages within Scripture that reflect on the nature of the physical world, we need to recognise a number of important points. Firstly, these passages in Scripture represent the reflections of a community of faith. The Priestly writer of Genesis 1 reflects upon the nature of the universe that he experiences, and the beliefs of the other religions around him, in the light of his own experience of God's self-revelation and that of the whole religious community of which he is a part. Secondly, these reflections must be consistent with the reality of both those physical and spiritual experiences. Thirdly, when we seek to interpret these passages we must do so recognising the way in which they originated, and in the light of our own experience both of the world and of the faith of the believing community of which we are a part.

4. What Sort of God?—Towards Taking Science Seriously

We discovered in our study of Genesis 1 that this account of creation presents or prompts important doctrinal statements concerning God's relationship with his creation. We saw that the ordering of creation depicted is at least consistent with cosmological and geological histories of the universe. But there are no proofs to be found here, for while modern cosmology presents a picture of purpose and fulfilment, faith takes us beyond this to see God's promise and fulfilment. Science may point us towards the God question, but it is faith that leads us to a personal God, revealed in Jesus Christ. Jesus Christ is not only the agent of creation, he is also the agent of salvation, fulfilling God's personal promise to heal relationships. The Incarnation speaks of God's deepest possible involvement with creation; the Resurrection is the hope of a destiny for all creation; the Ascension is the possibility of being caught up in eternity with God; and Pentecost marks out God's continuing involvement with his world now, with the possibility of new creation. Such an understanding comes by way of God's self-revelation, to which the discoveries of science can only be pointers. In turn, however, a scientific understanding of the world can certainly enable us to develop our reflections on these truths once they are glimpsed.

Science presents us with a rational approach to the universe. Human reason comprehends the universe and understands it to be rational. But then, this raises the question of the origin of such rationality. Do the laws of nature reflect the nature of God himself, or are they in themselves the universal, absolute 'givens' of the universe? But if we want to affirm the latter alternative, we have to observe that the initial conditions for the origin of the universe lie outside these laws, which only came into existence with the universe. Thus it is only a law for the initial conditions themselves that would explain how the universe came to exist in its present state. It is just such a law that scientists, such as Stephen Hawking, are looking for when they speak of a 'Grand Unified Theory' (G.U.T.) or a 'Theory of Everything' (T.o.E.). There is, however, a great deal of difference between a G.U.T or T.o.E. and the God who is revealed in Scripture as being involved in creation through his own freewill. Only a God who opens himself up to contingency can be truly immanent in his creation. The ultimate difference between a G.U.T. and God is that a G.U.T. is purely necessary and not contingent at all. If this is what we mean by 'God', it is a purely cause and effect, deterministic model of deity. But reflection upon the nature of the universe, with sub-atomic unpredictiblility and 'guided' evolution, and with characteristics such as beauty and hope, prompts us to think of a personal God, involved in the universe, who has taken contingency into himself. Such a God is intimately involved with creation and is affected by the freedom that he has given to his creation. In the end, such a God must be a suffering God.

Modern cosmology has not only raised the suggestion of design, but also of purpose. Paul Davies finds the Anthropic Principle to suggest that human life is 'truly meant' to exist on planet Earth, that the whole universe appears to have evolved with conscious human life in mind. Roger Penrose states that he cannot believe that the non-algorithmic nature of human consciousness is an accident conjured up by a complicated computation. It is the phenomenon by which the universe's very existence is made known.[25] Such conclusions force people to face the question of whether a universe that has seen the evolution of conscious human life requires the presence of a purposeful mind as its origin. In our investigations of the organic world we have seen that the growing complexity and organisation of living things is contrary to the second law of thermodynamics (see Chapter 3) and is a further indication of a finely tuned universe, as it would require the universe to have begun in a special state of low entropy. Increased complexity, especially in the form of conscious human life, suggests purpose, and purpose is suggestive of God.

When cosmologists speak of design they are not necessarily implying the presence of a designer; they can simply be describing principles and laws that are inherent in the universe. To speak of purpose takes us a step closer to a Creator, though this does not imply a personal giver of purpose. In fact much philosophical argument over the last 200 years would maintain that purpose is merely a way of describing what we observe, and scientists such as Richard Dawkins would see the 'blind forces' of natural selection accounting for the presence of human life. The step of faith lies in moving from design and purpose to belief in a Creator, whose mind and purpose are written into the evolution of human life. It is this step of faith, for the believing community, that is reflected in the doctrinal account of creation recorded in Genesis 1. While we have no proof for such belief, recent research in the physical and biological sciences would make such a step of faith at least more resonable.

We have left the deterministic, infinite universe of Newtonian physics behind, and as Christians we will need to come out from the bunker of private religious belief and engage in a dialogue with science. The new physics is raising metaphysical questions, which are the result of cosmological questions. The Church must not only address these questions, but also present the findings of modern scientific research to a wider audience, because many people's view of the world is still that of a Newtonian determinism. We have seen that science is discerning significant patterns in the universe, the big picture that reveals design and purpose. Newbigin is right to observe[26] that a machine is only fully understood when the purpose for which it was designed is known. We are right to present the broader, holistic view suggested by modern cosmology and significantly, from an apologetic point of view, recorded far earlier in Scripture, that the universe demonstrates design and purpose, which reflects the mind of God. A world that displays both autonomy and contingency discloses the character of God, and the experience of people down through the ages, recorded in the scriptures, witnesses to God's self-limiting love that gives freedom and looks for response.

It is therefore possible for the Church to accept the scientific understanding that the world is both rational and contingent and to bear witness to God who has declared his purpose in Christ.

5. *Towards Serious Preaching—Apologetics for Today*

As the former British Prime Minister, Margaret Thatcher, put it on the occasion of her departure from office, 'It's a funny old world' in which we now find ourselves. Science has now invoked a new theory of design, which at the beginning of the Enlightenment it had discarded. Western society which had become proud of a rationalism that dispensed with the need for God, now finds its people running after all sorts of irrational beliefs. A world that was convinced that science and technology would lead it to Utopia has now become disillusioned and unsure. And the Christian Church, which had largely withdrawn into the world of private faith, is now being forced to answer questions in the public arena of science. Here, I believe, is a vital opportunity for presenting the gospel of Christ, but it will mean serious study of both science and of the scriptures. We have the task of apologetics, a useful technical term that does not of course mean 'apologizing' for the Christian faith in a shame-faced or 'defensive' manner; it means making a positive defence (*apologia*) of faith by giving reasoned arguments for the way that Christianity can meet the intellectual questions as well as the emotional needs of people in the real world we live in. We will need to address questions about creation, evolution, the environment, suffering, stewardship of the Earth, desire for fulfilment, and the demand for proof, and I intend briefly to survey an approach to these issues.

But perhaps we need first to take notice of the alternative religions that people are seeking out in our spiritually hungry society. The last decade has seen the flowering of a syncretism of a wide variety of non-Christian religions, which are often referred to collectively as 'New Age', and also a re-emergence of the the older primal religions, which may be described as 'Neo-paganism'. New Age sees the material world as a projection of deity. There is no distinction between the natural and supernatural, but nature is seen as the ultimate reality whose member-parts are linked together in one organic whole. God is the impersonal life force, pure undifferentiated energy, and humanity is an expression of the One Self. While there is an individualistic search for the true self, and all moral standards are seen as relative, there is, nevertheless, a deep sense of concern for the environment.[27]

There are many parallels with the New Age movement to be found in Neo-paganism, and it may often be difficult to distinguish between them. Neo-paganism like New Age has many variables, including both polytheism and pantheism, in which all nature is divinity but manifest in a variety of forms. The reverence for nature is seen in the worship of the Earth Mother, Gaia or Freyja, and with this comes a concern for ecology. A stress on the feminine nature of reality, with the centrality of the mother goddess, has been an attraction for some strands in the feminist movement. There is an emphasis on the individual seeking entrance to power through various forms of ritual or meditation. In addition to the re-emergence of the pre-Christian primal religions, Neo-paganism has also been used in some cases as the base for involvement of people in anti-Christian satanic practices.

While there are genuine elements of spirituality in New Age and Neo-paganism, I consider that David Burnett[28] is right to attribute the large appeal they have in popular culture to a relativistic secularism where the equal validity of all beliefs is readily accepted, and where people feel free to do whatever they consider to be right and to follow any course that leads to self advancement. The dark side of all this is a self-centredness that leads to a seeking after any form of pleasure and excitement, and which for a minority has included the excesses of ritual cruelty and ritual sex.

Behind the interest that many are showing in these movements is the search for an understanding of the world we experience and for our place within the scheme of things; there is a search for personal fulfilment and well-being. We might then engage people who are on such a search through pointing to discovery of purpose in the fabric of the cosmos. We need to find the points of contact and address the questions and issues that are high on people's agenda. From my own experience as a Christian minister in discussions with both adults and school and college students who are outside the Church, I have found that the major issues are those surrounding science, especially creation, and suffering. It is these two issues that have been at the centre of all our deliberations thus far, and the conclusions at which we have been arriving might therefore be used as a basis for our presentation of the gospel.

In doing apologetics we will begin with creation, drawing on the suggestion of an Anthropic Principle woven into the fabric of the universe. We discover through this a sense of cosmic purpose and the central place of human beings within this purpose. We then need to tackle the creation narrative of Genesis 1 in the light of biblical scholarship and recognise that the difficulty raised by a creation in a literal six days was never the intention of the writer. When we take a serious look at this narrative we discover that it is first and foremost a statement of faith, whose purpose is primarily theological. It is a reflection upon the nature of the covenant God of Israel, who is presented as very different from the gods of the surrounding nations. The order of creation is seen to show a remarkable consistency with the discoveries of science that were made over 2,000 years later. I personally believe, and would want to say, that this in itself points to the inspiration of the Creator behind the Priestly writer's account. But more important is the central place accorded to human beings, whose self-awareness is seen to be in the image of God.

We might then tackle the issue of evolution, a real 'hot potato' for some Christians, while its denial is a stumbling block for belief to many outside of the Church. We need to address a number of questions here, most important of which are the place of human beings and the nature of God. Science presents us with a universe that has enormous dimensions in space and an equally enormous history in time. This history involves the slow but gradual evolution of the cosmos to a point where conscious, carbon-based human life might appear. The scientific evidence demonstrates a remarkable fine-tuning of the initial features of the universe to see such an end point to the evolutionary story of life. We can argue that the unfolding of a universe like this implies the need of guidance within the processes at work. In accord with this principle, the Bible presents us with a picture of a God who is intimately involved with his creation at every moment of its existence. If we consider the alternative model presented by creationism, we are presented with a God who creates a universe that already has a history of 15-20 billion years and who enters into creation to create separately each galaxy, star, planet, and living thing. Such a model appears to preserve God's transcendence, while reducing, if not denying, his immanence. I would thus maintain that the God revealed in Scripture accords more closely with an evolutionary model.

But an enquirer may then ask about the place of human beings. Biological and archaeological studies have shown that there are unique qualities to be found in *Homo sapiens* that we might sum up as 'civilization'. We have drawn attention in Chapter 4 to the two basic problems posed by the kind of separate creation of human beings envisaged by creationism. First, it assumes that God does not use the whole of creation in his purposes. Second, it would imply that our relationship with God is controlled genetically; if there had been no capacity in human genes for responding to external realities, a capacity acquired through inheritance and genuine development, then genes must have been created instantaneously for responding to God. The Bible excludes such a possibility, recognising the genuinely human aspects of response (John 1:11-12 and Heb 11:6). Moreover, the Bible suggests a spiritual unity of all humankind with Adam rather than a genetic one (Acts 17:26 and Rom 5:12-14); the point is that we are all caught within a web of sin and wrong-doing in a race of which Adam is the natural head. Within the movement of evolutionary development, there must have been a moment when *Homo sapiens* came to full moral consciousness for the first time, and moral beings could first have meaningfully obeyed and disobeyed the will of God. As we observed in chapter 4, recent studies in genetics points to *Homo sapiens* having passed through a 'bottleneck' in numbers during its evolutionary past, when the species may have been reduced to fairly low numbers for a time, and if so this would make the significant moment of moral choice even more critical for humankind as a whole.

In our 'apologetic' approach it will be more important to address the issue of purpose for humanity; why are we here? This is where Genesis 1 reveals that we are created for relationship with God, and worship of him. In the next two chapters of Genesis we find that humanity's relationship with God is fractured, through our own self-centredness. The result is that humanity is marred and fallen, and God's purposes are frustrated. This creates a sense of longing in humanity. Augustine expressed this truth when he wrote: 'You have made us for yourself, and our hearts are restless until they rest in you.'[29] Many people can identify a sense of dissatisfaction within them, and psychologists will often recognise that their subjects have an unresolved longing for a lost 'golden age.' Christian hope for individual lives and the whole cosmos is not, of course, a nostalgic return to some past paradise; as we have seen in chapter 7, it is a reaching forward to a renewed creation in the future. But human dissatisfaction, however poorly expressed, can be a stepping-off point for the discovery of the personal God, who longs for our fulfilment in relationship with him. In the Cross of Christ we see the redemption of this broken relationship. The Christian witness is to the fulfilment of our humanity in Christ, which is the experience of faith. I suggest, however, that we should not begin our apologetic by stressing the negative feeling of lack of satisfaction, but begin as does Genesis 1-2 with the positive purpose at the heart of the universe, in contrast with which we can feel the emptiness in human lives that is expressed in Genesis 3.

The other major issue that is raised by many people outside the Church is the question of suffering. At this point we will have to take great care over the model of God we appear to be presenting to people. If we emphasize the transcendent creator God, who is omnipotent and omniscient and who stands apart from his creation, we will struggle to answer this question. An understanding of the nature of God's involvement with creation is fundamentally important, and here the discoveries of modern science may help to point us in the right direction. Central to our understanding is to recognise that God in his freedom of will chose to create a universe that is contingent in itself. The picture of evolution from the biological sciences presents us with God's risk in such a creation, with mutations, extinctions, and fortunate survivors an integral part of the process. The God who is immanent within creation does not insulate himself from the risks that he asks others to bear, but will suffer along with his creation. In creating human beings at a distance from himself and with free will, he risks the pain of rebellion, while longing for the response of obedient love.

We have little problem in identifying where human sinfulness in such a free creation is the cause of the suffering of the innocent ('moral evil'), but cases of disease and the tragedy of natural disasters will be far more difficult. We cannot begin to deal with these problems without asking serious questions about how we believe that God acts in the world, and this also involves a scientific perspective. In his transcendence God has the power to intervene in human affairs, and in his immanence God is actually in the position where he is able to intervene. But if we propose that God does intervene on occasions, we are left with the difficult theological question of why he does not do so more often, and hence to ask what kind of a God would behave like this. I have suggested that we might keep the notion of 'intervention' for rare, defining moments of revelation.[30] Otherwise, the model of 'intervention' is not a helpful one in considering the continual action of God; it is too one-sided, and I suggest that we should be cautious in employing it. It would be better to think of a God who does new things on the inside of creation and in cooperation with it in a way that does not infringe its freedom, though I acknowledge a mystery about the way that this happens. It may not be possible easily to model the mystery, though I have suggested in chapter 7 that ideas of divine persuasion take us a long way.

Within the contingency of nature suggested by science, there is room for the emergence of 'natural' evil due to the distortion of living organisms at microscopic levels. Science demonstrates that the same processes that gave rise to the evolution of human life, namely the mutation of genes, also lead to disease and death. This is to be understood in theological terms as the risk God takes in endowing creation with freedom. In individual cases of suffering we will still of course have to wrestle with the questions of healing and wholeness, alongside pain and grief. There is no simple rational formula that can be applied to dissolve the mystery. In the mystery of suffering we will need to hold onto the model of suffering love that we see displayed in the Cross of Christ, where we find the Creator suffering with and on behalf of the world.

The discoveries of science also allow us to tackle a very different kind of so-called 'natural evil', the suffering brought about by events in the physical world such as earthquakes, volcanic eruptions, and extremes of climate. We recognise that these are necessary side effects of a world designed to produce the raw materials of life. Here it seems to me that we blame God too easily, and too readily speak of these as 'evil' in themselves. Their disastrous nature actually mainly stems from the moral evil of human irresponsibility. With the help of modern science we are able to predict where and when disasters of this kind are likely to take place. So countries that are rich in resources and technology could counter such anticipated problems and avoid the worst effects if they had the will-power to accept the economic costs; for example, houses need not be built on a major fracture in the earth's crust where earthquakes may happen, and farmers need not farm on the side of Mount Etna. Poorer countries cannot themselves take evasive action; unless developed countries are willing to share their wealth, living space, and expertise with others less advantaged, large populations will go on living—for example—on the coastal flood plains of Bangladesh. Thus, raising the moral question of the goodness of God also involves a moral issue for us.

Human beings are created with the ability to control creation with a freedom and power given to us by God. The question that remains will be our response. We are brought face to face once again with a God who, in his self-limiting love, gives freedom of choice to his creation, and who himself lives with the consequences of such an action. We have clearly found the God of love, revealed in his creation and in the Cross of Christ.

All of these are points of contact. They are a catalyst, an opportunity, they do not offer an alternative to God's self-revelation, but I believe that God has prepared the ground for us in such questions. We need to lead people from where they are to an understanding of the deeper truths about 'life, the universe and everything', which are to be found in Jesus Christ.

We will, of course, always come up against the demand for proof. This is the same as the demands that faced Jesus in his ministry (Matt 16:1-4). Jesus drew attention to the signs in creation, but then raised responding and trusting faith as the only possible proof available in the world. There can be no proof, but for the answering experience that comes with the step of faith and trust. Faith is not the belief that God exists, or that creation bears the imprint of purpose, or that the ideas of the Christian faith are correct. Faith is trusting in the promises of God, accepting them and receiving what they have to offer. What we are seeking to do through the area of apologetics is two-fold: to meet people where they are in their search for answers to their own life; and to demonstrate the reasonableness of the Christian understanding of the world, so providing an environment where God is seen to be worthy of faith and trust. We are working at that point of contact where someone is enabled to step from a secular world-view to a Christian world-view.

We need to keep in mind the theological objections that were made against the rational proofs for the existence of God at the end of Chapter 6, especially the point that the God who is the end of a philosophical argument will be far removed from the living God of biblical faith. We are presenting pointers toward God, which will help people to seek him and in love respond to him with self-sacrifice and worship.

6. Preaching from Genesis Chapter 1

Apologetics may be the right approach with people outside the church, but how do we teach believers who are within our churches? It might not always be helpful to our congregations to launch into an attack on the literal six days of creation, nor to uphold an unyielding position on such a literal understanding, in the face of science. This raises the question as to how we find a way of discussing Genesis 1 without assuming a position that will prevent some people from even beginning to listen. Our understanding of biblical criticism should inform our preaching, rather than be its content. Similarly, any knowledge of the world of science should help us to make immediate the scriptures, rather than be paraded before the congregation to show what books we have been reading. An approach that I have found useful is to tell, in story form, the background to the passage, and to move from there to discuss the relevance of the message for people today. Here then, is one way of tackling Genesis 1 and the issue of creation. The story might run something like this:

> The people of Israel had been in exile in Babylonia for a number of years, and their situation was depressing in every way. They were aliens in a foreign land, with a different culture, different religion, and different climate and environment from their own. On top of this they were prisoners with an existence that was not far from slavery. The understanding of their captors was that the gods of Babylon were victorious over the God of Israel, and they were often tempted into believing this version of the truth. They were living in mud-brick houses alongside the irrigation channel, called the River Chebar, in an inhospitable climate and land. They had been granted permission by their overlords to establish their homes, and they had sought to bring a degree of order and meaning to their existence. The local inhabitants made fun of their plight and derided their religion. Spiritually they were depressed. Their Temple in Jerusalem, the place where they had believed that God dwelt in a special way, was over a thousand kilometres away, and worse still, it was in ruins. Their view was that they were far away from God, and that their very condition demonstrated his impotence.

The messages of Ezekiel and Isaiah of Babylon must be seen against this backdrop. As prophets they declared that God was not confined to the land of Israel and the Temple in Jerusalem, but was with them in Babylon, and he was ready to forgive them and bring about a new Exodus. It is in this context that the writer of Genesis 1 began to reflect upon the faith of Israel. This priestly writer, or group of writers, reflected upon the traditions of their faith, the writings that the religious community had preserved and brought with them into exile, and upon the history of God's dealings with his people; they thought about the story of God's relationship with them over the years, from the Patriarchs to Egypt, from the Exodus to David, and from Solomon's Temple to the Exile. To this they added their experience of the world and the religious views held by their Babylonian captors.

The writers took all these experiences, and under the inspiration of the Holy Spirit a newly edited version of the Scriptures took shape. The very first belief that they wanted to express was that the covenant God of Israel was the God of all creation. Out of their experience they opened their major work with what we now know as Genesis 1.

This kind of story-telling may serve as a way into the text. The sermon may then unfold in different ways, but the preacher will surely want to include some aspects of the vision of God that the passage portrays. The writers, the preacher will explain, began with God as the one transcendent creator. They recognised the ordering of the universe as his plan, and they understood that his purpose was to invest human beings with a supreme place within creation. They brought some polemic against the religion of their Babylonian captors, asserting that it was the God of Israel who had created the sun, moon, and stars that the Babylonians thought of as being deities. It was their God who had created all the creatures of the sea, which included the 'chaos monster' of Babylonian myths. This God reaches a climax in his work with the making of human beings, in the image of himself; they are not the walk-on servile extras of the Babylonian creation story, but the crown of God's purpose in creation, invested with power, and entrusted as stewards. Creation is understood to culminate in the Sabbath praise of the Creator, the whole of creation reaching its ultimate fulfilment with the praise of God by the covenant community. And, we may add, the whole picture of this ordering of creation is consistent with a modern understanding of cosmology and geology, which may be seen as a confirming its origin in the inspiration of writers by the same sovereign God.

There are obviously many different emphases that might be made in preaching from this chapter, and a whole series of sermons might be produced. Themes that could be developed at greater length are: the primacy of God, the ordering of creation, the faithfulness of the Creator, the fruitfulness of his creation, what it means for human beings to be created in the image of God, the nature of our stewardship of the world and the implications that this has for our discussion of environmental issues. Continuing the 'story telling' approach, the preacher might relate how the writer of Genesis 1 was combatting and displacing the notions of creation that were widespread in the Babylonian religion all around him. There should then be scope for the preacher to do the same for today, describing and facing the various views of creation around us in our own world.

7. An Invitation to Get Involved

I have felt over the years, as I have talked and listened to people within the Church, that the reluctance to engage in a dialogue between Christianity and science lies mainly in a fear that the arguments of faith are simply not strong enough to keep company with the realities of the scientific world. If this were true, then as Paul said concerning belief in the resurrection, we would be the ones most in need of pity. For the Father of our Lord Jesus Christ is the God of creation, and is therefore the author of every discovery made by science. The world of science and the world of Christian spiritual experience are the same world, unless God be not God. This dialogue is not easy, and I can understand why some will retreat into the 'safety' of a dogmatic belief, denying the truth of any scientific statement or theory that disagrees with their deeply held views. While such an attitude may give apparent security to their belief, it fails to engage the world outside the Church, and worse still, may cause the Christian faith to be derided.

The people I have listened to and talked with outside the Church, or enquirers about the faith within Christian congregations, have no reticence when it comes to asking questions about the relation of Christian belief to the world that they learn about through science and their own daily experience. Their questions are difficult to grapple with, but they are worthy of our attention, for it is here that we are able to present the claims of Christ to a needy world. I am sure that Lesslie Newbigin was absolutely right when he wrote:

> The greatest intellectual task facing the Church is a new dialogue with science—a dialogue for which the way has been prepared by profound changes in science (especially in physics) during this century.[31]

Science asks why the universe displays purpose and looks for a theory of everything. We are able to point the world to the Creator who is the author of life, and whose ultimate purpose is declared in the life, death, and resurrection of Christ. Science points to the anthropocentric nature of the universe and asks what this might mean. We are able to point to the Creator who has created human beings in his own image. Ordinary people ask about origins, purpose, meaning, and suffering, and we are able to engage them with the realities of the scientific understanding of the world and thereby to lead them deeper into the truth of God revealed in Christ.

This book has been an attempt to provide the tools for such an encounter with the world outside the Church and to offer resources for teaching that will encourage Christians in their faith. I invite you to grasp with me the opportunity that I believe God has given us in this last decade of the twentieth century.

Notes to Chapter 8

[1]Isaiah 40:28 (New International Version).

[2]D. Adams, *The Hitch-Hiker's Guide to the Galaxy*, 51-52.

[3]S. Weinberg, *The First Three Minutes* (London: Andre Deutsch, 1979) 149.

[4]J. Barrow and F. Tipler, *The Anthropic Cosmological Principle* (Oxford: Oxford University Press, 1988).

[5]J. Barrow, *Theories of Everything*, (Oxford: Oxford University Press, 1988).

[6]Paul Davies, *Superforce* (New York and London: Simon & Schuster, 1984).

[7]P. Davies, *The Mind of God*, 204.

[8]J. Houghton, *Does God Play Dice?* (Leicester: I.V.P., 1988).

[9]R. E. Peacock, *A Brief History of Eternity* (Eastbourne: Monarch, 1989).

[10]A. Peacocke, *God and the New Biology*; *Theology for a Scientific Age—Being and Becoming*; *Natural and Divine*; see also his earlier books *Science and the Christian Experiment* (London: Oxford University Press, 1971) and *Creation and the World of Science* (Oxford: Oxford University Press, 1979).

[11]J. Polkinghorne, *One World—the Interaction of Science and Theology* and *Science and Creation*; see also The *Quantum World* (Harmondsworth: Penguin, 1986).

[12]D. Wilkinson, *God, the Big Bang and Stephen Hawking*.

[13]R. J. Berry, *Adam and the Ape*.

[14]E. K. V. Pearce, *Who was Adam?*

[15]R. Peacock, *A Brief History of Eternity* (Eastbourne: Monarch, 1989) 117ff.

[16]S. W. Hawking, *A Brief History of Time*, 122ff, 171-75.

[17]J. Hick, *Arguments for the Existence of God*, 33-36, 46, 108-16.

[18]Hawking, 175

[19]P. Davies, *The Mind of God*, 223.x

[20]Ibid., 232.

[21]D. Burnett, *Clash of Worlds* (Eastbourne: Monarch, 1990)

[22]L. Newbigin, *Foolishness to the Greeks—the Gospel and Western Culture* (London: SPCK, 1986) 45-50.

[23]Ibid., 50-51.

[24]Ibid., 56.

[25]R. Penrose, *The Emperor's New Mind*, 447.

[26]Newbigin, *Foolishness to the Greeks*, 73.

[27]See E. Barker, 'New Age Movement' in *A Dictionary of New Religions* (London: HMSO, 1989); W. Carr, *Manifold Wisdom—Christians in the New Age* (London: SPCK, 1991); R. Chandler, *Understanding the New Age* (Milton Keynes: Word Books, 1988); M. Cole, J. Graham, T. Higton and D. Lewis, *What is the New Age?* (London: Hodder & Stoughton, 1990).

[28]D. Burnett, 202.

[29]Augustine, *Confessions Book I,* trans. Henry Chadwick (Oxford: Oxford University Press, 1991) 3.

[30]See Chapter 7.

[31]L. Newbigin, *The Other Side of 1984—Questions for the Churches* (Geneva: World Council of Churches, 1983) 60.

Epilogue

'In the beginning . . . God'

Once there was a 'Big Bang' fireball, happening in finely-tuned conditions, resulting in the evolution of a universe that includes conscious, self-aware human life—
—in the beginning God, who created this world full of possibilities.

There is now a universe displaying design that is suggestive of purpose, and an Anthropic Principle that envisages the evolution of human life as central to that purpose—
—in the beginning God, who is the purposeful mind at the heart of the universe.

There is a rational universe, which is understood as rational by the rational minds of human observers—
—in the beginning God, who is the source of all rationality.

There has been evolution of life in all its complexity and variety, climaxing with the appearance of Homo sapiens, through the process of non-random survival and natural selection—
—in the beginning God, who has accompanied his creation, guiding its evolution at every faltering step.

There is a world in which freedom of choice is accompanied by suffering and death—
—in the beginning God, who in love has given freedom to his creation, and who in love will bring it to its final consummation in himself.

There is a Bible that witnesses to the creation of order out of chaos, light in the midst of darkness, the variety and richness of the physical universe and the living world, and human beings in the image of God, created for relationship with their Creator—
—in the beginning God, who has revealed himself in creation, in the record of Scripture, and specifically in Jesus Christ.

So we have a new beginning, a new worldview, and a new opportunity to be proclaimers of the central truth of all existence—
—in the beginning, and at our end, God.

'Christ is the Morning Star, who, when the night of this world is past brings his saints the promise of the light of life and opens everlasting day.'

—*The Venerable Bede,* A.D. 673–735

Index